The Enlightenment
A Beginner's Guide

ONEWORLD BEGINNER'S GUIDES combine an original, inventive, and engaging approach with expert analysis on subjects ranging from art and history to religion and politics, and everything in between. Innovative and affordable, books in the series are perfect for anyone curious about the way the world works and the big ideas of our time.

Beginners
GUIDES

The Enlightenment
A Beginner's Guide

Kieron O'Hara

ONEWORLD
OXFORD

A Oneworld Paperback Original

Published by Oneworld Publications 2010

Copyright © Kieron O'Hara 2010

The moral right of Kieron O'Hara to be identified as the
Author of this work has been asserted by him in accordance
with the Copyright, Designs and Patents Act 1988

ISBN 978–1–85168–709–1

Typeset by Jayvee, Trivandrum, India
Cover design by A. Meaden
Printed and bound in Great Britain by CPI Cox & Wyman, Reading, RG1 8EX

Copyright © cover photo The Metropolitan Museum of Art,
Purchase, Mr and Mrs Charles Wrightsman Gift,
in honour of Everett Fahy, 1977 (1977.10)

Oneworld Publications
UK: 185 Banbury Road, Oxford OX2 7AR, England
USA: 38 Greene Street, 4th Floor, New York, NY 10013, USA

Learn more about Oneworld. Join our mailing list to
find out about our latest titles and special offers at:

www.oneworld-publications.com

Contents

Preface

'The Enlightenment' is one of those terms that is often used, about which people have very strong opinions, yet its meaning is very hard to pin down. Some blame it for the bloody disasters of the twentieth century – Auschwitz, the Gulags, globalisation, Islamic terrorism. Others feel its legacy needs to be protected against a neo-barbarian onslaught, from supporters of intelligent design, animal rights fanatics, bloggers – and Islamic terrorists. For some it signifies the triumph of reason – but did reason triumph over ignorance or diversity? Has it brought tolerance, or hypocrisy? Does it support equality of women and men, non-white people and whites? Or alternatively is it a covert attempt to force women or nonwhite people to deny their own voices, reject their distinct inheritances and adopt European ways? Is it driving humankind to use science in an insane, unstoppable rape of our planetary resources, or are its discoveries the key to maximising human welfare?

The debates still rage. A short introduction cannot hope to resolve these issues, but it should be possible to provide some pointers. Where are the agreements and disagreements? Where the errors and misconceptions? What significance can we draw when we hear the term 'Enlightenment' used in social or political discourse? That is the aim of this book – a deliberately small book, a daunting aim for its author.

As the Enlightenment is such a distributed and heterogeneous group of phenomena, events and institutions, our survey will perforce have to be selective. As I will argue, the Enlightenment is an identifiable movement with underlying continuities, six aspects of which I will sketch in the opening chapter. In the next two chapters, I will briefly examine the progress of the Enlightenment and its distribution in space. The Enlightenment was about ideas, which the next five chapters will consider. Chapter four will sketch the intellectual origins of the Enlightenment, looking at its precursors and its founders. Chapter five will look at the philosophy of the era, including the central aspects of the philosophy of knowledge (epistemology) and the philosophy of mind. Chapter six will review the most abiding philosophical developments in political philosophy. Chapter seven will look at the new scientific views of nature, while Chapter eight will examine religious ideas. Next, chapter nine will look at the effects of the revolution in ideas on artistic expression. Chapter ten will consider the legacy of the Enlightenment in the present day and review attitudes, both pro and anti, and the final chapter will draw on all of these elements in briefly examining the significance of Enlightenment ideas during the last two hundred years.

This is a survey of a long period of time, which ranges over two continents and several kinds of artistic and political endeavour. As is clear from the table of contents, I have chosen to arrange material thematically rather than chronologically. Many names, not all of them familiar, crop up, and rather than interrupt the text for introductions I have placed the names of some of the more important figures in a list at the back of the book, which gives their dates and nationalities, as well as a very brief characterisation of their achievements. This, I hope, will serve to orient the reader as he or she moves through the text, and also act as a starting point for further study. The dates of birth and death of those not mentioned in the biographical section will be given in the text upon their first appearance. Throughout the book, names and titles have been anglicised, except where a non-English name is more familiar.

The major writers of the Enlightenment are relatively little-read in the twenty-first century. Some works remain popular – *Candide*, *Gulliver's Travels*, *Robinson Crusoe* – but many of the great philosophical and historical works, such as Locke's *Essay*, Hume's *Treatise*, Kant's *Critique of Pure Reason* or Gibbon's *Decline and Fall of the Roman Empire* are more referred to than read, while in the Anglophone world at least, remarkably few readers recognise the names of the greatest *philosophes*, including Diderot, Condorcet and Montesquieu. There are some excellent anthologies of Enlightenment texts, and in this book I have purposely leaned heavily on Isaac Kramnick's *The Portable Enlightenment Reader*, which happily remains in print, in order that the student might be able to find a selection of excerpts from a good range of Enlightened writers, scientists and thinkers in one convenient place. In the further resources section at the end of the book I will indicate which of my quotes can be found among the extracts collected in Kramnick. I also suggest secondary sources for the issues addressed in each chapter; each source appears once to avoid undue repetition, but many of them have wide applicability and are worth reading in a number of contexts. I also provide a list of important primary texts or useful anthologies of original pieces. Most of these are a joy to read, and I hope this little guide will open that enjoyment for the reader.

My thanks are due in particular to David Stevens, Marsha Filion, Dawn Sackett and an anonymous referee for comments and criticisms of previous drafts, all of which improved the book immensely. It should, but rarely does, go without saying that responsibility for remaining errors and infelicities lies solely with the author.

1
Introduction: aspects of Enlightenment

For a definition of Enlightenment, we do have a handy starting point. At the pinnacle of the age, 1784, one of the leading philosophers of the Enlightenment, Immanuel Kant, wrote a short piece entitled 'What is Enlightenment?' That piece is a splendidly concise summary of much of the preceding epoch, but nevertheless hints at some of the difficulties of definition.

Kant is commendably direct: his first sentence defines Enlightenment as 'man's release from his self-incurred tutelage'. The goal is intellectual freedom; people need to be liberated from authority. Kant's motto for the age is '*sapere aude*', often translated as 'dare to know!' So the search for intellectual freedom is a moral one, and failure to embark on it is owing to 'laziness and cowardice'. One *should* argue with authority, because one should claim 'the freedom to make public use of one's reason at every point'. That is not to say that we should be wrangling perpetually. We play various roles in life which quite properly restrict our freedom, but we have an individual core at the centre of our being which should dare to know, argue and find out. Kant gives the example of a clergyman who is obligated to the church to give orthodox sermons to his flock, but as a *scholar*, it is his duty to test such orthodoxy against his reason, to question and argue.

The Enlightened man challenges orthodoxy, argues against authority when his reason is compromised, and understands the limits to his reason dictated by the roles he plays in society. That is an important goal, but picking it apart exposes many of the tensions of the Enlightenment. For instance, the reader will no doubt have noticed its gendered language. Enlightened thinkers (of both sexes – even the important feminist thinker Mary Wollstonecraft) usually referred to *man* or *mankind* meaning all people, men and women, and it is certainly futile and anachronistic to condemn writers of a quarter of a millennium ago for lacking sensitivities we now possess. But their assumptions were indeed often sexist, and so the gendered language can also betray an unmotivated privileging of men's experience over women's. Kant, for example, asserts that the attempt to use one's own reason 'is held to be very dangerous by the far greater portion of mankind (and by the entire fair sex).' In this book, I shall generally use the gendered language used by the people on whom I am commentating, because to do otherwise would risk misstating key positions, and will leave the very difficult question of evaluating sexism to the reader, together with the additional question, if sexism be shown, of identifying whether it crucially undermines the arguments of the texts it appears in.

Kant is also unashamedly elitist. 'New prejudices will serve as well as old ones to harness the great unthinking masses.' He is very nervous of the idea that letting *all* individuals think for themselves is the best way to promote Enlightened values; he much prefers the idea that a radical prince (he is thinking of Frederick the Great of Prussia) should shepherd his people 'out of barbarity'. Only an Enlightened despot with a numerous and well-disciplined army, he thinks, can let his people argue. 'A republic could not dare say such a thing. … A greater degree of civil freedom appears advantageous to the freedom of mind of the people, and yet it places inescapable limitations upon it; a lower degree of civil freedom, on the contrary, provides the mind with room for each man to extend himself to his full capacity.'

Indeed, Kant denied that he lived in an 'enlightened age' at all (though 'we do live in an "age of enlightenment"'). The

Enlightenment, even for the foremost philosopher of the age, had not produced Enlightenment for the mass of people even by 1784. How, then, should a beginner's guide proceed?

The Enlightenment has very blurry borders, and no-one quite agrees on the fine detail, but there is a core that can be described. My hope in this book will be to guide the beginner around that core, so that she – or he! – can get to know the rough territory, and start to make her own judgements about the age.

In the following sections I will sketch out some representative Enlightenment positions, with the firm caveats that thinkers of other eras have had similar ideas, and that Enlightened thinkers could sometimes hold very uncharacteristic opinions. But, if one does not mind generalising enormously, one can provide a not inaccurate view of the key aspects of the processes and products of Enlightened thought.

Aspect 1: new sources of authority, particularly grounded in human capacities

Any kind of belief, be it scientific, religious, philosophical, political or common sense, has a justification, a *reason* why it is believed. In the Enlightenment, there was a broad and general shift in the accepted justifications of belief away from *authorities* and toward the *individual*, who was expected to take more responsibility for the beliefs he held. This attitude was at least partly due to the social changes brought about by increased literacy, and was not unnaturally concentrated in the towns – the social mix allowed more people access to a larger number of opinions jostling to be heard.

Older sources of authority such as the king, God, the Bible, or tradition lost their hold, and newer ones, such as experimental observation, reason and logic became more respectable. The past has no claim on the future. As Kant put it, 'An age cannot bind itself and ordain to put the succeeding one into such a condition that it cannot extend its (at best very occasional) knowledge, purify itself of errors, and progress its general enlightenment'[1] (seemingly neutral between a moral and a practical claim). Jean le Rond d'Alembert's take was that genuine *philosophes* 'respect that which they ought to, and prize that which they can. This is their real crime' – i.e. the real reason for their notoriety. The opinion of 'the people' also became important, as Jean-Jacques Rousseau's theories about 'the general will' were adapted by Robespierre and the French Revolutionaries.

To make all that clearer, let's take three examples. Many used to believe that the legitimacy of a ruler that made it obligatory for his subjects to obey him derived directly from God (the divine right of kings). In the Enlightenment the idea of a social *contract* emerged whereby subjects obeyed the king only in return for various services that the king was contractually obliged to perform, such as providing law and order, protection from want or outside invasion (see chapter six for more on this). So although royalism declined during the Enlightenment, it didn't disappear, while a royalist like Voltaire would rest his arguments on a strongly-argued rational case, not on the realities of tradition or power.

A second example is religious belief. Whereas in the seventeenth century one was expected to conform to the religion of one's country, and one could easily find oneself executed for holding the wrong beliefs, there was much argument in the eighteenth century that toleration of all religions was important, because God was less appreciative of someone getting it right, than of them making a genuine attempt to understand religious truth, even if they got it wrong.

Thirdly, science arose as authority, particularly religious authority or the authority of the great classical thinkers such as

Aristotle or Galen, declined (see chapter seven). Truth about the world was found not in the library or the Bible, but via investigation of the phenomena in the world, with experiment and observation. If observations went against authority, so much the worse for authority.

There were three important corollaries of this new attitude. First, the power of tradition was markedly reduced, and old habits and attitudes were almost automatically questioned. The eighteenth century was a period of self-conscious **modernisation**. Secondly, there was a general increase in **toleration**; people with opposing views should be able, it was felt, to live peacefully alongside each other, as long as those views did not affect other people materially. Pierre Bayle argued that people cannot be forced to believe, pointing out that each of us generally strives to obey God as best we can in good faith even though we diverge, and this is generally unproblematic. On the other hand, we can recognise when people are doing evil, and can deal with them accordingly.[2] A stronger argument, honed by John Locke in his 'Letter concerning toleration', was that the religious and secular spheres are and should be kept separate; the policing of conscience is simply beyond the competence and authority of the magistrate.

The third corollary of the new attitude was that the **individual** became more important as a political entity, correspondingly more time was devoted to studying and theorising the psychology of the individual, and individual **liberty** was increasingly seen as an important political goal. The work of Isaiah Berlin and others[3] reminds us that 'liberty' can be interpreted in many different ways, in the Enlightenment as much as in any era, but, however broadly construed, it was the watchword for many an Enlightenment thinker.

Mystery, in particular the mysteries of religion and folk-magic, became unfashionable. Alchemy and magic declined, and in the arts clarity began to reign. The dense, metaphorical poetry of the seventeenth century, represented in England by Donne and Vaughan, was replaced by the civilised, straight-speaking work of John Dryden (1631–1700) and Alexander Pope, and the acme of poetical achievement was when one's lines were 'what oft was thought but ne'er so well expressed'. The complex polyphonic music of Byrd or Palestrina from the sixteenth century was followed by the beautiful, joyous works of Bach and Händel.

The mysteries of religion were replaced by the assumption that God was basically rational and reasonable. The mysteries were really a way for the church to prevent ordinary people discovering inconvenient facts, and to obscure sensible ways of governing lives and nations. In Voltaire's short novel, *The Ingenu*, a noble and naïve Huron Indian transported to eighteenth century Paris notes that where matters are clear, there is no conflict – there are no sects in geometry. But then why would God make the truths of geometry clear and the truths of morality obscure? 'It is an absurdity, an outrage against the human race, an attack on the Infinite and Supreme Being, to say: "There is one truth essential to man, and God has hidden it." '

Aspect 2: confidence and optimism

This change in attitude towards authority coincided, not unnaturally, with another shift towards greater **confidence** about human powers of control. The example in particular of Newton's mechanics showed that exact theories of even very complex phenomena could be developed that not only explained but allowed one to intervene and alter the environment. Newton's advances were echoed in the world of politics by Locke, whose theories showed how a government could be tolerant while retaining power and legitimacy, and the example of the English government after 1688 proved it was possible.

The constraints of nature could be tamed by commerce, new transport and communications systems, agriculture, gardening and so on. The vast wilderness of America presented a big, but not insuperable challenge. This confidence often displayed itself as **optimism** about the future of mankind, in marked contrast to previous generations who tended to look back nostalgically to the glories of Greece and Rome whose remains were so visible, or to the Biblical world where man was closer to God.

Optimism developed into the idea of **providence**, that the world couldn't be any better than it was because God would surely not make an imperfect world. This view is generally associated with the German philosopher Gottfried Leibniz, but was certainly not unique to him. Pope's *Essay on Man* gave the philosophy its most concise formulation.

> All nature is but art, unknown to thee;
> All chance, direction, which thou canst not see;
> All discord, harmony not understood;
> All partial evil, universal good:
> And, spite of pride in erring reason's spite,
> One truth is clear, whatever is, is right.

Confidence about progress became optimism about ability. One could have total knowledge of a state of affairs so that all variables were explained. Precision became important, and tools, instruments and measurements became increasingly accurate. The irreducibility of complexity was not seen as an issue. **Abstraction** and, thanks largely to Newton, mathematics were important tools. **Expertise** and expert opinion were admired. Scientist Joseph Priestley made the connection between totalising and optimism explicit:

> [A]ll knowledge will be subdivided and extended; and *knowledge*, as Lord Bacon observes, being *power*, the human powers will, in fact, be increased; nature, including both its materials,

and its laws, will be more at our command; men will make their situation in this world abundantly more easy and comfortable; they will probably prolong their existence in it, and will grow daily more happy, each in himself, and more able (and, I believe, more disposed) to communicate happiness to others. Thus, *whatever was the beginning of this world, the end will be glorious and paradisiacal, beyond what our imaginations can now conceive.*[4]

Aspect 3: scepticism

The **balance** of **scepticism** and **confidence** could never reach equilibrium. Scepticism about the old authorities very quickly turned on newer ones; Bayle was unimpressed even with Newton, while Voltaire's *Candide, Or Optimism* (1759) parodied the optimism of the age as the philosophy of Dr Pangloss, the metaphyisico-theologico-cosmologist (spoofing Leibniz) who suffers terrible depredations (he catches syphilis that makes his nose drop off, is hanged, dissected, enslaved and whipped, in that order) while constantly intoning his view that 'all is for the best in the best of all possible worlds'.

One could be as sceptical of the fashionable nostrums of the Enlightenment as of the unfashionable mysteries and rituals of the Church – and many thinkers of the period were, but it did not have to lead to crippling inaction: James Boswell reports Dr Johnson arguing 'take the case of a man who is ill. I call two physicians: they differ in opinion. I am not to lie down, and die between them: I must do something.'[5]

One effect of the clash between scepticism and confidence was a split between, broadly, Anglophone thinking and Continental thinking that persists to the present. The American revolutionaries veered toward the sceptical and conservative in politics, while the French revolutionaries were characterised by confidence. As a direct result of their respective political histories, Americans even now instinctively want government kept out of affairs, while the French expect top-down solutions to social problems. Scions of the two political cultures have tended to detest each other, and still do to the present day.[6] Thomas Jefferson's *Notes on the State of Virginia*, which appears to be a factual description of the state in which he lived, was in part a riposte to the celebrated French naturalist Buffon, who had argued (not on the basis of first hand experience) that nature in the New World was inferior to that in the Old World, and that Americans were less virile than Europeans because of the dense forests and marshes in which they lived.

There was a warm but impermanent *rapprochement* after French support had helped America defeat Britain in the Revolutionary War. Jefferson was strongly committed to the ideals of the French Revolution, and is an important figure for those who stress the continuity of the American and French Revolutions. Nevertheless, the radicalism and single-minded confidence of the French Revolutionaries worried many Anglophone thinkers; even initially sympathetic figures like Wollstonecraft and Thomas Paine ultimately became troubled. In each case, their confidence in political and historical theory was shaken by real events. Historian Jonathan Israel argues that while scepticism and moderation towards theory may have been appropriate in the short term, it was the highly theoretical, confident radical theorists, not the sceptics, who furnished us with the treasured liberties of the modern age.[7]

Aspect 4: universal reason

The move away from authority meant that the individual needed the ability to find things out, and come to the right conclusions about the world. Scepticism about authority was fine, but it had no point unless something better could be found.

The 'something better' was reason, the ability to discover implicit truths from explicit evidence. A wealth of psychological theorising took place in the Enlightenment to show how people were able to deploy reason, and that in turn was an important factor in the confidence that was also characteristic of the era. Some argued that reason was a type of perception, analogous to eyesight.

Because reason was the driver, **truth** was a central value, and regarded as sovereign. One should not defer to authority until one had established to one's own satisfaction that the authority was indeed speaking truth. One should not avoid uttering or publicising truths even if they were inconvenient or dangerous. As d'Alembert put it, 'truth can hardly be too modest' and he went on to argue that the community of radical French philosophers and writers which grew up during the Enlightenment, *les philosophes*, formed a newly rational literary community.

It was also argued that reason was the same faculty in each person, which meant that the Enlightenment must be **universal** and global in scope. Indeed, for many thinkers, God, the Supreme Being, must be the ultimate deployer of reason precisely because reason was the supreme mode of thought. God's behaviour could therefore be at least partially understood even by an imperfect human, because the human could follow at least some of His reasoning. The cult of reason, both human and divine, contributed to Enlightenment optimism; many questioned or rejected the Christian doctrine of original sin, arguing that mankind was indefinitely improvable, or even perfectible, by deploying its reason effectively.

Admiration of reason was a threat to religion, especially Catholicism. The Protestant emphasis on the individual conscience could be squared with much of the more moderate Enlightenment thought, but traditional Catholic societies found their most treasured nostrums under attack. Gibbon is a good representative of the new advanced thinking, identifying the Romans' Christianity as a major factor in *The Decline and Fall of the Roman Empire.*

Aspect 5: self-interest, happiness and human nature

The rise of individualism led to a new favourable attitude towards purely personal good. The American *Declaration of Independence*, passed by Congress on 4 July 1776 and based heavily on the philosophy of Locke, enshrined in its second paragraph the 'self-evident' truth that individuals had inalienable rights to life, liberty and the **pursuit of happiness**. The philosophy of utilitarianism, whose major theorist was Jeremy Bentham, featured the promotion of happiness. **Pleasure** was no longer a vulgar pursuit, a rather lowly sort of good. It became something that people were expected to wish for, and which it was no-one's business to impede. Cultural differences still manifested themselves; a number of American thinkers visiting Paris found themselves appalled at the loose morals of the French *philosophes.*[8] Self-interest, as long as it was Enlightened, was not seen as necessarily destructive of social harmony; rather, it balanced the restraint of reason. As Pope argued,

> Two principles in human nature reign:
> Self-love, to urge, and reason, to restrain.

Philosopher David Hume went further, claiming that 'reason is, and ought only to be, the slave of the passions and can never pretend to any other office than to serve and obey them', while Rousseau painted a nuanced picture of a deeply interconnected mind:

> Whatever moralists may hold, the human understanding is greatly indebted to the passions which, it is universally allowed,

are also much indebted to the understanding. It is by the activity of the passions that our reason is improved, for we desire knowledge only because we wish to enjoy; and it is impossible to conceive any reason why a person who has neither fears nor desires should give himself the trouble of reasoning.[9]

Hume's fellow Scot Adam Smith expanded these ideas to the social and economic world, postulating that an 'invisible hand' helped a free market determine the 'correct' distribution of consumption of resources in production even while individual decisions were made on the basis of self-interest. Nevertheless, many thinkers believed that social virtues such as **benevolence** did contribute to the happiness of individuals, which helped them square the circle between individual wants and social needs.

A related idea was the importance of **nature**, particularly **human nature** taken as the common, universal part of human psychology, which was elevated above local idiosyncrasies of culture. The aim of many Enlightenment thinkers was to develop political institutions to bring out natural ways of living and thinking. Smith's markets removed obstacles to our 'natural' inclinations to trade and exchange; Rousseau was deeply opposed to most civilised societies precisely because they made us 'unnatural'. The cult of the 'noble savage' arose on the theory that 'uncivilised' men were closer to their genuine natures (any unfortunate warlike behaviour on their part was often put down paradoxically to the 'natural' inferiority of dark-skinned peoples[10]). Reason and experiment would help us discover the truths about both physical and human nature and their mutual influences; thinkers such as Montesquieu and artists such as the French novelist Crèvecoeur believed that human nature and consequently society were shaped by physical and social surroundings.

Aspect 6: attitudes of an educated minority

The noble savage, however, did not get it all his own way. For instance, although the philosopher and mathematician Condorcet pointed out that 'our trade monopolies, our treachery, our murderous contempt for men of another colour or creed, the insolence of our usurpations, the intrigues … of our priests, have destroyed the respect and goodwill that the superiority of our knowledge and the benefits of our commerce at first won for us in the eyes of the inhabitants,' he still hoped that 'the European population in [New World] colonies [will] either civilise or peacefully remove the savage nations who still inhabit … its land.'

Gibbon, like many Enlightened thinkers, disapproved and despaired of unorganised, charismatic religion, opining that 'the monastic saints, who excite only the contempt and pity of a philosopher, were respected and almost adored by the prince and people'. The 'extravagant' tales of miracles displayed 'the fiction, without the genius of poetry [and] seriously affected the reason, the faith and the morals of the Christians'.[11] These views of Condorcet and Gibbon are symptomatic; the Enlightenment was a very **top down** movement. It was an attitude, by and large, of a highly educated minority, often wealthy and with position in society, who felt the liberating force of Enlightenment, but were also conscious (and sometimes nervous) of the 'great unthinking masses' kept in darkness, through lack of education, money or manners, or perhaps merely through not being exposed to Enlightened views. It may be, as has been argued in the case of America, that Enlightenment ideas were simply too remote from the concerns of the agrarian majority – 'on the whole, various forms of Protestant Christianity served the emotional needs of most Americans better'[12] – and the same may be true in Europe.

Enlightened thinkers did not expect their own views to triumph without a struggle, and were keen to provide the conditions where they could flourish. Hence many thinkers developed theories of education.

Sometimes, paradoxically, tolerant elitism became a *lack* of toleration of the unenlightened. The great thinkers of the time were noticeably impatient of those who failed to 'get it', and often remarked on the inferiority (remediable or otherwise) of the working poor, or women, or non-white colonised peoples. As Leonard Krieger put it, they 'were in the anomalous position of writing on behalf of the whole society and at the same time castigating large sections of it for chronic abuses – governments for their inequities, aristocracies for their gratuitous privileges, and the masses for their servility.'[13]

Having said that, the Enlightenment was a very social movement, premised on more or less good-natured conversation, argument, discussion and the voicing of opinions. In England, the disputants tended to be the bourgeois and merchant classes discussing public affairs in the coffee houses of London (one of which, famously, evolved into the insurer Lloyd's of London), or in clubs which included the Lunar Society, a dining club of industrialists and intellectuals that met in Birmingham between 1765 and 1813, including Matthew Boulton (1728–1809), Erasmus Darwin (1731–1802), Joseph Priestley, James Watt (1736–1819), Josiah Wedgwood (1730–95) and William Withering (1741–99),[14] and which was visited by Richard Arkwright and Benjamin Franklin no less. In Edinburgh, intellectuals would often get together in clubs such as the Select Society, which included Adam Smith and David Hume, or the Poker Club. In France, however, the *philosophes* congregated in the houses, or *salons*, of well-connected Parisian ladies such as Madame d'Épinay (1726–83), Sophie de Condorcet (1764–1822, wife of Condorcet), Julie de Lespinasse (1732–76) or Madame Roland (1754–93).

As a result, they were drawn from a somewhat smaller social stock.

The different social *milieux* may be connected with the fact that the revolutionary or radical aspects of the British Enlightenment were muted (though not absent), while the French were much more inclined to 'think the unthinkable.' Gertrude Himmelfarb, for example, has argued that the British Enlightenment promoted the social aspects of virtue, while the French were much more interested in what she calls 'the ideology of reason.'[15] Certainly the more top down Enlightenment societies tended to produce more radical thinking.

Nevertheless, all across the Enlightened world people with no official status came together to talk of public affairs, to create what we now call the sphere of public opinion. This is central to our lives nowadays, but it was an innovation of the time, and helped revolutionise politics. It was this space that the *philosophes* filled – in England the coffee houses, in France the salons, in Scotland the societies of learned men. Journals developed to carry the debates, and branched out into periodicals such as *The Spectator* or *The Rambler*, or early versions of newspapers. Commerce, justice, philosophy, science were all discussed, as well as the high politics and diplomacy of the day. This arena was public, in so far as one was not concealed from one's fellows, yet private in so far as one could not be held to account for what one said. The importance of public opinion both for democracy and for fostering the revolutionary forces of the age cannot be overstated.[16]

The public arena changed politics in a number of ways. Public opinion acted as a counterweight to decisions or debates at court, and implicitly addressed the interests of a wider class of people. Rent-seeking by ruling classes, widespread in the seventeenth century, came under attack from the public who felt they would benefit from, for instance, fewer wars, or lower tariffs. By giving voice to the bourgeois classes, it automatically put them on the political radar even though they were often nominally powerless, and this gave immediacy to the debates on government legitimacy which carried on throughout the Enlightenment (see chapter six). Furthermore, since the public in this sense was relatively wealthy and educated, there could be no objection that 'the mob' was being brought into politics. It took many decades before the majority of people could take their place as part of public opinion – the development of the public sphere was an important step towards democracy, but it was only one step, and the direction of influence was still mainly top down.

This top down aspect also meant that Enlightened thinkers were often self-consciously one or two steps ahead of reactionary governments and princes, and consequently were rarely secure, especially in dictatorships. They developed circumlocutions for their more radical thoughts, and relied heavily on **irony**, often saying the precise opposite of what they really intended to say. Voltaire was the master of this, but see also Gibbon's apparent criticism of the heretical Bishop Demophilus (Damophilus) of Constantinople, which conveys only admiration.[17]

The social context

One final point to be made particularly with respect to the sixth aspect of the Enlightenment (though it is relevant to any discussion of the Enlightenment couched as the process of transmission of a set of ideas) is that ideas have contexts which are often more explanatory of their spread or otherwise than their intellectual force. The history of ideas can look like a list of great men, women and books, and indeed in this Beginner's Guide it is appropriate to focus on the names, ideas and works with which the reader will hope to become familiar. However, it does not follow from this that the great do their work in a vacuum, that ideas are transmitted by sheer intellectual force alone, or that other more humble processes do not have a part to play.

American historian Robert Darnton has been at the forefront of the movement to uncover the unconventional and irredeemably social aspects of intellectual history, aiming to incorporate the spread of not only books but 'unofficial' communications ranging from rumours and jokes to pamphlets and wills, as well as the actual working practices of contemporary publishers. The result is an understanding of the wider culture of communication within which the intellectual debates discussed in introductory books like this one take place.

This work has been extremely important and influential, and is one reason why the aspects of Enlightenment discussed above are not entirely philosophical, but also incorporate more generally diffused attitudes (e.g. scepticism) or social structures (e.g. the Enlightenment as a 'top down' phenomenon). Nevertheless, when we are looking at ideas, it is important to focus on their content as much as their context, and also to remember that context includes the disputes and controversies that help define and refine ideas. These are what the *philosophes* actually believed were important, of course. Furthermore, whereas the clash of ideas in open debate is at least visible and traceable, the undercurrents of the wider communication culture – though clearly relevant – are dogged with uncertainty and even invisibility.

Hence in this book, there will be a concentration on ideas and intellectual debate, but it should not be forgotten that there are powerful, if not fully understood, social undercurrents. Accordingly, I will end this chapter with a brief discussion of one publishing project as much social as intellectual, whose influence was as much to do with the philosophy *behind* it as the philosophy and ideas contained *within* it.

The quintessence of Enlightenment: *L'Encyclopédie*

How did the Enlightenment work? The 'Enlightenment' metaphor (in French, *Siècle des lumières*, in German, *Aufklärung*) was meant to be taken seriously. The thinkers of the Enlightenment did claim to have brought light where previously there was darkness and replaced mystery with clarity. Knowledge should not be hoarded, but rather shared. It was a public good, not a private possession. This was perhaps the most revolutionary idea that issued from the Enlightenment – one fundamental to the organisation of Western democracies today.

With that thought in mind, a notable development was the encyclopaedia, the history of which shows an amalgam of subversive intention, commercial possibility, respect for the individual reader and faith in the progress of science and knowledge, which between them cover the breadth of Enlightenment myth and reality. An encyclopaedia brings together information from a number of sources, and presents it in a clear way; it also aims for universality, in that, though one is not expected to read it cover to cover, all that one needs to know is contained therein. Encyclopaedias had existed for a long time, but those of the Enlightenment altered the model to increase accessibility. The languages they were written in changed from Latin to the vernaculars used by the increasingly prosperous and influential middle classes. Publication was often via several volumes, on the subscription model, so that the outlay would be spread over a manageable period of time. And the trend was for short articles organised alphabetically, rather than longer articles organised thematically (which made individual pieces of information harder to find, demanded greater commitment from the reader, and negated the modern ideal of the encyclopaedia as 'ready reference'). The alphabetical arrangement of short articles also made updating possible – supplemental volumes often followed completion of eighteenth century encyclopaedias – which implicitly supported Francis Bacon's view of science as an open-ended activity, rejecting the idea of the mere preservation and curation of a pre-existing 'complete' body of knowledge.

There were many great examples of Encyclopaedic writing, by individuals and by collaborating groups. Ephraim Chambers (c1680–1740) created his 'universal dictionary' or *Cyclopaedia* in 1728 (two volumes), which wrestled with hypertextual problems by ordering the articles alphabetically while pioneering the use of cross-reference and showing how all knowledge could be classified into a hierarchy of forty-seven disciplines. The oldest English-language encyclopaedia currently in print, the *Encyclopædia Britannica* (1768–71, three volumes) appeared at this time, edited in Edinburgh by William Smellie (1740–95). More specialised publications followed. Buffon became a revered celebrity with his *Natural History of Animals, Vegetables and Minerals* (1749–78, thirty-six volumes), which classified the biological world minutely, with an eye to geographical influences, while Johnson's *Dictionary* (1755) was not superseded until the publication of the *Oxford English Dictionary* over a century later.

For some encyclopaedists, ideology counted for more than the spread of knowledge, and the movement was used as a kind of Trojan horse to smuggle in articles with more political spice. Bayle's *Historical and Critical Dictionary* (1697) looked at ideas and their originators, and deliberately cultivated a measured evaluation to show the value of tolerance. Almost the whole work was sceptical of its subject matter, but Bayle was able to use the encyclopaedia format to hide subversive thoughts away in footnotes. Meanwhile, Voltaire's *Philosophical Dictionary* (1764) remains an essential and entertaining read. Organised largely around religious and philosophical concepts, it is basically a series of short discursions on toleration and justice. Its title should certainly not be taken literally – for instance, the section on 'Chinese catechism' is an essay in dialogue form about the relationship between ethics and religion, and mentions Chinese catechism precisely zero times. For Voltaire, the encyclopaedic form was heaven-sent – he was able to publish a number of his shorter pieces (the various editions of his *Dictionary* differ substantially in content) without having to relate them to any kind of central narrative, anonymously and safely. He also used the survey form as a vehicle for his brilliant irony; for instance, the article on 'Abraham' begins by enumerating a number of mythical Asian and Arabian figures, including Abraham himself, before disingenuously reporting that fortunately, the Bible 'having manifestly been written by the holy ghost himself', we need not doubt Abraham's existence (which would have been an extremely shocking thing to do). Voltaire, without expressly stating that Abraham was a mythical character, was able to hint not so subtly that 'if we followed the methods of our modern history books it would be quite hard to believe' in the Biblical Abraham.

Of all the encyclopaedic works of the period, the most celebrated was *L'Encyclopédie*. This appeared in Paris between 1751 and 1772, and originally had the modest intention of being a translation of Chambers' *Cyclopaedia*. But under the editorship of prominent *philosophes* Denis Diderot and d'Alembert, its scope widened. With Diderot taking the lead, twenty-eight volumes (eleven consisting entirely of illustrations) were published, followed by five supplementary volumes edited by other hands, and a two-volume index. In all over 70,000 articles were included, many by Diderot and other Enlightenment luminaries, including Voltaire, Montesquieu and Rousseau.

It fell to Diderot himself to summarise the project in the *Encyclopédie* article on 'Encyclopédie'. Such an undertaking, he claimed, could only take place in a philosophical age 'because [it] constantly demands more intellectual daring than is commonly found'. The aim of setting out the total state of current knowledge is revolutionary, for two reasons. First, everything has to be debated and examined, and vested interests have to be challenged; the duty of an encyclopaedia editor is to leave nothing unexamined. And secondly, an encyclopaedia puts everything on show. Those who benefit from the scarcity of knowledge would prefer an encyclopaedia to be 'an enormous manuscript ... carefully locked up in the king's library, inaccessible to all other eyes but his'. Surely, they would say, France's superiority over other nations depends on its monopoly of knowledge about industry and the arts. Surely, rather than enlightening foreigners, it would be better to keep them in darkness, or even to reduce other nations to barbarity. To this rhetorical question, Diderot replies that it is one's duty as a member of the human race to spread Enlightenment everywhere, if the word 'humanity' is to have meaning. He believed, but did not feel bold enough to add, that the spread of knowledge would help drive out superstition and prejudice. For instance, in *L'Encyclopédie*'s 'figurative system of human knowledge' (a hierarchical scheme analogous to that of Chambers), religion appeared as a mere branch of philosophy (and therefore subject to reason) on the same level as black magic and divination.

L'Encyclopédie was banned by the authorities after the first seven volumes. But we have already remarked on the strange, hypocritical world of 'keeping up appearances' in monarchical France. Thus, the government of the ineffectual Louis XV banned *L'Encyclopédie* in order to please the church, but did not enforce the ban in order to please his mistress Madame de Pompadour. This may also have pleased Diderot, but he was not so pleased by his publisher, who, feeling threatened, cut a number of the more radical passages.

It is a matter of controversy as to how revolutionary the encyclopaedists believed themselves to be, but a matter of record that *L'Encyclopédie* contributed substantially to the revolutionary dynamic in eighteenth century France (Robespierre called it 'the introductory chapter of the revolution'). The writers were a diverse group of experts and polymaths, but the existence of *L'Encyclopédie* immediately set up an alternative moment of authority against the government and the Catholic Church.[18]

The whole point of the Enlightenment was that spreading knowledge would shake the foundations of what became disparagingly known as the *Ancien Régime* – and *L'Encyclopédie* shows that to be absolutely and definitively true. But the foundations shook at different rates, and in different places; in the next two chapters, we will look at the Enlightenment's development through time and space.

2

The genesis and progress of the Enlightenment

The duration of the Enlightenment

The aspects of Enlightenment which were sketched in the previous chapter could all be felt over long periods of time at various strengths, which makes it impossible to locate the Enlightenment in time exactly. Consequently, there are many different opinions about its duration. Leonard Krieger begins his historical survey in 1689 and Gertrude Himmelfarb in 1700 while Norman Hampson begins his account in 1715. Roy Porter argues that in England at least, the attitudes characteristic of the Enlightenment were detectable about 1660, while Christopher Hill finds them as early as the late sixteenth century. Theodor Adorno and Max Horkheimer begin their classic critique of the Enlightenment with a discussion of Francis Bacon. Maurice Cranston dates the key 'moment in history' as the publication of Montesquieu's *Persian Letters* (1721). Jonathan Israel looks at the rise of radicalism in Holland from around 1650, after which 'everything, no matter how fundamental or deeply rooted, was questioned in the light of philosophical reason'.[1] Most are agreed that the French Revolution marks the end – but does that mean the fall of the Bastille (1789), the Terror (1793), the *coup* of 18 *Brumaire* (1799), or the final defeat of Napoleon at Waterloo (1815)? In some parts of the world the Enlightenment was only beginning at this time. In South

America, the Venezuelan liberator Simón Bolívar (1783–1830), leader of the struggle for independence from Spain, was versed in Voltaire, Locke and Adam Smith – a revolutionary on the conservative American model rather than the ideological French model. Yet his political career began when he returned to Latin America from Europe in 1807, well after decline had set in in the Enlightenment's homeland.[2]

Judgements as to its duration vary depending on what different writers want to prove. French chauvinists tend to mark the beginning later, after the unenlightened reign of Louis XIV and the first works of Montesquieu when the intellectual and political momentum moved to France. Those who wish to emphasise the radical ideas underlying it like to move the date earlier, to include the progressive Dutch thinkers such as Spinoza. The more conservatively inclined, as well as British and American commentators, tend to go for a date in the middle. My inclination is to follow suit, as the emerging Enlightenment consciousness seems to have been galvanised by the boost it received from Newton, Locke and the Glorious Revolution.

The ideas that grew into 'the Enlightenment' were already nascent in European thought, but they spread when they were seen to be practical. Key to that were an event, and a publication. The publication was Isaac Newton's *Principia*, in which it was argued that the description of all motion, no matter how complex, could be reduced to applications of three universal laws (see chapter seven). This triumph of reason over complexity appeared in 1687, although it took a short time for its value to be registered. I take my starting point therefore to be the event that appeared to show that reason could triumph in politics, and that history could be steered in a forward direction, the Glorious Revolution in England of 1688, which ended the long argument about whether monarchs of England had a divine right to rule, and resulted in the replacement of inept would-be autocrat James II by a regime responsive to a wider range of interests headed by the Dutch William III. To end the period, I nominate the French Revolution, which began in 1789. Quite apart from the nice symmetry of the Enlightenment beginning and ending in revolution, it was, as I shall argue, the French Revolution that showed how reason could fail, and that history conditioned by reason need not result in progress.

The development of the Enlightenment

In chapter one we characterised the Enlightenment in six aspects:

1. A reliance upon the natural faculties of the individual to understand the world, society and our fellow man, at the expense of tradition, authority or (Biblical) revelation.
2. An increasing confidence about human control of the world, optimism about progress and a belief in the providence of a reasonable and benevolent God.
3. Scepticism, including scepticism about (1) and (2) above.
4. The importance of reason, of universal principles over local ones and of truth as a value.
5. A focus on personal goods such as happiness and Enlightened self-interest, based on theories of human nature.
6. A focus on the beliefs of the highly educated minority.

These are characteristic of the Age of Enlightenment, but of course at different times, in different places, they varied in intensity and perceived importance. For instance, Norman Hampson argues that early in the period the intellectual can-do optimism of Locke and Newton prevailed, but by the mid-century a more negative scepticism had taken over.[3] On the other hand, Jonathan Israel argues that the moderate Enlightenment is a betrayal of the early radicalism developed by a coterie of thinkers in Holland influenced by Spinoza; Locke was the chief culprit.[4] Thirst for change accelerated through the eighteenth century, especially after the success of the American Revolution, and the two developments were not merely coincidental. The importance of scepticism grew as the desire for change outstripped the understanding of technocrats and the grounds for optimism. What had begun as a drive to modernise society and government morphed into a hardened ideological rejection of the past.

We can, then, discern three broad phases of the Enlightenment, during which the six themes varied in importance.

1. An early phase, from about 1688 to round about 1740 or 1750 when optimism was at it height. Aspects (1), (2) and (4) predominated, (3) and (5) were also present. This was a period dominated politically by traditional forms of government, monarchies and aristocracies, where the Churches remained strong and the Enlightenment spirit was concentrated in the middle classes.
2. A middle phase, from about 1750 to shortly after the American Revolution, where reaction began to set in, and scepticism spread to the tools of the Enlightenment itself, as well as earlier periods. An important event prompting this development was a major earthquake in Lisbon, indicative of a number of issues to do with the implementation of Enlightened thought, which I will discuss in more detail in the next chapter. Aspects (3) and (5) began to predominate. In particular, (2) began to decline. This middle phase may have been kicked off by a revival of religious enthusiasm detectable across a series of nations, and by a growing perception that the legacy of Locke and Newton was ossifying into a complacent rationalism. Politically, things changed, as the spirit of the age began to be absorbed by the

ruling classes, and experiments in government took place, often with the autocratic support of Enlightened despots such as Frederick of Prussia, Catherine of Russia and Joseph of Austria.

3. A final phase, from about 1780 on, when (2) was reborn as an ideological desire for change and (4) also reappeared. With the growth of democratisation, (6) became less marked. The American Revolution recharged the Enlightenment, before its climactic end in the French Revolution.

While I look at the Enlightenment thematically, rather than tracing its development through time, the fluctuating context of individual contributions ought always to be borne in mind. Ideas have different levels of acceptability and purchase in different societies at different stages in their history resulting in an uneven distribution, which we will briefly review in the next chapter.

3
Enlightenments?

The Enlightenment did not spread uniformly through space and time. Different societies responded differently, and at different rates, while many of the major thinkers moved, or were moved, between countries. Those nations with strong traditions of liberty, such as the Netherlands and England, found themselves playing host to exiled geniuses whose own societies were too hot for them. Meanwhile, some individual monarchs, particularly Frederick the Great of Prussia and Catherine the Great of Russia, were enthusiastically Enlightened and enjoyed the company of the most advanced thinkers.

Nevertheless, as Israel has cogently argued, it is a mistake to focus too much on the diversity, and to ignore what he calls 'core intellectual issues'.[1] Divisions into national, cultural or religious types of Enlightenment are misleading, and yet easy enough to make in a movement that was spread over several nations and through a century or more of intellectual, political and social activity.

Only the most active men of letters would have had up-to-the-minute understanding of all the debates, but equally, when we consider the size of sales of the major works of the Enlightenment (there were eight editions of *Candide* in 1759 alone, and the first English translation appeared within six weeks and sold 6,000 copies; even a work as expensive as the *Encyclopédie* had 4,000 subscribers) it is clear that a sizeable public would have known of the arguments, even if not from the most up to date perspective.[2]

Geographically, the Enlightenment emerged from a rough triangle marked out by London, Paris and Amsterdam. The speed of its spread depended on social conditions, communications between the periphery and the centre, the different attitudes of governments and literate publics, religion – and even on chance: the American Enlightenment was kick-started when a gift of books including works by Newton and Locke arrived at Yale University in 1714.[3]

The Enlightenment was European in origin, but if any single nation could reasonably be said to be its crucible, it has to be England.[4] Many of the key early thinkers were English, including Bacon, Hobbes, Newton and Locke. The revolution of 1688 showed that political change could be progressive. The relative freedom of English society meant that intellectual life was keen and rewarding, and many major Enlightenment philosophers including Montesquieu, Voltaire and Diderot were great admirers of at least some aspects of English thought and political life. During the eighteenth century, more great thinkers appeared, and the English were masters of the new form of literature, the novel.

Whether it is football, cricket, the car industry or Enlightenment, the English are great at innovation, less good at implementation. England was changed but not transformed by Enlightened thinking. The 1688 settlement, the strong tradition of liberty and the relative political weakness of the court meant that speculation and debate could not be restrained by the centre. Its place as a trading nation meant that many Enlightenment nostrums were absorbed in that lively commercial life which prompted so much theorising of property, trade and tolerance. Many great English thinkers were associated with practical developments; for instance Joseph Priestley and Richard Arkwright.

Liveliness was one thing, destructive instability quite another. We can see how chaotic life could be from novels such as Defoe's *Moll Flanders* or Henry Fielding's *Tom Jones*, but few wanted to overturn the social order. The English were determinedly prosaic during the century; their poetry was clear, language growing more uniform, architecture 'solid, proportional according to the rules, masculine and unaffected',[5] painting was either elegant (Sir Joshua Reynolds, Thomas Gainsborough), or lusty and populist (William Hogarth), musical talent was imported. The periodical essayists Joseph Addison and Sir Richard Steele were responsible, in their development of the journalistic craft, for ensuring that men of letters were men of the world. They also implicitly defined the ideal life and manners of a civilised man. The same point was made negatively by the 3rd Earl of Shaftesbury, who wittily debunked the whole idea of enthusiasm.

Furthermore, the eclectic English were quite happy using Enlightened methods and assumptions to either forestall or attack Enlightened ideas. The eighteenth century produced four great reactionary thinkers based in England (two were Irish) who flourished using Enlightened styles of thought. Jonathan Swift was an unrelenting sceptic and reactionary, but his great novels were impressively humane as well as pitilessly satirical. In *Gulliver's Travels*, his famous metaphor for the pointlessness of the religious conflict of the preceding century was the war between the miniature people of Lilliput and Blefuscu about which way up they should eat their eggs, while the windy philosophising of the Enlightenment was lampooned as the Academy of Laputa, where brilliant arts and sciences had no practical value whatever. Edmund Burke supported the American Revolution, but outraged his Whig colleagues with his brilliant deconstruction of the events in France. Demographer Thomas Malthus predicted impossible pressures on food supplies as populations grew – though he fully accepted that it was the successes of political, scientific and agricultural reforms that made the population grow in the first place. Samuel Johnson, essayist, critic and lexicographer, dominated Enlightened society, helped standardise the English language, and used highly Enlightened methods and vocabulary to argue for very traditional High Tory beliefs.

On the other hand England's greatest revolutionary thinker Thomas Paine found his homeland very uncongenial – he was ignored rather than oppressed and few listened to his message for better pay and working conditions. He emigrated, and was able to take part in both the American and French Revolutions, narrowly avoiding execution in the latter (his enemy Robespierre was executed first). Though his life was neither happy nor successful, there is no doubt that his influence on figures such as Thomas Jefferson and Benjamin Franklin would have been far less had he remained on the quarrelsome and conservative English scene. Other British thinkers who wished to challenge accepted wisdom, and who found a period of residence abroad helpful, included Gibbon (Lausanne) and Hume (Paris).

If we look to England for the origins of the Enlightenment, it is to France that we go for its pioneering edge; perhaps the moment when the baton was passed was the publication in Paris of Voltaire's admiring paean *The English Letters* (1734). A brilliant class of *philosophes* emerged in the salons of aristocratic Parisian ladies, who brought together thinkers, writers and artists to discuss philosophy and foment revolutionary thoughts. French society in the monarchical period was much less functional than England's, and managed to be both top-heavy (there were many aristocrats, and the monarch lived an extravagant life in the palaces of Versailles and the Louvre), and grossly unequal. The doctrine that evolved from the *salons* was much more radical than the cautious commercial chit-chat that emanated from the English coffee houses, perhaps because it was correspondingly further removed from what we might call 'ordinary life'. It was wide-ranging, involving many fields of thought including science, aesthetics, morality and theology, but it was at bottom political. Theories of equality, liberty and of the legitimacy of the ruler abounded. As Krieger notes, the shift in the Enlightenment's centre of gravity from London to Paris meant a move from English relativism to French certainties, which travelled better and could be encoded in simpler messages and slogans. Israel has similarly argued that the radical element of Enlightenment, more closely associated with France, was easier to defend, communicate and implement because it wasn't hedged around with compromises in the way that more moderate ideas were.[6]

Les philosophes, for many, define the Enlightenment. Thinkers such as Voltaire, Montesquieu, Diderot, Rousseau, Condorcet and d'Alembert are paradigm cases of the Enlightenment intellectual, while some of the more advanced British thinkers such as Hume and Gibbon were successes in Paris. Style was almost as important as content – whereas English prose of the period tended towards plainness and simplicity, the French applauded wit and cleverness. *Les philosophes* in general, Voltaire in particular, made philosophy fashionable, and the relatively low-born man or woman could be accepted in the best houses in Paris as long as he or she was suitably brilliant. Nevertheless *les philosophes* often looked explicitly to England for inspiration – in politics, both Voltaire and Montesquieu studied the English constitution and took it as the basis of their political theories. A sceptical Englishman might question the value of theory when two such great men, thinking about the same set of social arrangements, could come to two opposite conclusions.

The American Enlightenment was marked by conservatism, though as in France it ended in revolution.[7] Enlightenment forces coexisted with two other major influences on opinion. First, pre-revolutionary America was a British colony. Colonial societies often breed resentment against the colonisers for obvious reasons, but in America the colonials were recent imports and the native Americans were denied a voice. This led to a somewhat schizophrenic attitude, where colonial Americans looked to England for a cultural lead, while being conscious and proud of differences. And secondly many of the colonists had arrived from a protestant/puritan background, which meant that the Enlightenment had to make a settlement with protestant thought. Political scepticism was common, with many writers doubtful about the ability of government to solve problems, but the religious scepticism that was marked in Britain and France was almost absent in America (Benjamin Franklin being an exception) outside the slave owning states, although sceptical writers such as Hume, Gibbon and Voltaire were well-known and their clear and readable prose admired. A rational, Enlightened, yet still religious establishment centred on Harvard and Boston was countered by more intuitive religionists elsewhere. Even now, Massachusetts is regarded as one of the more liberal states, and the East coast is trying to rebuff further waves of anti-rationalist arguments staking the claims of religion against science.[8]

Only in the revolutionary era did America's lasting contribution to Enlightenment materialise. Revolution was a response to English misrule and European inegalitarian monarchism, an attempt to restore liberties (rather than, as in France, create them anew). In the post-revolutionary age, the combined brainpower of the founding fathers used reason to provide a firm basis for the society that was already in place, rather than to explore new possibilities of social interaction and politics. Great men wrestled with great political issues, and figures such as Jefferson and Franklin, and works such as the *Declaration of Independence* and the *Federalist Papers* (by Alexander Hamilton, James Madison and John Jay) remain salient to the present day.

Much of the inspiration for the Americans came from Scotland, where an Enlightenment somewhat different in form from the English variety built up slowly through the eighteenth century. Scotland would appear to be a highly unpromising cradle of Enlightenment, a dour, cold, theocratic place with a stern and unforgiving religious tradition, but the two fierce campaigners whose Reformation established Calvinism in Scotland had done important groundwork. John Knox (1510–72) had called for a national system of education, while long before Locke had had the idea George Buchanan (1506–82) had argued that political legitimacy stemmed from the people. The Presbyterian Church was organised, as a result, on highly democratic principles. Furthermore, the inept seventeenth century Stuart kings had instilled the spirit of independence and rebellion in the Scots. In the lowlands a politically aware and independent-minded people, however intolerant its church, would be able to exploit Enlightenment thought in its own way. Knox's educational ideas were enshrined in the Act for Setting Schools of 1696, which established a school in every parish in Scotland, which meant that by the time the Enlightenment had matured, Scotland was the most literate and numerate nation in Europe. Perhaps because of this, the Scottish Enlightenment was concerned less with changing the world, and more with understanding and classifying it.

Scotland joined with England and Wales to form Great Britain in 1707, and there was a great deal of commerce between Edinburgh and London, but the Scots nevertheless retained their own identity. Scottish thinkers were serious about improving society through the application of reasoning, and were markedly less sceptical (with the notable exception of David Hume) than their English counterparts, but in their empiricism and practicality they also differed from *les philosophes*. Their contribution to the advancement of science and the developments that led to the industrial revolution was enormous. The Scots were a vital inspiration for the Americans via the privileging and theorising of 'common sense', especially in the work of philosopher Thomas Reid. Common sense, it was argued, was a more reliable guide than clever philosophical use of paradox and sophistry. After all, even the philosopher who claimed to doubt the existence of the carriage galloping towards him would seek to avoid falling under its hypothetical wheels.[9]

The Netherlands (or United Provinces) had fought its way to independence from the Spanish Habsburg dominions in 1581, and so was still, at the beginning of our period, a relatively new state, yet it was particularly important as a crucible for the Enlightenment. Without natural resources, and under severe diplomatic and political pressure after its struggle for liberation, good government was essential for the fledgling state. It survived on trade and prosperity, which required liberty that was in turn exploited by many who fled their own countries to live, work and publish there. Holland became the centre of the European publishing trade. Descartes, Locke and Bayle were only the most famous of those who preferred freedom and exile, while an even longer list, including Voltaire, Montesquieu and Rousseau, felt it expedient to publish works there – ironically, Holland's one real home-grown genius, Spinoza, had work banned and distributed in secret, and attracted no significant Dutch following.

But Holland was generally speaking an environment for rather than a first-order contributor to Enlightenment. As early as 1730, the republic was losing confidence in its superior position; economic crises, natural disasters and a perceived loss of moral leadership made the Dutch turn in on themselves, and play less of a role in wider European movements. Indeed, a popular point of view was that the adoption of 'French' manners had sapped Dutch virtue, and the country turned conservative, hoping to reinvigorate its commercial culture.[10]

These were the main centres of Enlightenment, but other countries took part. Germany produced a number of leading figures, including Kant, Goethe and the Bach family, but was politically fragmented (the smallness and pettiness of Germany's independent statelets is satirised in Voltaire's description of the domain of Baron Thunder-ten-Tronckh in *Candide*), and having been terribly ravaged by the Thirty Years' War (1618–48) took decades to recover. Frederick the Great of Prussia was perhaps the most Enlightened of all the Enlightened despots, but he also suppressed German culture, which was just beginning to emerge, artificially promoting French literature, music, philosophy and manners. The move from Enlightenment to Romanticism received a strong push from Germany, with Goethe as a literary pioneer and Kant a leading influence on nineteenth century philosophy. Two important monarchs, Empress Maria Theresa and Emperor Joseph II, ruled the ragbag Austrian empire from Vienna, and they adopted the principles of the Enlightenment enthusiastically as a method of imposing some kind of order on their heterogeneous lands. They were keener on the modernising aspects of the Enlightenment than its scepticism, and their chief opposition came from a highly conservative nobility in Hungary, Central Europe and the Balkans. The Austrian contribution to music, through Haydn and Mozart, was most important.

In Eastern Europe, only French-speaking aristocrats were able to appreciate the new philosophy – few works were translated into Eastern vernaculars. Catherine the Great of Russia was a keen follower of trends, inviting Diderot to stay in her court and buying Voltaire's library after his death, while Stanisław II of Poland and Lithuania (r.1764–95, d.1798) modernised his country – until Enlightened Catherine, in cooperation with the Targowica Federation of conservative Polish nobles who disapproved of Stanisław's redrawing of the constitution, partitioned the Polish-Lithuanian commonwealth of 1795, deposing Stanisław, whose fate was virtual imprisonment and death in St Petersburg.

Italy's, Spain's and Portugal's contributions to the Enlightenment were patchy. In Italy, French culture predominated, against a flowering of local folk arts, while the undoubted glories of the classical and Renaissance civilisations, there for all to see, were equally obviously dead and arguably superseded by the modern learning. Nevertheless there were important thinkers, including the historical theorist Giambattista Vico (whose work was unrecognised at the time) and the penologist Cesare Beccaria. In Spain the higher echelons of society were sympathetic to its aims, and Charles III (King of Naples and Sicily 1735–59, of Spain 1759–88) in particular was a reforming, if untalented, king. But the deep-seated opposition of the Catholic Church, and the intellectually moribund state of the capital Madrid meant that momentum for modernisation and reform never built up.

Portugal is a different case entirely, a peripheral presence until 1755, when a random event pitched it into the forefront of the consciousness of the age.

Watershed: the Lisbon Earthquake

The Lisbon Earthquake soured the age's optimism, undermined belief in providence, produced a fine example of a benevolent despot, showed why benevolent despotism is not enough for progress and for good measure inspired the Enlightenment's most famous work of literature.

Portugal, like Spain, was labouring under two great handicaps in the first half of the century. It was fiercely religious, with a militant Catholic hierarchy which disdained the new learning and censored study of mathematics, philosophy, logic and the sciences; the curriculum at the prestigious University of Coimbra was based around canon law, civil law, theology and medicine. And secondly, its ideology of nobility preferred rent-seeking to the contributions that commerce and business could make to society. The important thing was to be a gentleman, versed in the arts of warfare, not tainted by trade.

Appearances were deceptive thanks to the institutionalised theft and greed of empire. An earlier, somewhat more entrepreneurial, generation of Portuguese had been explorers and travellers, creating a great trading empire upon which the home society lived parasitically. Gold had been discovered in Brazil in the 1690s, and Portugal was active in the slave trade, but the fruits of all this were not distributed widely – poverty and ignorance were widespread, and the expropriated raw materials were usually re-exported across Europe, where artisans in other more active societies (Dutch diamond cutters, Italian goldsmiths) added value. The king of Portugal, meanwhile, took twenty per cent of all precious imports.

On 1 November 1755, a massive earthquake shook the Eastern Atlantic, hitting Lisbon badly. Three shocks flattened many buildings; then smouldering fires and candles set off an inferno; finally a giant tsunami destroyed much of the waterfront. The casualty rate is not known, but a reasonable estimate is 25,000 people killed, about ten per cent of the population. The Catholic establishment blamed the disaster on the sinfulness of the people – but this was one of the most religious places in Europe, the quake happened at 9.30 a.m. on All Saints' Day, and many people were killed as they crowded into their churches. The red light district, in contrast, was untouched.

One of Portugal's few Enlightened figures, an official called Carvalho, took charge in the administrative vacuum, bullying the hapless King José I into giving him *carte blanche* to remodel the capital in the teeth of Catholic opposition. A city planned on Enlightenment principles and aesthetics grew up slowly, while Carvalho took the opportunity of his emergency powers to wage war on the religious opposition. Single-handedly, now ennobled as the Marquis of Pombal, he dragged Portugal into the eighteenth century.

The Lisbon earthquake was famous for decades, and helped shape the Enlightenment in a number of ways (in its cultural effect it has been compared to the Hiroshima bomb[11]). In the first place, it undermined the legitimacy of the Catholic Church. The dreadful response of the Portuguese churchmen – they actively blocked and mocked the rebuilding effort – enabled Pombal to marginalise them. The Church did not have a coherent response to obvious questions. Why had the quake trapped so many in churches? Why did it take place on an important religious festival? Why didn't it affect bustling, commercial London or heretical Amsterdam? The most plausible explanations were natural – this was a natural disaster, without malice, direction or purpose.

Secondly, it also shook the confidence of many Enlightenment thinkers in providence and the essential goodness of God. Could it really be argued in the face of the terrible suffering in Lisbon that the deity was moral, just and logical? The earthquake undermined faith in a rational God, and precipitated a backlash against Enlightened optimism. Some, such as Rousseau, were prepared to question whether a good God would be inclined to forgive human folly: 'Should it be ... that in order to interdict an earthquake, we have only to build a city there?' The definitive Enlightenment response, though, was Voltaire's *Candide* (some scenes of which are set in the earthquake) which entirely repudiated optimism and providence.

Thirdly, the post-quake events undermined the theory of Enlightened absolutism. The Voltairean (and, later, Kantian) idea that a suitably determined and Enlightened monarch could best implement Enlightened ideas was taken up by Pombal, who quickly became King José's most important minister. Almost single-handedly, he turned Portugal into a more tolerant place, supported industry and education, created several liberal reforms, such as the abolition of slavery (in Portugal only, not in the colonies where it was a mainstay of the economy), the elimination of legal restrictions on converted Jews, and the promotion of equality of the citizenry before the law.

There is no doubt that life in Portugal improved. But the conduit for Pombal's power was the King himself, and government was not restructured around liberal constitutional principles such as those described by Locke and Montesquieu. Pombal turned a cack-handed attempt on the King's life into an excuse to torture and execute his powerful enemies. The Enlightenment had not been institutionalised, and when the King died his heir Queen Maria I (r.1777–1816), about as reactionary as it was possible to be (she was known successively as Maria the Pious and Maria the Mad), undid most of Pombal's reforms. Absolutism could only work if all monarchs were Enlightened. The accidents of dynastic succession could not be the basis of an Enlightened world. Enlightenment could go backwards as well as forwards.[12]

The Portuguese episode in particular demonstrates the close links between the fates of ideas, institutions and informal social structures. Bearing this in mind, we will now move on to look at the ideas themselves, beginning with the intellectual context inherited from the seventeenth century in which the Enlightenment began.

4
Glimmers of Enlightenment

Precursors

To set a date of 1688 is not to say that Enlightened attitudes came out of thin air at that time, nor that the *philosophes* and other thinkers did not explicitly recognise their intellectual antecedents. In particular, the arbitrary timeframe should not make us ignore the contributions of Francis Bacon, René Descartes, Thomas Hobbes and Baruch de Spinoza.

Francis Bacon provided an important step by expounding an experimental method for the development of knowledge. In his *Novum Organum* (1620) he advocated a practical accumulation of knowledge by collecting as large a body of observations as possible, and then tabulating and classifying them to see if any generalisations suggested themselves. This is a caricature of traditional experimental science (although Charles Darwin, for one, saw himself as a Baconian in this way), but his influence was important, for example in the formation of the Royal Society in 1660.[1] He was explicitly cited as an intellectual forerunner by d'Alembert, who enthused that 'we owe our tree of knowledge mainly to Chancellor Bacon'.

René Descartes also prefigured many of the Enlightenment's attitudes, particularly in his faith in reason. He made advances in a number of areas of thought, particularly mathematics where the Cartesian system of coordinate geometry ($x^2 + y^2 = r^2$ etc.) is a vital tool for understanding any n-dimensional space. He created the easily used notation where the square of x is written as x^2. In physics, he made important advances in optics, and discovered the law of reflection, that when light is reflected off a surface, the outgoing beam makes the same angle with the reflective surface as the reflected beam.

His best-known work was in philosophy; his *Discourse on Method* and *Meditations* remain classics – in many ways they are the first modern works of philosophy. In these works, he changed the epicentre of philosophical thought away from metaphysics – the study of the nature of reality – to epistemology – the study of how we know things. In other words, philosophy changed from uninformed speculation about life, the universe and everything, to the informed study of human thought processes. His aim was no less metaphysical; he wished to use reason to prove the existence of God, but his method was to focus on what we know. His strategy was to establish something about which we could be certain, and from that deduce God. His certain proposition was *cogito ergo sum*, 'I think, therefore I am.' If I am wondering about whether or not I exist, then I must exist, because I am that thing doing the wondering. However uncertain we might be about the world, we have to be certain about that. Simply by inference from that basic statement, Descartes deduced the existence of the whole world, and God with it. A corollary to this basic thought is that our minds and bodies are, in some sense, separate entities. We can be uncertain about the existence of our bodies, but not about some of our mental functioning (wondering whether we exist, for example). So Descartes deduced that the physical world (including our bodies) and minds were made of different kinds of 'stuff', and went further, to argue that animals were basically complex machines, made entirely of physical 'stuff', and it was possession of a mind that made humans unique amongst living things. The existence of God also entailed that minds were created already furnished by Him with innate ideas that enabled us to understand the world correctly. This mind/body distinction remains implicit in much Western thought even now, although the basic objection, noted almost immediately by critics, remains: if the mind and body are totally distinct, then how, except by some supernatural agency, does the mind influence the body at all? Descartes anticipated the objection, but his answer was unconvincing.

Descartes' focus on reason as opposed to faith as a method of assuring ourselves of the existence and goodness of God was sincerely felt, but too radical for the Catholic Church, which placed his work on the index of banned literature in 1663. Despite his religious purpose, he posed awkward questions. He privileged reason: he argued that God is good and omniscient, and that therefore if we can work something out by pure reason it must be true, because God would not have created the world so as to undermine reason. But that raises the issue of whether reason is valid independently of theology. Does $2 + 2 = 4$ because God says it must? If so, that means that God could make $2 + 2 = 5$ if it suited His purposes, and reason must be contingent and changeable – does that even make sense? If not, then it seems that God is subservient to the laws of arithmetic – and therefore not all powerful. If we can understand God through the exercise of our reason, which Descartes hoped to do, then it seems to follow that God is a slave to reason. Descartes' view of God dehumanised Him – rather than the jealous, feeling God of the Bible, Descartes defended Him as an abstract principle, the first cause of motion.

D'Alembert, in applauding 'the illustrious Descartes' as another precursor of the Enlightenment thundered that 'in spite of all the sagacity he employed to prove the existence of God, he was accused of denying it by clergymen who perhaps did not have any faith at all'. He was impressed at his achievements in 'shak[ing] off the yoke of scholasticism, public opinion, and authority; in a word, certain prejudices and barbaric attitudes'. D'Alembert noted the double-edged nature of Descartes' sceptical approach, but remained admiring: 'If he finally believed that he had explained everything, at least he began by doubting everything; and the arms that we use to combat him do not belong to him any the less because we turn them against him.'

Transgressive as their philosophies were, Bacon and Descartes were soon succeeded by two more thinkers who gained even greater notoriety. The English political philosopher Thomas Hobbes was unambitious, empirical and commonsensical, while Dutch metaphysician Baruch de Spinoza carried on the Cartesian work in a more continental vein. Each was marginalised in his own time; each enormously influential.

Spinoza took the Cartesian mechanistic philosophy to a logical conclusion. He was not convinced by the division of the world into the physical and the mental, and argued instead that the universe had to be basically simple, a unity in which both thought and matter inhered. It followed that there was only one substance, which must, therefore, be God, and matter and thought – in particular, people – could therefore only be attributes of God. Everything that happened necessarily had to happen, so there were no contingent events, no free will, no miracles. Good and evil could not exist in this theory as moral absolutes.

Hobbes studied down-to-Earth politics in an age of great political upheaval in England. Perhaps no-one apart from Machiavelli has thought so clearly and deeply about the nature of power, but Hobbes went further than his predecessor's essentially Renaissance outlook in two ways. First, he did not take power as a given; it *required legitimacy*, and needed to be balanced against the natural rights of man. The aim of much of Hobbes' thought was to try to harness power for good ends, without neutering it in a self-defeating way. And second, he attempted, like Spinoza, to be systematic. Impressed with Galileo, whom he knew, he tried to make politics into a deductive science with the certainty of geometry.

His work provided rational grounds for citizens to obey their rulers, but insisted on the establishment of the legitimacy of rule, primarily by the ruler's guaranteeing the lives of the citizens. His conclusions did not endear him to the rulers of his day, whether the Stuart monarchs of England and Scotland (who disliked the idea of popular consent) or the Parliamentarians who briefly created a republic in 1649–60 (who opposed Hobbes' continued support for absolute rule). The basic postulates of his system were mechanistic – all human actions could be explained as compositions of elementary motions of body and mind – and strongly pessimistic about human nature, arguing that an individual's power depended on how far it exceeded those of others in his society, and that the use of power necessarily hindered others.

His method began with a characterisation of the *state of nature*, a description of what life would be like without organisation, law or what we might loosely call civilisation. This became an extremely important intellectual device in the Enlightenment (see chapter six); only d'Alembert of the major *philosophes* noted that the divergence of opinions on the state of nature meant that it was not a reliable method of deriving political truths. In Hobbes' formulation, the dangers of the state of nature meant that sovereignty would be legitimised by an effective *contract* between the people who would prefer effectively organised society to the violence of nature, and so contract to create a sovereign in whom would be invested certain of their rights. The Hobbesian model moves away from the code of the warrior or the aristocrat, with overarching ideas of honour or glory.

Founders

Two thinkers contributed significantly to creating the conditions for Enlightenment. John Locke was an English philosopher whose theories of mind and politics were, and still are, enormously influential. Unlike many political philosophers he was more than a theorist – he took an active part in the 'Glorious' Revolution against King James II the success of which gave great authority to his writing. He can be credited with creating a practical, tolerant and principled politics and holding out the possibility of the end of arbitrary rule. Sir Isaac Newton needs little introduction, the English physicist and mathematician whose achievements are legendary; his theory of gravity and three laws of motion are perhaps pre-eminent, and are still the basis of modern engineering.[2] He will be discussed in more detail in chapter seven but his theories, derived from deep thinking about the nature of motion, showed that the exercise of reason could produce mastery of nature. He was idolised by his contemporaries; we might cite not only Alexander Pope's famous epitaph ('Nature and Nature's Laws lay hid in Night. / GOD said, "*Let Newton be!*" and all was Light'), but also the futuristic design for a cenotaph for Newton by the French architect Étienne-Louis Boullée (1728–99), an incredible sphere 500 feet in diameter, containing empty space and illuminated by pin-pricks in the sphere representing stars.

There were also transitional figures whose careers straddled the beginning of Enlightenment. Fontenelle was a failed poet and dramatist who nevertheless inveigled himself into French literary society and popularised the new Cartesian sciences. His *Conversations on the Plurality of Worlds* (1686) was immensely influential in undermining the authority of the Catholic church on metaphysical matters. Gottfried Leibniz was a German philosopher and polymath who followed in the tradition of Descartes and Spinoza (and indeed is often grouped with them as 'the seventeenth century rationalists'), and produced a number of important mathematical innovations (see chapter seven). Philosophically, his contribution was something of a dead end; he developed Spinoza's notion of 'substance' as we shall see in chapter five, but his theory did not gain much support. His reputation has suffered posthumously, partly because of his failure to found a philosophical school, and partly because of Voltaire's lampoon of him as Dr Pangloss.

One more preliminary figure needs to be mentioned, less of a household name than some of the others: French philosopher Pierre Bayle. Bayle was a sceptic, and, after some years of wavering Protestant faith, launched a total attack on any attempt to understand the world. His major work, *A Historical and Critical Dictionary*, is a compendium of destruction of all mankind's *hubris*. He was happy to launch into older thinkers such as Aristotle or Epicurus, but also enjoyed demolishing more recent and respected figures such as Descartes and Spinoza, and even allies, including Locke, Leibniz and Newton (who was almost untouchable). He extended scepticism deep down – whereas Descartes had been sceptical, doubting everything, in order to discover the self-evident truths that would underlie and ensure the reliability of our understanding of the world, Bayle's aim was to show that understanding was underpinned by nothing. His only response to the idea of a self-evident truth (such as 'I think, therefore I am') was to raise the possibility that something could be self-evident and yet false.[3] In this far-reaching scepticism, Bayle, though a neglected figure now, was central to the Enlightenment's *Zeitgeist*.

By 1688 a set of intellectual processes and debates were in place, ready to be harmonised and integrated to create the Enlightenment proper. The continuation of the debates, in philosophy, politics, science and religion, are the topics of the next four chapters.

5
Philosophy

The Enlightenment was a time of unfettered thought, when the power of the human mind began to be appreciated and its limits had not yet been glimpsed. Philosophy was the growth industry of the time and in this chapter we will set out some of the more important ideas, in particular in the key areas of metaphysics, knowledge and psychology. These ideas, abstract as they are, soon fed into the area of politics, where Enlightenment thought really excels; we shall move on to discuss political philosophy in chapter six.

Metaphysics

Metaphysical questions – what is the nature of the world? – were a preoccupation of the seventeenth century, and it was in this respect perhaps more than any other that Enlightenment thought drew on its antecedents. One of the major questions was that of *substance*: what is the world made of? Hobbes was an out-and-out materialist, believing that life was merely motion of the limbs, so that robots or machines could be correctly said to exhibit a type of artificial life. Descartes had similarly strong views, but held that people were important exceptions to the rule. Although animals and automata were completely subject to physics, men's souls animated their bodies, interacting through the pineal gland where the soul comes into contact with the material parts of the human. The pineal gland theory hardly withstood serious analysis and was quickly dropped by the Cartesian school, and the Cartesian picture because a *dualism* of two substances, mind and matter – formalising a position to which Western thought, influenced by Christianity, had been tending for many centuries. The philosophical problem bequeathed to the Enlightenment was how to reconcile the two – if they are different and separate, how do thoughts influence action, or actions thoughts? This has a metaphysical side (what are the causal relations between the two?) and also raises a question about knowledge (where does the mind get its information about the world from, and how can it be reliable?).

Spinoza's response to the problem, like Hobbes', was to try to reduce the two substances to one. We, and everything we see, are all aspects of the divine which is inherent in everything. But the idea that there should be just one type of thing, whether this took the form of Hobbes' materialism or Spinoza's pantheism, was ultimately unconvincing because of its failure to square with the perceived facts. In particular, everything cannot be matter, because thoughts are immaterial; but everything cannot be thought, or mind (even the mind of God), because thought has no *extension* – it does not take up space in the world.

Leibniz tried to follow the anti-dualistic logic to its bitter end in a number of works, in particular *Monadology* (representing Leibniz' thought fairly is hard, given the vast quantity of unpublished work that he left; *Monadology* was written in 1714, and published posthumously). He tried to solve the substance problem by suggesting that individual elements of substance, which he called *monads*, were basic, and had no extension. But *aggregates* of them did. Each monad was simple, had no constituent parts, was immortal and there were infinitely many of them. Aggregated, they made up objects and persons; individually, each one was a soul. Each one of us is made up of monads, and each monad is a soul; for a creature with a soul (like a person), one of these monads takes priority, and is *the* soul of the person.

It seemed to Leibniz that monads couldn't interact, because if they acted upon each other they would have to change. This was particularly problematic as it seems that knowledge of the world requires perception, which appears to require change and interaction between monads. But Leibniz insisted that, if monads were to remain simple, they needed to be *windowless*. Fortunately, thanks to God's benign nature, each monad reflects the world with a pre-established harmony. This harmony means that monads appear to perceive, but in fact are merely in tune with the wider system, in the same way that two perfectly tuned clocks may seem to influence each other (one of them strikes twelve when the other's hands both point upwards), but actually do not.

This harmony helped Leibniz deal with the problem of evil in the world. He used the pre-established harmony as a proof of the existence of God (if it wasn't God who established the harmony, what else could have?). And he went further: God could have established any old harmony, but instead, being God and good, He created a world that had the greatest excess of good over evil. He could, admittedly, have created a world with no evil, but then that would have less good – much good comes about through remedying and overcoming evil. For instance, free will is a great good, but it implies the possibility of sin. If God made sin impossible then will would not be free. This, concluded Leibniz, is therefore the best of all possible worlds – the argument that Voltaire parodied in *Candide*.

A contrary tradition, through Copernicus, Kepler, Galileo, Bacon and Newton, was the development and privileging of science. I shall discuss the Enlightened view of the natural world in chapter seven, but a couple of properties of scientific thought had a philosophical influence. Firstly, physical theory expunged almost all traces of animism from European thought. It may be, as Newton thought, that God was needed to 'kick-start' the universe, but once it was started the laws of motion meant that it could trundle on without further supernatural intervention. Natural events needed no rationalisation in terms of God's purpose – they could be explained totally in terms of their physical conditions. Science could not explain *why* things are as they are, but it could explain *how*.

Secondly, the seventeenth century witnessed a profound change in humankind's understanding of its place in the world. Copernicus discredited the idea of the Earth as the centre of the universe, and civilisation was shown to be a by-product of squabbling communities on a small planet orbiting an undistinguished star. That new sense of insignificance, expressed in works such as Swift's *Gulliver's Travels* and Voltaire's *Micromégas* (who is eight leagues tall, and from the star Sirius; he finds events on Earth extremely trivial), led, ironically, to a new confidence in the possibilities for humankind – 'as if it were of any consequence to the Being of Beings whether a few assembled bits of matter were in one place or another'.[1]

George Berkeley, Bishop of Cloyne in Ireland, resisted the removal of God from philosophy. His major philosophical works were written when he was relatively young, and he published little of note after his greatest work *The Dialogues of Hylas and Philonous* in 1713. In the dialogues, Hylas is a representative of science and common sense, while Philonous provides Berkeleyan criticisms. Berkeley delves into the relevance of the distinction between mind and matter, and although he is most usefully seen as part of the English tradition of Locke and Hume, his thinking also makes sense in the rationalist context of Descartes and Leibniz.

Berkeley's argument hinges on adopting Descartes' absolute and complete distinction between mind and matter. Something is either mental or physical, and cannot be both. Our ideas of things – say, an image of a tree – are clearly mental; this is the burden of Hylas' and Philonous' first dialogue. The tree is physical, while memories, images or perceptions of the tree are mental. From this, Berkeley concludes that we cannot infer the existence of the physical tree; indeed, we cannot infer the existence of anything in the physical world because of the separation between mind and matter. All that we know are our perceptions. Therefore existence is intimately related to being perceived; if something is not perceived by someone, then it does not exist.

This appears to lead to some bizarre corollaries. Not only would things in an empty room disappear when the door closed and magically reappear when it opened again, but the landscape seen from the window of a carriage would flit in and out of existence as it became visible and was then hidden again behind a line of trees. There are interesting questions about what is a *bona fide* perceiver: would it have to be a person that perceives, or could it be a cat? A mouse? A fly? Fortunately, there is a quick answer to the issue, which is that stability is created everywhere by the omnipresence of God. God, if no-one else, is in the empty room, and continues to perceive the objects within it even when the door is closed. Berkeley argued that the existence of God is essential for the common sense picture of reality to be maintained.

David Hume gave this line of thought his own twist in his *Treatise on Human Nature* (1739), arguing that our perceptions of reality could never tell us about what laws regulated events 'behind the scenes', as it were. If we consider a statement that events of type A cause events of type B, there is nothing we can have perceived about A and B to suggest the causal relation. All we could possibly have seen is that events of type A are followed shortly afterwards by events of type B, and on that basis have developed expectations of what will follow A, expectations that, expressed more formally, become theories of a causal connection. But our observations do not support the theories; as Hume puts it, 'we cannot penetrate into the reason of the conjunction'.[2] Our investigations into the world cannot lead us to any satisfactory knowledge that goes beyond what is present in our perceptions. The world, for Hume, is inherently unpredictable, although we as a matter of fact tend to be drawn towards good predictions, not because of our reason, but because that is how we are constituted. If we try to supply a reason for believing that B-type events follow A-type events, we shall fail. Such reasoning is called *induction*; we assume a connection between events that are closely conjoined. Hume's argument that induction was unjustified (not necessarily false) is a severe blow to our normal habits of thought. Indeed, he maintained that our reason for believing in the principle of induction was based on its having been a reliable method of reasoning in the past – in other words, the principle of induction was justified by an application of itself, and so was circular.

The Prussian philosopher Immanuel Kant wrote that Hume's presentation of the sceptical argument awakened him from his 'dogmatic slumbers', and prompted the research that led to a series of formidable works, of which the most well-known, if not the most read, is the *Critique of Pure Reason* (1781).

Kant argued that philosophers in the past had been conflating two separate distinctions. The first was a distinction between two types of knowledge which were called *a priori* and *a posteriori*. *A priori* knowledge can be discovered, or confirmed, purely by reflection; logic and arithmetic are truths of this kind. I do not need to do any experiments to show that $5 \times 17 = 85$. *A posteriori* (or empirical) truths, on the other hand, do need investigation and some sense perception for confirmation; these include ordinary everyday statements such as 'the cat is on the mat', and also scientific ones such as 'the Earth orbits the Sun'. Because of this, we can be certain of *a priori* truths, but not quite certain of *a posteriori* truths, because we can never be 100% certain of the evidence of our senses.

The second distinction is between *analytic* and *synthetic* sentences. The former are true purely by virtue of their meaning, and therefore to be judged by analysing the concepts in the sentence – so for example 'a bachelor is an unmarried man' is true, because the concept 'bachelor' is exactly the same as the concept 'unmarried man' and if you know the meaning of all the words in the sentence you automatically know that it is true. Synthetic sentences are all other types, requiring experience for understanding. Kant argued that philosophers had led themselves into error by illicitly conflating the analytic and the *a priori* on the one hand, and the synthetic and the *a posteriori* on the other.

Most of the time this was unobjectionable. But Kant argued that because analytic truths could be judged by *a priori* analysis of concepts, it was also incorrectly assumed that synthetic truths could *not* be judged *a priori*. For instance, he claimed that arithmetic and geometry were *a priori*, but actually synthetic; they could be determined by reflection, but experience is needed to understand them. Against Hume's scepticism, Kant maintained that what Hume had shown without realising it was that the principle of causation was not analytic, and was therefore synthetic. He had then gone on mistakenly to assume that knowledge of causal relations must be *a posteriori*, and therefore uncertain. Kant's point was that causality was another example of the synthetic *a priori*; it needed experience to understand it, but its truths could be determined *a priori*.

Kant is fiendishly difficult to grasp, but the idea of the synthetic *a priori* prompted a revolution in philosophy which dominated the nineteenth century. It opened up a picture whereby the world supplied the sensations with which we gain knowledge, but the mind ordered them into significant concepts and relations. Causation (for instance) could not be observed; it was *imposed* on sensation by our mind's sensemaking capabilities. Other such impositions included space and time. The real objects of the world, which Kant called things-in-themselves, were unknowable in principle. So Hume's scepticism was half-right, but according to Kant's theory many of the contradictions or philosophical difficulties that we find ourselves in are the results of failing to see that metaphysical ideas such as space and time are not properties of the world itself, but rather ordering principles created by us. The philosophy of Kant was enormously influential – and still is today – and he began the German dominance of philosophy that lasted throughout the nineteenth century.

Philosophy of knowledge

As is readily seen from the above, metaphysics quickly become entangled with theories of how we gained knowledge and how far that knowledge could be relied upon. The seventeenth and eighteenth centuries were a golden period for the development of science and our understanding of the world – but also an important time for investigation of how we gain that understanding. Knowledge about knowledge is the philosophical discipline now (but not then) called *epistemology*.

Bacon raised many important epistemological questions by distinguishing between faith and reason. If I believe something on the grounds of faith, that means that I trust the source of the belief. If I believe something on the grounds of reason, it means I have worked it out for myself. We can work many things out for ourselves, but some truths, if truths they be, seem dependent on faith. In particular, belief in God seems to depend on faith, and Bacon's own view was that the triumph of faith was greatest when the belief was least plausible. The paradoxical element of this was taken up by Bayle, whose *Dictionary* took the idea to the extreme, artfully showing how bizarre faith-based thinking could be.

Consistent with his division of substance into mind and matter, Descartes maintained a distinction between knowledge gained from reason and from the senses – although in his case, he was much more interested in the former than the latter. His epistemological contribution was to refine the concept, and argue for the importance, of *certainty*. For Descartes, certainty could not be imposed from outside (i.e. take the form of faith), either by habit, prejudice or revelation. One should achieve certainty using one's own capabilities. Reason is located in each individual, and because my reason is autonomous, others should not think for me. Descartes doesn't even seem to believe that others should think *with* me; I should be totally independent of other thinkers, and work everything out for myself.

Given Cartesian separation of mind and matter, it was not clear how one could gain knowledge of the world at all. After all, knowledge required some form of interaction between matter and the mind, with some aspect of the world being recognised and appreciated by a mind. Descartes himself suggested there were different sources of knowledge of which the most important were *innate* ideas implanted in the mind by its very structure, independent of sensations; innate ideas included our idea of God as well as mathematics, logic and metaphysical concepts such as identity or substance.

Between them, Bacon and Descartes stripped away many sources of prejudice and bias, and set the scene for the great epistemological work of Locke. Natural reason, for Locke, is the 'touchstone' that helps us determine what is true and what false, and to identify errors often made as a result of poor education at a time when, as Condorcet puts it, the 'pliant soul can be shaped at will'. Reason should replace deeply-held but false nostrums with certainty.

In the first book of his *Essay Concerning Human Understanding*, Locke argued strongly against innate ideas, pointing out that what appear to be innate – for example the difference between colours and tastes – could be furnished by developing sense organs in the womb, or may appear at an early, pre-speech, phase of life. Instead, he elaborated the influential idea that the mind is a *tabula rasa*, a blank slate upon which experience impresses 'that vast store, which the busy and boundless fancy of man has painted on it with an almost endless variety'.[3] Our ideas, said Locke, come either from sensation, or from our perception of our own minds operating. All ideas come from experience. Even things we have never experienced, such as a winged horse, are created from a fusion of ideas we have already derived from experience; in this case, we can compose the ideas of wings and horses to produce the idea of a winged horse even though we have never seen one.

The problem with this self-contained philosophy is that it leaves open the problem about our knowledge of the world – if all we are genuinely acquainted with are ideas, experiences or sensations, how do we know that the ideas have any connection with things outside our heads? It may be that all our ideas are misleading, and that nothing comes from experience. Locke didn't have an answer to this, but neither did he care much. He was impatient with speculative metaphysics, wasn't too interested in the big metaphysical questions of substance, and simply chose not to worry overmuch about the problem.

Locke's advance on Cartesian thinking was in identifying a limit to certainty; he was satisfied with the certainty achievable in mathematics, and thought that thinking hard about the natural laws of morality would allow some certainty there. Science produces truths that are not certain, but very probable. Ideas about space and time and the 'real' nature of objects were all, said Locke, very uncertain indeed – a view stemming from his lack of interest in metaphysics. One's belief in a proposition must be proportionate to the evidence for that proposition; we must accept the possibility (perhaps small) that we are mistaken about the world. We have to act on uncertainty all the time, and so it is unavoidable. It is a reason to avoid dogmatism, and to tolerate what we believe to be wrong opinions in our fellow men. So, for Locke, scepticism leads to tolerance and forbearance.

The view that the contents of our mind have their ultimate roots in experience has proved extremely influential in philosophy and science under the name *empiricism*. The problem about the relationship between experience and the world remains troubling, and the theory itself doesn't work completely as many philosophers of science have argued since, but it has proved fruitful nonetheless. Berkeley, as we have seen, was drawn to conclude that to be is to be perceived, and the separation empiricism implicitly makes between the 'real' substance and appearance has always tempted thinkers in the direction of scepticism: if all we have access to are the appearances of objects, why do we need to bother with the underlying but inaccessible substance?

David Hume, strongly influenced by Bayle,[4] dug deep into Locke's philosophy to investigate the sceptical crisis of empiricism. His attempt to develop a Lockean combination of scepticism and common sense succeeded only in detaching philosophy from daily life. His *Treatise of Human Nature* paints a picture of man searching for knowledge and truth, prompted by nature to believe what he sees and hears but without intellectually satisfying justification. Man had to believe – that was the nature of his constitution – but the application of any philosophy led to scepticism. When someone received an impression (or, as Hume would say, an idea – see below for Humean terminology) of, say, a table in front of him, he obviously believed that there was a table there – but he could not prove it, and if he took philosophy seriously his reason would lead him to reject the inference from the impression of a table to the table itself. Even the supposed certainties of mathematics and logic could be doubted: 'in all demonstrative sciences the rules are certain and infallible; but when we apply them, our fallible and uncertain faculties are very apt to depart from them, and fall into error.'[5] All that meant, for Hume, was that it was impossible for anyone to be a philosopher all the time.

So feeble are our reasoning abilities, argued Hume, that were we forced to depend on them humanity could not survive. People were forced by their physical constitutions to make judgements which could not be justified wholly satisfactorily about matters of fact, morality and philosophy. Reason was much less of a guide about any of these matters than experience, habit and our own nature as thinking beings. No less a philosopher than Bertrand Russell asserted that 'David Hume's philosophy ... represents the bankruptcy of eighteenth-century reasonableness.'[6]

He soon became *persona non grata* in France, where he was criticised by philosopher Baron d'Holbach and Diderot because of his rejection not only of old thinking, but of the new as well. We have already seen how his philosophy prompted Kant's critique of pure reason. In his native Scotland, the incredibility of scepticism strongly influenced the 'common sense school' of realism championed by Thomas Reid, who reversed the argument and claimed that, as scepticism about the world was impossible as a way of life, it must be false. An examination of what 'normal' people believed and would continue to believe in the face of any philosophical argument (i.e. common sense) was therefore moulded into a philosophy of opposition to scepticism supported by the goodwill of God. Hume (and others, including Joseph Priestley) noted the common premises of scepticism and common sense philosophy, and pointed out that Reid was actually saying more or less what Hume had said, though with different emphasis. But the common sense school flourished, and became influential in America, brought over by a Scottish President of Princeton College (which later became the University), John Witherspoon (1723–94), a signatory of the *Declaration of Independence*.[7]

Not all thinkers took scepticism negatively. Condorcet, a mathematician by inclination and an optimist at heart, managed to turn Hume's argument into a call for empirically-based social science. He accepted that Hume had proved that no knowledge could be certain. But all that showed was that the probabilities of scientific claims were less than one, as Locke had argued. This was already agreed about claims about people and society, so the upshot of Humean scepticism was that social science was as well- (or ill-) grounded as physical science. For Condorcet, the way to bring reason back into human society was to determine and understand the probabilistic laws of human interaction, enabling us to discard habit and custom, which held social progress back.

Philosophy of mind

When it came to human psychology, Enlightenment philosophy tended towards individualism. The Cartesian bedrock of 'I think, therefore I am' rested all human knowledge upon the evidence vouchsafed to an individual. This led most philosophers to feel that the foundations of someone's understanding of the world were more likely to be found within the person than in the outside world, or the community of which the person is a member. This individualism sat rather neatly with the requirements of scientific investigation (the scientist should not take matters on authority) and commerce (sellers and buyers should fix their own prices). Following Hobbes' line of thought about a state of nature, most assumed that man had a 'natural' disposition which was changed or affected by the arrival of social arrangements. Far fewer thought there were any social bases for psychology; Diderot emphasised the natural gregariousness of mankind, while Hume pointed out that virtually every human action involved cooperation with others.

The most influential philosophy of mind of the eighteenth century was linked to Locke's empiricism: the mind was a *tabula rasa* receiving ideas from the world which were imprinted on it.

Ideas were often simple and unanalysable; complex ideas were created out of combinations of simple ideas. Hume made a distinction between impressions – immediate sense perceptions – and ideas, which are more abstract. This class of ideas might include memories of impressions, as well as complex concepts and thoughts created out of a myriad of simpler ideas. In each case, the bedrock of our thoughts is our experience.

The *tabula rasa* theory was extremely influential in two ways. First of all, it led to a view, closely associated with the French philosopher Helvétius, that people were born mentally equal, whatever life threw at them afterwards. The way the blank sheet was filled determined differences in psychology and intelligence and therefore the key to improvement was education. Genius, argued Helvétius, was a matter of chance – the right experience at the right time could make all the difference and a well-designed education would increase the probability of useful experience. Conversely, stupid people were made stupid by a bad education. Social hierarchy was a matter of chance; breeding was nothing. The only significant difference between the Lord of the Manor and the peasant in the field was the greater extent of the resources devoted to the former's education.

Secondly, the *tabula rasa*'s very simplicity pulled the rug from under complex motivational theory. The pursuit of happiness came to be seen as a prime reason for individuals' actions. The hope was that happiness would play the same role in political and psychological thought as gravity did in Newton's physics.[8] As Rousseau put it in his *Discourse on Inequality*, 'self-love is a natural sentiment which prompts every animal to watch over its own conservation and which, directed in man by reason and modified by pity, produces humanity and virtue.'

This idea fed into political philosophy; the individual's pursuit of his or her self-interest or happiness was seen, in particular by Adam Smith and Montesquieu, as a way of enlarging the public good.[9] Some, such as the influential poet and satirist

Bernard de Mandeville and on occasion even Voltaire relishing the paradox, saw individual vice as part of public virtue, as when rich men's greed supported a vast industry of artisans, vintners, publicans and farmers. If there were no thieves, policemen and locksmiths would be poor. This was too much for many, including d'Holbach who thought that the common good would only be served by people who tried directly to serve it.

Towards the end of the Enlightenment, Jeremy Bentham formulated a basic theory of mind in this tradition, which contained the 'greatest-happiness principle' that psychological goodness was *equivalent* to pleasure or happiness, and conversely that whatever was psychologically bad was painful. Human action therefore should be calculated in order to maximise pleasure and minimise pain (although ignorance, either of one's own best interests, or of the course of future events, meant that people would often fail to achieve their benevolent aims). This simplistic view of motivation (which still has currency today[10]), became the focus of the important political doctrine of utilitarianism, of which more below.

However, a number of thinkers noted that people often did things for pleasure that could not make them happy in the long term. Francis Hutcheson, who taught Adam Smith at Glasgow and prefigured many of Bentham's ideas, argued that man was not only essentially social, but essentially loving, and that his own happiness would depend inevitably on the happiness of others[11] (the psychological dimension of love is often unaccountably absent from individualistic theories[12]). D'Holbach drew a distinction between happiness (good) and pleasure (not necessarily good); happiness was a kind of long-term glow that was also connected to doing the morally right thing, while pleasure was enticing short-term enjoyment. He therefore denied that supposedly sexually promiscuous South Sea Islanders were happy, because they behaved immorally. Johnson's short novel *Rasselas* argues that unconditional or permanent happiness can never be achieved, and that it is the lot of mankind to strive, while Kant denied that happiness could or should be the ultimate goal of human behaviour. Many thinkers found it hard to depart from the Christian model of an ultimate reward for 'correct' behaviour, and the more atheistic or materialistic thinkers found this led to disagreeable complexity in their theories.

Education

Locke's *tabula rasa* theory had obvious implications with respect to training and education; it implied that (a) the purpose of education was to write truths upon the *tabulae*, and (b) morally, children were innocent, and not tainted with the evil of original sin. Locke's essay 'Some thoughts concerning education' (1693) brought Enlightened principles into European homes, and was also influential in carrying them to America, where a conservative education system developed generations of stern, serious people who avoided frippery, took part in public affairs and had useful skills. Locke advised 'parents and governors always to carry this in their minds, that children are to be treated as rational creatures.' This meant sparing the rod, the 'most unfit of any [instrument] to be used in education', in order to give a child mastery over his own inclinations so that he could listen to and obey the voice of reason telling him what ought to be done, while simultaneously ensuring that his 'spirit [is] easy, active and free; and yet, at the same time ... restrain[ed] ... from many things he has a mind to'.

Locke was pragmatic about education. Latin was 'absolutely necessary to a gentleman', but of no real point for those destined for a trade, a point later taken up by Joseph Priestley who argued that education should have the proto-utilitarian purpose of creating people capable of being active in the world as good and thoughtful citizens, and men of business. Education was seen, in Roy Porter's phrase, as a panacea to problems of poor behaviour, as a way of ensuring the spread of reason, and explaining, via its absence, the failure of real people to act reasonably.[13]

Another way of looking at this is that education can make people easier to control, which was an assumption shared with the Jesuits, who used to boast that given the boy they could form the man. This controlling idea was very rarely expressed explicitly by the Enlightened *philosophes*, but its most extreme form emerged in arguments by Anglicans in the slave states of colonial America that education in Biblical matters would make slaves more docile. The slavers had a different view of things however, and were nervous about the possible consequences of educating slaves; after a revolt in South Carolina, it was forbidden to teach slaves to write.[14] The Jesuits too overestimated the extent of their influence over children; Voltaire, the Marquis de Sade, Condorcet, Diderot, Beccaria, Buffon and Bayle all received excellent Jesuit educations, while the Jansenists, equally dedicated Catholics, produced d'Alembert and la Mettrie.

The most important work of the later Enlightenment was Rousseau's *Emile* (1762), influential, like so many of his works, on the French Revolutionaries, which questioned Locke's assumption that children were little empty adults to be filled with good sense and denuded of the impediments to reason. He insisted instead that childhood was a special stage in life. 'I find nothing more stupid than children who have been much reasoned with.'

> Nature intends that children shall be children before they are men. If we insist on reversing this order we shall have fruit early indeed, but unripe and tasteless, and liable to early decay; we shall have young savants and old children. Childhood has its own methods of seeing, thinking, and feeling. Nothing shows less sense than to try to substitute our own methods for these. I

would rather require a child ten years old to be five feet tall than to be judicious. Indeed, what use would he have at that age for the power to reason?

Rousseau also had ideas about virtue and society which impinged on the childhood idyll. In his *Discourse on Political Economy*, written about the same time, he expressed the somewhat scary idea that 'from the first moment of life, men ought to begin learning to deserve to live'. The state should inculcate virtue in children, who should be encouraged to see themselves as existing only in relation to the state. The two halves of Rousseau's ideas, the idyll and the anthill, are difficult to reconcile; in many ways, the history of Enlightened political thought, on to which we will now move, is driven by attempts to achieve that reconciliation.

6
Political theory and the road to revolution

It will already be clear from chapter five why Enlightened philosophers soon found themselves in the political sphere. Theories of substance, mind and knowledge would be dragged into the seminal debates of the age, out of which most of our modern ideologies emerged. In this chapter, we will look in particular at the political sphere, beginning with the major debates and moving on to the ways in which theory informed politics, until history's first great ideological conflicts broke out. In a sense, the innovation of the Enlightenment was to provide enough theory and ideology to make ideological conflict possible.

In this respect the Enlightenment was shaped by the theological disputes of the previous century in two ways. First, the intellectual competition spurred concentration on education, argument and the development of young minds. Secondly, more importantly, the religious wars that followed led to weariness with bloodshed, and the growth of tolerance as an ideal.[1] Hobbes argued that bloodshed was a function of a *lack* of authority and prescribed a strong central government to keep the peace, but he had remarkably little sense that people within a nation, whether sovereign or subject, might have *competing* interests that needed to be balanced. Enlightenment philosophers were more subtle.

Liberalism

The cradle of the Enlightenment's dominant political philosophy was the commercial hub of Northern Europe, in particular
England and Holland, and in many respects early Enlightenment
liberalism was a codification of already existing social attitudes
which evolved out of a tolerant kind of Protestantism. Trading
nations flourish or collapse depending on how many goods and
services they can produce and sell, irrespective of the colour or
creed of the purchasers. Furthermore, trade is more successful in
stable, predictable conditions when people can make investment
and purchasing decisions with reasonable confidence. Religious
wars, civil wars and persecutions were inimical to trade. The
early liberals opposed the wars of religion, partly on humanitarian grounds, partly because of their pointless destructiveness.

The early liberal preference for tolerance and trade had a
number of obvious corollaries. It favoured the growing middle
classes over aristocratic and monarchical interests, which were
rent-seeking rather than value-creating. A system of protection
of private property, preventing it from being arbitrarily
impounded, was important, which also required respect for
contractual agreements and the rule of law within a society
(especially by its rulers). Locke's conception of liberty was influential (though not undisputed); laws to curb what we would
now call anti-social elements were essential, but liberty consisted
in the freedom to do whatever was not prohibited by law. A
person was understood as an individual, and someone should be
able to escape their situation in life if their hard work warranted
it. For all these reasons, early liberalism opposed the feudal
arrangements of medieval times, and in reaction became self-
consciously 'modernising'.

The new liberals were also prepared for their opinions to
be overturned through reasoned argument. This reasonable
rationalism is strongly associated with forms of government

associated with deliberation and discussion, especially Parliamentary democracy, and inimical to the certainties of those driven by their religious faith. Locke argued that it was essential to 'distinguish exactly the business of civil government from that of religion and to settle the just bound that lie between the one and the other.' Revelations of religious truth needed to be examined critically. Locke, and many others including for instance Shaftesbury, were very opposed to 'enthusiasm', the blind and uncritical belief in revealed religious truth.

Liberalism is associated, in fact if not in logic, with Locke's empiricism as outlined above, and as such has tended to have similar problems. Most glaringly, liberalism shares the 'interior' perspective of empiricism, assuming that we perform actions because of the benefit that they give us (later economists would phrase this as our trying to 'maximise utility'). But then the problem of Hobbes' *Leviathan* – how can we ensure the social or public good if people consider only their private pleasure? – raises its head. Liberals have tended to argue that public and private interests coincide, at least in the medium to long term, as long as we are sufficiently reflective. Those, like Locke, of a religious persuasion could also suggest that God would act as a punishing magistrate if need be, so potential transgressors would have to take into account benefit not only in this world, but also in the next. Nevertheless this optimism has always been a point of tension in liberal philosophy (see chapter ten).

The French debate on liberty

Locke's achievement in placing liberty as the central issue of political philosophy sparked a debate in authoritarian France. 'Liberty' was seen by most *philosophes* as the supreme political good, but they disagreed radically over what it actually meant even though several (not all) of the participants took Locke as their reference point. They also diverged over what kinds of political structure could secure liberty – could the aristocratic system be purged of its inequalities and cruelties, or was a parliamentary system necessary?

Voltaire was an admirer of Locke and Bacon, and followed them in advocating non-interference with civil society and in particular religious tolerance. An early stay in England (following a spell in the Bastille) made a great impression on him, and he praised the way that 'in England everyone is allowed to go to heaven in his own way'. Reason and science were forces for good, and he proposed a centralised government that could disseminate ideas while eliminating intolerance and superstition. Such a government, capable of imposing modernisation on a society, would have to reside in a single figure, unencumbered by reactionary forces such as the church or law courts, an absolute but benign monarch – a position that reveals his debt to Hobbes and explains why he was welcome in the court of Frederick the Great.

In Voltaire's view the legitimacy of absolutism was strongly connected with modernisation. An absolute monarch had duties to Enlighten his people, which was a departure from previous absolutist thinkers such as Sir Robert Filmer, Mazarin or Richelieu. In the words of Austria's Emperor Joseph II, 'everything for the people, nothing by the people'. Diderot held a similarly absolutist point of view at least while editing the *Encyclopédie*, hoping that a strong government would implement scientific development, but while he shared Voltaire's Baconian optimism about science, he did not have similar faith in a monarchy, and would have preferred a technocratic government to appoint experts to solve social problems.

Montesquieu followed Locke's account of liberal scepticism about the motives of governments, and advocated a division of powers between the executive and legislature with independent judicial oversight; the dangers of centralisation outweighed any benefits provided by a Voltairean system. His major intellectual innovation was to insist on experimentation and description prior to political theorising, following the new inductive practice in the sciences. He did not simply reason about what would be a good system, but rather, in his masterpiece *The Spirit of Laws*, tried to formulate social laws that would explain what constitutional arrangements would complement the 'natural genius' of a particular society. That was not to say that he eschewed universal principles – for instance, he held that 'justice is eternal and does not depend on human conventions'[2] – but it was on experience rather than philosophical grounds that he based his argument that any monopoly of power was liable to be bad. His original theories were republican, but extensive travels in actual republics in Italy and Holland disillusioned him. A tour of England led him to admire the settlement of 1688, and to advocate constitutional arrangements with British-style moderation. Gertrude Himmelfarb describes Montesquieu as 'more representative of the British Enlightenment than of the French'. He is certainly a missing link.

'Moderation' was Montesquieu's highest term of praise, and his political judgements always included an appreciation of context. Other thinkers preferred more abstract discussions of sovereignty and power, often using numerically-based categories of government that dated back to Aristotle – rule by a single person (monarchy or tyranny), by the few (aristocracy or oligarchy) or by the many (constitutional government or democracy).[3] Montesquieu, in his mature thought, focused instead on institutions and methods. So although he retained republican affections, he thought it was an impractical ideal and rejected it.

His preferred option was monarchy, but he enlarged on the differences between an absolute monarchy, such as France, and a constitutional one, such as Britain, which with its checks and balances turned out to be a much better guarantor of liberty than

a republic where little stood in the way of the will of the majority. Montesquieu's notion of separation of powers was eventually adopted by the Americans, but his point about Britain was
not that the executive, legislature and judiciary were strictly
separate (they were not and are not), but rather that the three
constituted, in the British context, effective brakes on each
other's powers, brakes which were not applied so rigorously
that the business of government ground to a halt. His
sensitivity to local conditions meant that he could not advocate
wholesale adaptation of the British system to France; he studied
French history deeply in order to establish the most 'French'
institutions between which powers should be distributed. He
foresaw important roles for the nobility, the clergy, the
chartered cities and the *parlements* (local law courts which had
the duty of approving and interpreting legislation laid down
centrally).

Montesquieu's work was highly influential in the areas of
civil liberties and civil punishments, especially among practical
constitution builders such as Franklin, Jefferson and even
Catherine the Great. However, moderate constitutional monarchism faltered after his death in 1755 because the situation in
France was so dire that political views tended to polarise.
Everyone wanted change, and checks and balances could never
be applied constructively. Furthermore, his focus on the past,
and on the institutions which had traditionally played a large part
in French affairs meant that in the fraught political situation he
seemed insufficiently 'modern' and progressive. Voltaire, in
contrast, argued that the clergy and the institutions controlled by
the nobility were the most egregious barriers to liberty, and in
particular that the *parlements* acted only in the interests of
their class, actually making French law more oppressive than the
king intended (for instance, King Louis XV had wished to
revoke the authorisation of torture, but the *parlements* would
not allow the revocation). Much of Voltaire's public life was

spent exposing injustice, cruelty and inhumanity in the *parlements'* prosecutions.

D'Holbach, on the other hand, was unimpressed with England on his visit, which seemed to him less the home of liberty than anarchy. His experience suggested to him that liberty required order and virtue as prior states. His ideal was a state where virtue flourished, and where people did the right thing. This idea of an ethocracy, governed by ethical behaviour which would promote happiness rather than mere pleasure, unconnected with any church or other body, was an intriguing notion, especially as other thinkers, notably Rousseau and Robespierre, were keen on the promotion of virtue. However, much as d'Holbach enjoyed building an imaginary state in his works, he had little practical plan to implement one.

The rights of man and the categorical imperative

The idea that people had natural rights appeared prominently in Locke's *Two Treatises on Government* (1689), and supported the typically Enlightenment feeling that just because social relations had been organised in a particular way for time immemorial, that was no argument that they should continue. There were limits to what even a legitimate government was entitled to do to its citizens. People had their own dignity, and, to borrow Jefferson's words, 'the mass of mankind has not been born with saddles on their backs, nor a favored few booted and spurred, ready to ride them legitimately, by the grace of God.' Jefferson wrote that a few days before his own death (the fiftieth anniversary of the *Declaration of Independence*), but he had been a prime mover in getting the idea of natural rights into the public arena since an early paper he had written for the radicals in the colonial Virginia Assembly. In this important polemic he brought a great deal of new theory to bear on the English constitution, and was able to show that Americans had the natural right to govern themselves.

On 4 July 1776 the *Declaration of Independence* appeared, authored mainly by Jefferson (as head of a five-man committee including Benjamin Franklin and John Adams) and amended during debate in Congress. America declared itself independent with great statements of the centrality of human rights and self-government, using the language and concepts of the liberal tradition of the Enlightenment.

> We hold these truths to be self-evident: that all men are created equal; that they are endowed by their Creator with certain inalienable rights; that among these are life, liberty, and the pursuit of happiness; that to secure these rights, governments are instituted among men, deriving their just powers from the consent of the governed; that whenever any form of government becomes destructive of these ends, it is the right of the people to alter or to abolish it, and to institute new government, laying its foundation on such principles, and organizing its powers in such form, as to them shall seem most likely to effect their safety and happiness.

The self-evidence of the truths meant they were clear to anyone using their unhindered reason. The natural rights were endowed by a Creator; no specific idea of God is relied upon but this is not an atheistic document. There is more than a nod to the developing psychology of happiness. The rights are inalienable – that is, they cannot be given away or sold. A government that does not support these rights is illegitimate.[4]

The austere nature of Kant's intellect meant that he would never make as pragmatic a contribution to political philosophy as Locke or Jefferson, but his important work in moral philosophy, notably his *Groundwork of the Metaphysics of Morals* (1785) and *Critique of Practical Reason* (1788), began an important tradition in which just, equal and fair treatment, was the main moral requirement. Morality, he claimed, had no meaning outside itself – it wasn't *for* anything. It was self-contained and amenable to reason, because (applying his own metaphysical ideas) it was another example of the synthetic *a priori* – one needed experience of the world to understand moral statements, but one could work out their truth purely by reflection.

His thinking led to the formulation of what he called the *categorical imperative* that stated that moral laws could not be nor should be limited: 'act only according to a maxim by which you can at the same time will that it shall become a general law'. If we are thinking morally, we have to think entirely generally – there can be no exceptions. If one person is to be punished for committing a crime, then anyone who commits the same crime should be punished similarly. Equally, the outcome of a moral action is irrelevant to whether it is moral or not; in its most extreme form this entails that telling a lie is wrong, even if by telling a 'white lie' you can do some good. Most importantly, every man should be treated as an end in himself; you should not use people solely as means for particular ends, even if those ends are good. Hence Kant ends up with a highly abstract statement of something that sounds like the rights of man, and an emphasis on generalities such as duties, rights and obligations, as opposed to moral particularities such as trust.

The French revolutionaries adopted their own *Declaration of the Rights of Man and the Citizen* at the beginning of their revolutionary process in August 1789. The National Constituent Assembly, which had taken on the task of representing all interests in France and writing the new constitution with the reluctant agreement of Louis XVI, created a preliminary document that remains a bold and authoritative summary of Enlightenment thought. In particular, it changed the terms of political trade from the balancing of corporate interests (the clergy, the nobility) to the assertion of the universal, natural and inalienable rights of the individual. There were several influences, most obviously Locke's natural rights and Rousseau's general will (see below), but also Montesquieu's idea of the separation of powers (overridden later in the Revolution) and of course the American *Declaration of Independence* (Jefferson was in Paris at this time).

It is a short document, containing some seventeen clauses and a preamble, but has remained influential; it is part of the constitution of the current French republic. It is highly egalitarian, asserting equal rights for everyone irrespective of their status in society; the particular rights it focuses on are to liberty, property, security and resistance to opposition. The nation is the source of all sovereignty and authority, and the law is the expression of the general will which must be applied equally and fairly, and not arbitrarily. Anything not forbidden by law is allowed, and no-one can be arrested or accused of anything except where the law determines it. The police must act in the interest of the nation, not of any particular clique. Taxes must be assessed equally on all citizens proportionally to their means. Free communication of ideas is a key aspect of liberty, and all opinions are to be tolerated. Most if not all of the proposals are uncontroversial nowadays, though they were highly charged implicit criticisms of the monarchical constitution. Nevertheless, the document is arguably incomplete as a statement of human rights; it makes no mention of slavery, or indeed of women (Condorcet and others had argued that women's rights should be included explicitly, but were overruled).

Utilitarianism

Given the substructure of Enlightenment psychology, one did not need to subscribe to the rights of man to be radical. The English philosopher Jeremy Bentham famously argued that the rights of man were nonsense, and the imprescriptable rights of man 'nonsense upon stilts'. He was a subscriber to the view that the aim of action was happiness, and that the happiness of the individual was his most important interest. Liberty was of less interest to Bentham, except in so far as it promoted happiness, and he argued that security was much more conducive to supporting happiness than liberty. Nevertheless his minimal psychological theory led him to radical and progressive conclusions (some of which he reached after the Enlightenment had faded), including the equality of women, animal rights, free trade, the right to divorce and the legalisation of homosexuality.

From his own greatest-happiness principle Bentham derived a variant of liberalism that still commands respect today. Rather than trying to articulate complex theories about which states of affairs were good and which bad, he extrapolated from the happiness principle to argue that politically (and morally), one state of affairs was better than another if the sum of happiness was greater in it than in the other. The aim of the legislator should be to coordinate everyone's individual pursuit of happiness in order to maximise the general public happiness. This does not necessarily mean that traditional rights and liberties are not supported by utilitarianism; rather, the ground for making judgements about them has changed. A moral wrong such as theft or murder, is not wrong on the basis of some deep moral truth, but specifically because it tends in almost all circumstances to reduce the total sum of happiness. The purpose of punishment should be to reduce crime, not to exact revenge on the criminal.

As has often been pointed out, he hardly invented this philosophy which he termed *utilitarianism*. Helvétius described the psychology in *On the Mind* (1758), Cesare Beccaria's *On Crimes and Punishments* (1764) applied the principle to law, Joseph Priestley's *First Principles of Government* (1768) applied it to politics, taking 'the greatest happiness for the greatest number' as a criterion for moral correctness was defended in Francis Hutcheson's *Inquiry Concerning Moral Good and Evil* as early as

1725. All these appeared prior to Bentham's own important works, which began with *Fragment of Government* of 1776. Nevertheless, Bentham's development of the theory, and his argument that it was a sufficient purpose for government, was powerful and simple to grasp and established it in political discourse.

Utilitarianism is an instance of the more general principle of consequentialism, that the consequences of an action, not its intention, are the important moral parameters. This was hotly debated at the time, and is still a key topic in moral philosophy today.[5] The advantage of Bentham's use of the happiness principle is the simplicity of the resulting idea, but if the happiness principle is replaced by something more complex and realistic, the picture is muddier and complexities re-emerge similar to those of Lockean natural law theories. D'Holbach tried to redefine happiness as the reward for virtuous behaviour, for example, but this variant is clouded by the need to bring in prior judgements about what virtuous behaviour might consist of, which require difficult moral reasoning. Furthermore, even very sophisticated and rigorous moral theorists disagree about what constitutes virtuous behaviour, and so the determinacy of happiness-based utilitarianism is lost as well.

Opponents of utilitarianism maintained (and maintain) that the philosophy seems to license immoral behaviour. It may be that the public happiness will be served by the execution of an innocent man for a crime. A criminal could be punished by the jailing of his wife or children, even if they were innocent of involvement. For many thinkers, such as Condorcet, this was not acceptable, and they preferred to extend Locke's thoughts about natural rights by insisting that the individual's rights had always to be respected, and could not be ignored in favour of those of the community. Consequentialist methods for incorporating such deeply held moral intuitions gradually evolved over the next century, but are beyond the scope of this guide.

The beginnings of economics

The constant theorising of the nature of the individual and of his relation to the world and wider society around him led to the first inklings of economic science. There was little consensus; Locke regarded the protection of property and the enforcement of contract as central to a functioning society, while Rousseau thought the invention of property undermined the simple relationships characteristic of primitive societies, and that laws to promote justice and peace were a sham to cover the perpetuation of social divisions by giving social force to unequal distributions of resources. A number of thinkers, including Mandeville and Voltaire, allowed themselves to be persuaded that low wages for the poor were a good thing, while the wealthy Helvétius thought, presumably without much evidence, that the poorest people were the happiest.

It was left to Diderot, a man of modest means whose sympathy for the poor never left him, to point out that however brilliant Helvétius was, his opinion of the happiness of the poor was hardly *au point*. The introduction of free trade in France in the 1760s led to speculation, shortages and profiteering, and Diderot led the way in opposing economic liberalisation on the pragmatic ground that it had not worked. He did not agree with Voltaire that the production of luxury goods for the wealthy was socially beneficial by providing employment for poorer artisans, while his ally d'Holbach argued that conspicuous consumption (as we would now call it) persuaded people to spend more money than they really had, and – remembering his distinction between happiness and pleasure – that they would focus their energies on frivolities, rather than in the virtuous behaviour which produced true happiness.

Perhaps surprisingly, the revolutionary Condorcet saw free trade as liberating. He hoped that the sugar industry in Africa would 'destroy the shameful exploitation which has corrupted and depopulated that continent for the last two centuries', and argued that trade monopolies were 'a tax imposed upon [the people] in order to provide their governments with a new instrument of tyranny'. Free trade, for Condorcet, was an essential leg of freedom as well as helping spread wealth more widely.

The moral arguments were informed by a more fundamental debate about the nature of economic interaction. At the beginning of the period *mercantilism*, the idea that money was a store of value that happened to be more durable than things valuable in their own right such as food or clothing, was a common view, supported by Locke among others. Demand for products was understood to be relatively slow-moving (as we would say now, *inelastic*) It follows that a nation's prosperity is based on its capital, and it is the duty of government to ensure a positive balance of trade by promoting exports, placing high tariffs to protect against imports and granting monopolies to favoured traders, as well as 'investing' in imperial ventures to use colonies to preserve favourable terms of trade, as sources of cheap labour, natural resources and export markets, and to absorb surplus labour from the home market in times of unemployment.

Mercantilism eschewed psychological theory; rather it was highly influenced by political considerations of national independence and security, and it came under critical scrutiny as the Enlightenment unfolded. French economists, particularly Condorcet's mentor Controller-General Turgot, developed the theory of *physiocracy* which suggested that wealth came from nature, and hence that agriculture should be fostered to support prosperity. A happy corollary of this theory was that peasants and agricultural labourers became more valued by their rulers. Scottish economists and thinkers, though, generalised the physiocrats' argument to produce a powerful and influential alternative to it. Hume in a series of essays criticised the idea that money had any intrinsic importance; rather it was a measure of value of fundamentally more important things, including agriculture and raw materials but also the skills and abilities of a nation's population. Demand could be elastic, and money would be its measure.

Perhaps the most important book published by any Enlightenment thinker was Adam Smith's *An Inquiry into the Nature and Causes of the Wealth of Nations* (1776), an impressively broad vision of a self-regulating free market. Smith showed how the division of labour (not an original idea) turns 'every man … in some measure [into] a merchant', selling a good, a service or a skill, and promoting growth. Famously, he pointed out that although it would take one man a long time to make a pin, dividing the labour up between many people resulted in thousands of pins being made much more cheaply. Others, including Diderot in some of the craft chapters in the *Encyclopédie*, had made this argument, but none in more detail; Smith devotes the first book of the *Wealth of Nations* to the topic, because, *contra* the physiocrats, he believed that labour, not land, was the most important economic resource.

The other innovation for which Smith is famous – again, building on the work of others – is the idea of the 'invisible hand'. Where a market for goods is allowed to operate unhindered, demand and supply will fluctuate, but price and profit will help produce the 'right' level of a good. If there is a shortage of something, its price should rise, which will tempt more producers to produce it; if there is a glut, the resulting low price will deter producers. This will not necessarily produce equilibrium, but the regulation will be beneficial. For instance, if producers' decisions took a long time to take effect (as for example in agriculture, where planting decisions are made months before the goods reach the market), prices should stay high in times of shortage, which will help ration the good in question. The invisible hand steers supply across the whole economy, even though all of the economic decisions to buy and sell goods and services are made on the basis of self-interest and local knowledge. The invisible hand is another example of nature, not tradition, helping determine individual decisions.

All of this is rooted in Smith's psychological theories that people are conditioned to exchange and save. People who try to behave altruistically are often ineffective whereas if self-interest can be aggregated properly, the results are genuinely beneficial. 'It is not from the benevolence of the butcher, the brewer or the baker that we expect our dinner, but from their regard for their own interest. We address ourselves, not to their humanity, but to their self-love.' The importance of individual action and responsibility in economics, and the attractions of a strong yet distant government, seem to have been most appreciated in Scotland, a remote part of Britain whose government was very little concerned about it, and in America, where suspicion of government was deeply ingrained.

Smith was not an amoral free-marketeer – a caricature which made him the poster-boy of twentieth century neo-liberalism and a hate figure for collectivists. He saw markets as an important part of a society made up of many ties and bonds, only some of which were of economic importance, and also thought that the operation of markets would help diffuse socially useful ideas about work and cooperation. His *Theory of Moral Sentiments* explores the moral judgments people make even as they consult their self-interest. In his two great works, Smith analyses 'self-interest', arguing that it is very distinct from selfishness, and even more distinct from the desire to aggrandise oneself at the expense if necessary of everyone else. He also does not make the mistake of several of his commentators of assuming that self-interest is the single motivation for people's actions.

Instead, Smith weaves a subtle web of insights about the complex relationship between our understanding of our own interests, and the informal pressures from wider society. Although we do address our own interests, Smith argued that we have ineradicable sympathy with others which makes it very hard to be 'purely' selfish, and which ensures that most societies do contain a degree of cooperation and moral behaviour. We often act, says Smith, in order to impress an 'impartial spectator'; we gain an understanding of the requirements of morality from our interactions with other people. Markets are an important part of the socialising process, as well as being useful mechanisms for allocating resources across a complex society in which many people have highly specialised occupations.

Conservatism

During the Enlightenment, there were many proudly unenlightened reactionaries, often in the Catholic Church and in aristocracies feeling threatened by a newly-empowered middle class. More principled conservatism, the intellectual or emotional justification of resistance to change, was rarer, but could be found in America and Britain, where liberty had been entrenched by the revolutions of 1776 and 1688, and conservatism had a noble principle to defend, namely the Lockean notion of liberty.

Scepticism was an important Enlightenment theme, and conservatism (which after all is scepticism about theories of radical change) developed in important ways. The notion of an Enlightened conservative, undogmatic and sceptical equally of traditional and progressive claims to truth, is not oxymoronic. For example, James Boswell often reports Johnson as having drawn conservative conclusions on the basis of an open-minded examination of a position followed by reasoned analysis, in true Enlightenment fashion; his argument that laws and institutions derive their authority from 'manners' and not reason is itself a reasoned argument from the premise that if the law is not revered then social unrest will follow. Similarly, a founder of

German conservatism, Justus Möser (1720–94), defended his notion of gradual reform of institutions to an educated public, and developed a journalistic career alongside his day job as a legal official for an Osnabrück princeling. The conservatives of the eighteenth century tried to make the case that reason and tradition were not incompatible, and that a balance was required between the two.

Hume criticised the Lockean theory that governmental legitimacy depended on its keeping an implicit contract with its citizens. He was not prepared to support Locke's rationalist picture, but it was also important to Hume, as an Enlightened sceptic, to demythologise the origins of authority, so he could not go back to the discredited theory of the divine right of kings. He argued that the origins of political authority would not be found either in human reason or divine will, and instead examined lived human experience and history. His *History of Great Britain* (1754–62, later, and now more usually, known as the *History of England*) decoded current discussion about liberty and rights, and he was able to show that 'liberty' was a relatively recent idea, and its rise, in tandem with Locke's theories and the 1688 revolution, depended both on the creation of restrictions to the monarch's power and on the strong, stable and fair government which the Stuarts had never been able to provide. The rule of law provided the vital backdrop to liberty.

Although social conventions arise unplanned by human reason, they were not thereby ruled out from being socially useful. Indeed, no convention could have survived at all if it were injurious to society. Morality developed through human interaction and social order – it may seem that there are 'natural' laws of morals, but actually they depended on accidents of history and institutions. Historical experience, not pure reason, will tell you what rules are consistent with an orderly society. This chimes in interestingly with Bacon's views in a different context of how we can be misled by reason and why experimentation and observation are correspondingly important.

Burke, in his great work, *Reflections on the Revolution in France*, discussed in more detail below, adopted a similar position to Hume's, although his own scepticism was not as thoroughly worked out. His conservative writings highlighted the inability of reason to cope with the complexity of society, the unintended consequences of its application, and the lack of motivation for demanding a rational justification of every institution or convention. '[P]olitics ought to be adjusted, not to human reasonings, but to human nature; of which the reason is but a part, and by no means the greatest part.' Reason is difficult to apply and prone to error; if moral behaviour demanded reason, then society was in trouble because it would be too hard to achieve.

The Enlightened aspect of Burke's thought reveals itself in the claim that the value of traditions, customs and prejudices which in functioning societies usurp the idealised role of reason are neither God-given nor justified by myth, but rather demonstrated by their functional success over a long period of time of actual usage in a genuine society. He supplied reasoned arguments for (mild) superstition and prejudice; this was not mere counter-Enlightenment, but an application of Enlightened principles of reason and analysis to political and moral behaviour. He was particularly appreciative of the role of religion in society, but advocated tolerance and respect particularly for those religions socialised by tradition. 'I would give a full civil protection, in which I include an immunity from all disturbance of their public religious worship, and a power of teaching in schools as well as temples, to Jews, Mahometans, and even Pagans; especially if they are already possessed of those advantages by long and prescriptive usage, which is as sacred in this exercise of rights, as in any other.'

His comprehension of the Enlightenment is shown by his first major work, *A Vindication of Natural Society* (1756), in which

he satirically guys progressive thought in a cod argument for the
rational redrawing of society, using the same arguments used
against religion and the church ironically to attack government
and other bases of 'artificial' societies. So successful a satire was
it that it was taken seriously by many and he had to release a
second edition with an explanatory preface pointing out the
dystopian aspects of his work. He was an enthusiastic early
adopter of Smith's ideas, with a temperamental disapproval of
regulations as by definition restrictions on liberty. And as with
Smith, his liberal economic philosophy sat alongside sympathy
for the intangible connections which held society together;
Burke would not have approved of twentieth century-style
market fundamentalism which disregarded the effects of social
change. Trade, manufactures and exchange must co-exist with
civilising and moral institutions, traditions and practices, or else
precipitate descent into barbarism. And this social responsibility
also applied to early imperial ventures; much of Burke's early
fame rested on his failed attempt to impeach Warren Hastings
for abusing his position as the Governor-General of Bengal. His
opposition to the bad behaviour of the British in India was
pungently expressed. 'Every rupee of profit made by an
Englishman is lost forever to India ... England has erected no
churches, no hospitals, no palaces, no schools; England has built
no bridges, made no highroads, cut no navigations, dug out no
reservoirs.' He used similar arguments to warn the British
government against its unreasonable behaviour in America.

In America, conservatism was culturally more acceptable
than in Europe, and fitted more easily into the mainstream of
Enlightenment thought. For instance, John Adams was able to
craft a conservative position from a combination of scepticism
and stoicism that has echoes of Franklin or the Voltaire of
Candide, as well as an admixture of earlier writers, in particular
Machiavelli, although his very typically American antipathy to
British Tories prevented him from including Hume, whom he

thought merely cynical, in his influences. Man was morally imperfect, and Adams argued that history would include cycles of progress and decline, and that optimism was therefore foolish. Following Montesquieu he believed that virtue was essential for a functioning society, and could be corrupted by luxury, and that the purpose of politics therefore was to craft political institutions that would dampen down man's natural greed, and protect the different classes from each other – protect the rich from the envy of the poor, and the poor from the exploitation of the rich. Democracy was not that institution for Adams, because when a majority realised that it would have the power to gratify its desires, it would be unrealistic to expect self-denial.[6]

The state of nature, social contracts and democracy

Adams was not alone in thinking 'democracy' a dirty word, implying an unstable system where a large number of uneducated, landless and unpropertied people ('the mob') would have political power, and could not be restrained from redistributing property and wealth to a ruinous degree. Many major Enlightenment thinkers, including Voltaire, went along with this view which dated back to Plato and Aristotle. The reverence for science and reason promoted a cult of expertise in which it was hoped that rational and technocratic fixes could be found for most social problems; consulting the people seemed like a self-defeating indulgence.

The first blows for democracy were struck by Locke in his *Two Treatises on Government* of 1689 and 1690. He began by demolishing arguments for the legitimacy of monarchical rule, pointing out the absurdity of assuming that any real monarch was in any sense the heir of Adam. There were many monarchs, but Adam surely could only have one heir! The negative argument of the first Treatise is supplemented by a positive argument about legitimacy in the second, which makes play with a Hobbes-like notion of a *state of nature*. Locke assumes that men in such a state have reason, but merely no common superior; liberty, but not licence. Some social arrangements, including private property, equality and the principle that no-one ought to harm others in terms of life, health, liberty, or possessions were legitimised by being 'natural', i.e. possibly existing in the state of nature.

However, a state of nature is not stable. In order for more complex societies to flourish, government is essential, and – again following Hobbes – can only be imposed with the acquiescence of a society. Government legitimacy lies with a *social contract*. The rights that people possess cannot be denied by government, but rather it has an obligation to protect those rights. This idea improves on Hobbes, by giving political power a moral dimension beyond a mere display of force; as Camus put it, after Locke 'power is no longer what is but what should be'.[7] The contract as Hobbes conceived it was compatible with tyranny if people were desperate for protection, but in Locke's version of the theory consent was required not only at the outset but at all times afterwards. Merely creating a government did not absolve the need for constant legitimation. Sons do not inherit contractual obligations from their fathers; new consent is needed. Locke, of course, was well aware that the social contract was never actually signed in any actual country in the past; it was a thought experiment – *if* people in a state of nature *would* have signed a contract which described what a government did, *then* that government was legitimate.

Ironically it was Rousseau, a great democrat who genuinely preferred the company of lower-born people, who provided the intellectual means to morph democracy into tyranny. His major political work, *The Social Contract* (1762), argues for the superiority of small states (such as his own native Geneva with which he conducted a love-hate relationship – *The Social Contract* was banned there), on the model of the ancient state of Sparta. The famous opening sentence of the book, usually translated 'Man is born free, and everywhere he is in chains,'[8] sets out the tension between liberty and equality.

In his exploration of this paradox, he argued that Hobbes and Locke had failed to realise that in a state of nature, human nature would be different. Life would only be 'nasty, brutish and short' (Hobbes' famous description) in a state of nature if we lived there with our 'civilised' personalities. A genuine state of nature, to which we as humans would be adapted, would be pleasant (his novel *The New Héloïse* and opera *The Village Soothsayer* made the case artistically). People were driven from their natural state by social pressures – natural disasters, or growing populations – and thereby forced into unnatural relations of government and governed. How can people preserve their freedom while at the same time allowing themselves to be governed? How can liberty and authority co-exist?

The answer most Enlightened thinkers adopted here, based on contractarian ideas and rumination on the state of nature, was that people would consent, freely, to binding laws. One does not lose freedom by agreeing to be constrained. Rousseau's particular solution was along these lines, but went somewhat further as he expected the individual to immerse himself in the community, conceived as a 'general will'. If an individual retained any rights while so immersed, there could be no superior agent who could resolve disputes between the individual and the collective. Hence there should be no intermediating institutions between the will and the individual. 'Each of us puts his person and all his power in common under the supreme direction of the general will, and, in our corporate capacity, we receive each member as an indivisible part of the whole.' To the modern eye this looks like an unlikely recipe for retaining liberty. The 'general will' is the will of the collective, and those who refuse to obey it should be forced to do so. 'This means nothing less than that he will be forced to be free.'

Rousseau tried to undo the paradox by arguing that 'the passage from the state of nature to the civil state produces a very remarkable change in man, by substituting justice for instinct in his conduct, and giving his actions the morality they had formerly lacked.' It is only then that a man could use his reason and appeal to moral principles such as justice. Rousseau's admiration of the general will meant that he neither upheld the more realistic and conservative ideals of Locke such as the preservation of private property, nor saw the need for constraining institutions such as the checks and balances advocated by Montesquieu. The potential for abuse is frightening; even Kant, a democrat who admired Rousseau, understood that this philosophy would be very likely to descend into the tyranny of the majority.

Rousseau's democracy is a metaphysical one. The general will cannot be determined by majority vote or even consensus but the citizen must abide by majority votes because they were the only way to interpret it. In other words, the citizen does not obey the will of the majority, but the majority *interpretation* of the general will. The general will is the interest of the community; individuals' wills consist of a self-interested part and a part which follows community interests, and so if individuals get together and debate, their self-interest would as it were be cancelled out by the opposite self-interest of some of their fellows. However, Rousseau also understood that communities exist within communities, and each of these can have their own general will. His solution was to ban all sub-communities, and to insist that 'each citizen should think only his own thoughts'. The 'little platoons' of which Burke wrote, churches, unions, political parties, and interest groups, would be superseded by the state representing the general will and the individual. This is not liberty as most would understand it. Condorcet's twist on

Rousseau's ideas, to replace the idea of the 'general will' with that of 'public reason', was an attempt to find an Enlightened solution to the problem because man's reason, not his will, was driven by the truth.

Most theorists saw freedom as an absence of constraint, but Rousseau added an important element that we hold dear today, the right to determine the rules by which one is governed and the magistrates who police those rules. Condorcet similarly included a democratic element to his theory of public reason; his problem was how to enshrine reason institutionally. Reason is best produced by a small, elite body (ideally using the social arithmetic that Condorcet had pioneered), but it is then important to stop that body simply becoming one more vested interest (like the *parlements* of *Ancien Régime* France). Hence the elite administration should be elected by several provincial assemblies of citizens. The theory of public reason was ultimately his downfall. Its supposed elitism, coupled with his opposition to the execution of Louis XVI, resulted in Condorcet's imprisonment (he died shortly afterwards in prison, perhaps by suicide in order to escape the guillotine). His capture, ironically, was facilitated by his aristocratic accent, which marked him out from the peasants among whom he hoped to remain concealed.

Gender

Democracy usually includes a tacit agreement that people are to be treated equally by the system, however unequal they are in capacity. But some people are more equal than others, and Rousseau's contention that the purpose and vocation of women was to delight men, expounded at some length in *Emile*, is contradictory to modern eyes.

Gender relations were the topic of much discussion, pitting two contradictory Enlightenment tropes against each other. The

Lockean idea that people's minds began as *tabulae rasae*, blank slates to be filled, downplayed innate gender difference, putting it down to differences in education and culture. On the other hand was the Rousseauvian idea that there was a distinct human nature, essentially associated with the person, and which was different for differently-constituted persons – specifically, men and women. Of course, this 'nature v nurture' debate is still ongoing.

Locke was somewhat inconsistent where women were concerned; in the vanguard of considering individuals as individuals, he assumed a traditional hierarchical model of the household. The following passage seems as contradictory as anything by Rousseau.

> But the husband and wife, though they have but one common concern, yet having different understandings, will unavoidably sometimes have different wills too. It therefore being necessary, that the last determination (i.e. the rule) should be placed somewhere, it naturally falls to the man's share, as the abler and the stronger. But this, reaching but to the things of their common interest and property, leaves the wife in the full and true possession of what by contract is her peculiar right, and at least gives the husband no more power over her than she has over his life.[9]

A wife enters into a voluntary arrangement with her husband from which she can withdraw, and she remains an individual, not the property of her husband. But if she and her husband disagree, then he gets the casting vote. And if you have the casting vote in a two-person democracy, you always get your way.

Rousseau described the genesis of gender relations through various stages of civilisation in his *Discourse on the Origin of Inequality* (1754). In the state of nature sex was promiscuous and opportunistic without long-term commitment, but as more cohesive societies developed, it became a stronger force, generating romantic love and fidelity. Fidelity, warned Rousseau, even if beneficial in itself (and it was not his, nor many of his fellow *philosophes*', long suit), generates infidelity, suspicion, desire and jealousy. Romance brings people together as lovers, but divides them as rivals, strengthening and undermining society at the same time.

Women are weaker than men, argued Rousseau, and so love was more important to them. Men can establish dominance by force, but women ('the sex that ought to obey') must use their charms. Because women (and their children) are dependent on men for shelter, food and protection, they need to dominate via cunning and selective granting of sexual favours. Self-control is essential, because women have more intense sexual desires, which leads to the idealisation of modesty and chastity. Society needs exclusive sexual relationships to function.

Rousseau translated this argument, somewhat self-servingly, into the political realm: men should rule the world, and women should rule men, but he was not the only writer to equate manliness with strength, decisiveness and effectiveness in the public realm. Jefferson's original *Declaration of Independence* argued that 'manly spirit bids us to renounce forever' government by the British (though Congress deleted these words from the final version). Meanwhile, Gibbon attributed the fall of the Roman Empire partly to its effeminate relaxation into oriental luxury, and partly to the pernicious effects of Christianity, when 'all the manly virtues [were] oppressed by the servile and pusillanimous reign of the monks,' though these criticisms are not always thought through; in the thirty-seventh chapter of *Decline and Fall*, he singles out 'the infirm minds of children and females' as particularly prone to lapses in reason, yet all the examples he gives are of men![10]

The positive aspects of the Enlightenment – science, reason, mechanism – were seen as 'masculine'. Even proto-feminist

Mary Wollstonecraft accused her opponents of arguing effeminately, and preferred to put forward 'manly' arguments dressed in 'manly' prose, which has caused problems for many of her commentators in modern times.

Despite the Enlightenment's free-thinking, rebellion against sexual stereotyping often caused hardship, as for example in the career of Catherine Macaulay. An important intellectual and radical, she was fêted for her counter to Hume's Tory history, appeared in a ubiquitous engraving as Libertas and was immortalised as History in a 2m tall statue. However, her unconventional relations with men, her love of publicity and her supposed vanity made her a target for satirists. Rumoured to be having an affair with a man thirty years older than her, she suddenly married a man twenty-six years younger; the ensuing scandal has more than effaced her quite considerable intellectual contribution. She spent her last years in America where, away from the small world of English letters, she befriended many of the leading revolutionaries, including George Washington.[11]

It was unsurprising that the same arguments and reason that produced the Rights of Man would also trigger challenges to the neglect of women's rights, but ironic (or telling) that they appeared after the Enlightenment was already crumbling, with Mary Wollstonecraft's *Vindication of the Rights of Women* (1792) in England, Olympe de Gouges' *Declaration of the Rights of Woman and the Female Citizen* (1791) in France (two years later she became a victim of Robespierre and the Terror), and Judith Sargent Murray's 'On the equality of the sexes' (1790) in America.

Race

The Enlightenment seemed from the inside to be a largely European process of advancement for light-skinned humans. In

America, the European colonial and ex-colonial population made the political pace; the polite fiction of the slave-owner's paternalistic eye and his innocent, child-like, grateful slaves was always a rather desperate one, while the natives at the frontier were treated morally and politically like rather disagreeable natural conditions, on a par with harvest failure, bad weather or disease. Even those who espoused cultural relativity blithely assumed that one needed to be white in order to enjoy its fruits. Many implicitly believed that providence itself worked in favour of whites; Norman Hampson cites the example of one thinker who compliments God on His forethought in making fleas black, so they can easily be seen on the skin.[12]

Swift's *Gulliver's Travels*, intended as an indictment of European and specifically British mores and politics, nevertheless depicts the loathsome Yahoos as distinctly negroid.

> The beast and I were brought close together, and our countenances diligently compared, both by master and servant, who thereupon repeated several times the word *Yahoo*. My horror and astonishment are not to be described, when I observed, in this abominable animal, a perfect human figure; the face of it was flat and broad, the nose depressed, the lips large, and the mouth wide. But these differences are common to all savage nations, where the lineaments of the countenance are distorted by the natives suffering their infants to lie grovelling on the earth, or by carrying them on their backs, nuzzling with their face against the mother's shoulders.

Swift is not attacking the 'savage races' in his work; the Yahoos are (and were taken at the time to be) meant to stand for European brutality and coarseness. He makes no explicit assumption of European superiority over other races – but his archetype for the lower instincts of mankind is non-European in physiognomy. His description tallies with contemporary scientific opinion, as for example the definition of 'Negro' in the

Encyclopaedia Britannica, which describes, as objective fact, supposed 'negro' behaviour.

> Vices the most notorious seem to be the portion of this unhappy race: idleness, treachery, revenge, cruelty, impudence, stealing, lying, profanity, debauchery, nastiness and intemperance, are said to have extinguished the principles of natural law, and to have silenced the reproofs of conscience.

As with gender issues, thinkers in the Enlightenment were pulled two ways. On the one hand there was the idea of the 'noble savage', totally natural and untainted by corrupt civilisation. On the other was reverence for cutting-edge European culture and aggressive racial stereotyping, for example of Africans as fundamentally unintelligent (Kant: 'this fellow was quite black from head to foot, a clear proof that what he said was stupid') or of 'Orientals' as decadent, effeminate and sensuous. North Americans were seen as the best and most noble, of the lot – which didn't stop their genocide.

Some, like Swift, thought that adverse social or geographical pressures were responsible for non-white people's supposed degeneration. Montesquieu classified everyone into five groups, of which the 'African' was crafty, indolent, negligent and governed by caprice (he also 'anoints himself with grease'). Buffon similarly thought that temperate climate zones were ideal for raising people, that white people were a standard from which others had slipped, and that European climate, food and education would make everyone white and civilised after a few generations. Jefferson's nominal opposition to slavery appears to have co-existed not only with his owning slaves, but also his believing Africans to be fundamentally inferior; hence perhaps his failure to develop any practicable scheme for freeing the enslaved. He apparently could not imagine a society where freed slaves could easily intermingle with the free-born white population. To be fair his original draft of the *Declaration* contained a ringing condemnation of slavery ('this execrable commerce'), and of George III (r.1760–1820) for failing to stop it, all of which Congress deleted, but equally George's sin was one of omission – he did not force Americans to enslave anyone. Jefferson more usually condemned slavery for its bad moral effects on the slavers, rather than for the sufferings of the enslaved.

Racism often lived alongside the belief, sometimes observed more in the breach, that all men were equal, and the result was a complex, not always edifying, set of attitudes. Hume blithely assumed that 'negroes' had little or no higher intellectual capacity, yet also railed against the inhuman practice of slavery, of which the more radical *Declaration of the Rights of Man and the Citizen* makes no mention. In fact, many of the leading campaigners against slavery and racism subscribed to a theory of degeneracy – they felt that though non-whites were inferior and savage, this was not their fault.[13]

The campaign against the slave trade had its roots in the writings of many people in the Enlightenment, but it has to be admitted that the abolitionist movement really gained momentum towards the end of our period (the Committee for the Abolition of the Slave Trade was founded in 1787), and many if not all of the leading lights had religious, not Enlightened, objections. Indeed, in America itself it was largely the unenlightened radicals and dissenters who were most opposed to slavery. The moderate Anglican Church, which took seriously the Enlightened writings of Locke and Samuel Clarke (1675–1729), tried hard to accommodate the opinions of slavers. Anglicans were wont to argue that religious instruction would make slaves harder-working and more docile, although slavers were usually and probably correctly suspicious of that idea.[14] Opposition to slavery in the Enlightenment tended to be literary and philosophical, and rarely translated into effective political action. The careful compromise that is the American Constitution tiptoed round the issue; too strong a condemnation would have caused the secession of the slave states of Georgia and South Carolina and possibly others. Moderate liberalism on the Lockean model never threatened what was recognised by most at the time as a moral outrage. Diderot and Adam Smith had the most 'modern' disgust against both slavery and empire, and win our admiration most frequently on this topic.

Enlightened absolutism

Political debate and practical politics traded on a tacit distinction between democratic processes and democratic outcomes. There was suspicion of processes which would grant 'the mob' a say in affairs commensurate with their numerical superiority, to say nothing of the enfranchisement of women or non-white people. But thinkers were keen to ensure democratic *outcomes* that were just and which did not favour particular rent-seeking classes. It was thought by many, including Voltaire and Kant, that the way to do this, ironically, was to have a sovereign who, free from too much democratic accountability, would be powerful enough to enforce just outcomes. Recall Kant's argument in 'What is Enlightenment?' quoted at the beginning of chapter one, which expresses in its least diluted form the top-down aspect of Enlightenment.

The first half of the Enlightenment was an Age of Kings, kings who were inward-looking and conventionally inclined to pursue personal and national aggrandisement, but the second half was the Age of the Benevolent Despot, who supported Enlightenment and wished to implement it, often in return for some flattery from a *philosophe* or two. The enthusiasm went right to the top – Frederick the Great of Prussia's *Essay on Forms of Government* (1777) circumscribed the role of the monarch and contained not a mention of divine right. The services that the monarch should provide consisted in:

> ... the maintenance of the laws; a strict execution of justice; an
> employment of his whole powers to prevent any corruption of
> manners; and defending the state against its enemies. It is the
> duty of this magistrate to pay attention to agriculture; it should
> be his care that provisions for the nation should be in
> abundance, and that commerce and industry should be
> encouraged.

Frederick was adamant that the monarch should not abuse
his position, and argued that 'he and his people form but one
body, which can only be happy as far as united by concord' – in
other words, that the interests of the sovereign are identical
to the public good. Furthermore, the monarch should be
hands-on, and as far as possible should not delegate.
Frederick's use of a Lockean contractual argument is particularly
interesting.

> Princes and monarchs, therefore, are not invested with supreme
> authority that they may, with impunity, riot in debauchery and
> voluptuousness. They are not raised *by their fellow citizens* in
> order that their pride may pompously display itself, and
> contemptuously insult simplicity of manners, poverty and
> wretchedness. Government is not *entrusted to them* that they may
> be surrounded by a crowd of useless people, whose idleness
> engenders every vice. (My italics)

Frederick employed a similar premise to argue for religious
tolerance, universal and proportionate taxation, and that serfdom
was 'barbarous' and an 'abuse'.

As Pombal's experience in Portugal showed (recall chapter
three), if the right person gets him- or herself into a position of
power at the right time, he or she could do a lot of good.
Frederick was alive to the problems of having the wrong person
in power, but makes no suggestion as to how to prevent that

happening. Montesquieu's notion of the separation of powers would have mitigated the risks of the regression such as happened in Portugal after Pombal's fall, but equally would have stood in the way of Prussian-style transformation. Furthermore, in the absence of a revolution, separation of powers could only be implemented by an Enlightened ruler, who would by this very action make his own job so much harder. Only England functioned well with a limited monarchy; Poland's elective monarchy was controlled by powerful nobles who had so weakened central power that it was partitioned three times and eventually wiped out. Little wonder that the American Revolution, which cut through this Gordian knot, was influential.

In the second half of the Enlightenment, a cluster of monarchs emerged who actively aspired to the role of Enlightened despot. Philosopher kings and queens were in fashion, among kings and queens at least. As well as Frederick the Great, there were Joseph II and Maria Theresa of Austria, Catherine the Great of Russia, Gustavus III of Sweden, Stanisław II of Poland and Charles III of Spain, not to mention many a German princeling who followed the crowd, and powerful ministers like Pombal in Portugal. Some of these monarchs were more Enlightened than others. Maria Theresa was a motherly Catholic, although she banned capital punishment, pioneered inoculation against smallpox and reformed the condition of serfs. At the same time she was religiously and morally intolerant, expelling the Jews from Prague. In their desire to do good and to transform society these despots differed enormously from earlier cultured, dominant figures like Louis XIV. Perhaps only Peter the Great from the early part of the century would have appreciated their aims, though their methods would have seemed enormously effete to the old ruffian.

It probably goes without saying that the freedom and rights that the monarchs talked about tended to be observed more in the breach. Inequalities continued to be tolerated, and bureaucracies continued to govern in their own interests. Foreign policy was unprincipled and hard-nosed, especially now the spread of empire meant that the powers were distributed across the globe, defending territory and trading monopolies in the Americas, Africa or Asia. 'When one has an advantage,' asked Frederick, 'is he to use it or not?' 'He who gains nothing, loses' wrote Catherine, pithily. Power and opportunity were the drivers of foreign policy in the Enlightenment, perhaps nowhere more obviously than in the Partition of Poland by Prussia, Russia and Austria in 1772. All three powers needed a base in Eastern Europe – so they took one.

Enlightened thought, with its concept of inalienable human rights and the theoretical equality at some level of all people, was inherently inimical to serfdom, the condition of semi-slavery where a villager was born into service of his or her lord. Yet cheap labour is useful in and of itself, and also a source of military force, so Enlightened absolutism was particularly tested in this regard. The attitudes of three despots make an interesting contrast. Joseph II conducted a long campaign to abolish serfdom in his extensive empire, but failed to break the passive resistance of the nobility. The somewhat cannier Frederick the Great of Prussia fulminated against it, but accepted that the practice must linger.

> No man certainly was born to be the slave of his equal. We reasonably detest such an abuse; and it is supposed that nothing more than will is wanting to abolish so barbarous a custom. But this is not true; it is held on ancient tenures, and contracts made between the landholders and the colonists ... [W]hoever should suddenly desire to abolish this abominable administration would entirely overthrow the mode of managing estates, and must be obliged, in part, to indemnify the nobility for the losses which their rents must suffer.

Meanwhile in Russia, Catherine nominally opposed serfdom yet presided over its growth. The vast size of the nation made it virtually impossible for central government to maintain contact with the peasantry, and as in the Austrian empire the nobility was an important intermediary with no incentive to promote change. A serious problem with top-down change in the Enlightenment was that without good communications, rulers were dependent on regional bigwigs and nobles to implement change, and when they were reluctant to cooperate there was relatively little the ruler could do.

The revolutions

Benevolent despotism was clearly a dead end, and when *philosophes* visited the courts of the despots (Frederick played host to Voltaire and Catherine to Diderot) they tended to be disappointed. Of much more importance for the elevation of democracy as an ideal were the revolutions in 1776 and 1789. Democracy in America was something of an afterthought, and the system that the victorious revolutionaries imposed was indebted to Britain's own representative system, albeit with a broader franchise. Several conservative thinkers, notably Burke, were supporters of the American Revolution because it, unlike the perverse colonial government, preserved political continuity.

The American constitution was a beacon of rational politics developed over a long period of deliberation after self-government had been won, drafted at a convention in Philadelphia in 1787, and ratified in 1789. The publication of the constitution resulted in much high-quality political debate, in particular a set of pseudonymously-written newspaper articles (under the name 'Publius', after a Republican Roman consul) that became known as the *Federalist Papers*. Actually written by James

Madison, Alexander Hamilton and John Jay, they tried to design a representative government strong enough to levy taxes and defend the nation, subtle enough not to be ensnared by factions yet not powerful enough to threaten hard-won liberty. They rejected the label 'democracy' (in the Aristotelian sense of rule by the many) altogether, and excluded 'the people in their collective capacity' from lawmaking. The authority of the government would be derived in a Lockean way from regular votes of the people, but its institutions would be controlled by the government, not the people. The democratic element was firmly representative, so the people would not make decisions, but instead would have a say in who the decision-makers would be. The 'people', at this stage, included neither women nor slaves. Montesquieu was invoked to ensure that no arm of government had enough power to become over-mighty, while the great republican thinkers of Ancient Greece such as Pericles and Demosthenes also cast a long shadow over the debate. Madison was the leading light and, having drawn his major insights from Hume, saw the use of reason to govern passions as the key problem in politics; the constitution was an attempt to do just that.

Even as the Americans were creating a system for institutionalising moderate conservatism, the moderate centre of the Enlightenment was shrinking as a result of pressure from two directions. Hard questions were being asked of moderates – if humanity is perfectible, and there is no original sin, why can humankind not govern itself? Meanwhile, radicals, especially in oppressive states, suspected that American-style compromise would not work in a European context.[15]

Ironically, the moderation of the American Revolution encouraged the more extreme of the French thinkers by providing a successful revolutionary example; had it been more extreme it might have been more disruptive, and less beguiling. The notion of a democratic republic was seen, in the France of

Louis XIV and Louis XV, as a pipedream that could only happen on the small scale, such as in the city states of Ancient Greece, or Rousseau's idealised Geneva, but the overthrow of British power in 1776, and the success of the new American Republic emboldened the democrats against liberal constitutionalists such as Voltaire and Montesquieu, neither of whom lived to play his part in the debates of the 1780s. The sheer size of America excited thinkers such as Condorcet who realised that a revolution throughout France was not only possible but feasible. Jefferson, in Paris from 1785–9, was cautious, advising reform and worrying about the naïvety of the French citizenry and the dangers of conservative reaction.

Few of the living *philosophes* were opposed to revolution. Although Diderot wanted revolution, he characteristically (though anonymously) questioned the right of the American rebels to be in America at all. In so far as they were the American population they had a right to change their government, but as their society was established on the displacement of the native American population and supported economically by the exploitation of African slaves, could they really argue that America had been legitimately appropriated at all?

In America, democratic thinking was almost a *post hoc* method of rationalising the Revolution, but the discontent in France meant that philosophers had wondered all along about how to empower the people to some degree. The Marquis d'Argenson (1694–1757) suggested in his *Considerations on the Ancient and Present Government of France* (published posthumously in 1764) that democratic consultation could be used to support the king. The king, being king, naturally had the interests of the nation as a whole at heart – in fact the two were inseparable – but as an individual he might easily be unaware of the situation of the poor.

The Abbé Joseph Sieyes provided an important contribution at the outset of the revolution with a series of pamphlets in

1788–9 drawing on some of the major thinkers of the time, most obviously Adam Smith, following d'Argenson in wanting to harness the democratic spirit without bringing the whole edifice of government down. Again, representation was the means, but only because France was too large to convene direct forums. A series of bitter political and economic disputes had led to the king to go some way along the path d'Argenson advocated, and to consult the three estates of the realm, advisory bodies which were intended to represent the main social groups. Sieyes, perhaps frustrated by the lack of constructive engagement with his ideas from the privileged estates of the church and aristocracy, railed against privilege and in his great pamphlet *What is the Third Estate?* answered his own question with the word 'everything'. Everything that needs to be done can be done by the third estate (which contained everyone except the aristocracy and the clergy); the first two estates had separated themselves off from the nation and had become 'foreign'. He was not entirely sure what should replace the current situation, but he was very sure that the current arrangement of privileges could not be justified.[16]

The reaction: Burke, the Americans and de Maistre

The French Revolution was foreseen by very few, and it developed a fearsome momentum of its own. An early phase beginning in 1789 provided some necessary restraint on the hapless French monarch Louis XVI, but within four years the political process became irretrievably radicalised. The monarchy was abolished in 1792, and Louis put on trial at the end of that year for high treason, found guilty and executed early in 1793 (his Queen Marie Antoinette followed later that year). A power struggle in the new National Convention between the parties of the Jacobins and the Girondins (who opposed the executions) ended in the complete triumph of the Jacobins led by Maximilien Robespierre, a disciple of Rousseau who wanted a system which would implement the general will of the French nation. In a febrile atmosphere in 1793–4, thousands of political prisoners, including most of the Girondins' leaders and ultimately most of the Jacobins, were killed in pursuit of purity and virtue; at the end, in July 1794, Robespierre himself was toppled, and guillotined the day afterwards. The Terror, as this period was called, was a frightening episode that fatally interrupted the flow of revolutionary events and ideas, and the revolution died as Napoleon crowned himself emperor.

There was an immediate response to the events in France which created the dialectic between revolutionary politics and conservatism which lasted at least until the collapse of the Soviet Union in 1989, and arguably is still present in political thought. The most famous and distinguished reaction (actually a reply to a sermon by cleric and philosopher Richard Price) was Burke's *Reflections on the Revolution in France*, which appeared as early as 1790, yet eerily foretold the breakdown of French society well before the September massacres or the Terror. The work is a key conservative text – to take one example, Russell Kirk's authoritative *Conservative Reader* includes six passages from the *Reflections*, and three from other pieces by Burke, far more than any other writer.

Although Burke supported the American Revolution, he despised the French one, and correctly predicted the anarchy that would follow. He believed that the revolution of 1776, like 1688 in England, was caused by futile resistance to rational political change by blinkered British governments, whereas 1789 was a complete overhaul of a moral system. The American Revolution was made both more likely and more necessary by British misrule, and was probably the best course of action because it fitted the temper of the American people and preserved most institutions, traditions and practices; the French Revolution overturned everything, on the say-so of fallible reason. Burke denied that any narrow class of politician would be able to represent the spread of interest and opinion in France.

Burkean conservatism, however, is not merely an appalled reaction to the Revolution, but contains within it several Enlightenment assumptions and patterns of reasoning. For instance, Burke applied Enlightenment ideas about human nature to culture. The French Revolutionaries had focused too much on universal human nature, and so assumed that they could build a system from scratch that was fair, tolerable and appropriate for the whole of French (and ultimately European) society. Against this, Burke argued that the culture in which one was born was a vital determinant of personality that meant that human universals would be outweighed by cultural specifics (a position supported, incidentally, by Rousseau). One was brought up surrounded by familial structures of varying strengths, governments of varying power and intrusiveness, arts and crafts, property rights, geography and – not least – religious beliefs and customs that were passed down and which shaped one's personality. This would be true across societies as well as between them. It followed that thinkers in Parisian salons could not dictate the ideal conditions for any society, even their own.

It also followed that the whole idea of the social contract, as developed in the tradition from Hobbes to Locke to Rousseau, was flawed. The fatal disanalogy was that one chooses the conditions to which one will be bound when one signs a contract but one does not choose one's society, family, culture, values, language, religious background or economic, social and educative inheritance. It is impossible to factor these out of any description of, or political mechanism for achieving, the good life for an entire society. Burke wrote before the collapse of the Revolutionary ideals, but he certainly anticipated the clashes of interests that occurred. The bourgeois revolutionaries failed to speak for either the aristocrats or the radical Parisian wage-earners known as the *sans-culottes* (who played a decisive role in the Terror). Society was a plural, diverse group of people with no single 'point of view', which therefore required compromise and brokerage between the different interests. Therefore the best way to ensure that individuation of culture was catered for in politics was not to try to engineer institutions and outcomes, but rather to observe and preserve the institutions and traditions that had grown up organically alongside society. Scrapping these would lead to calamity, as so much social regulation is informal and not rule-based. Burke was not at all surprised at the murderous chaos into which the French Revolution descended.

Some of the most surprising passages in the *Reflections* concern the decline of chivalry in France, and the attacks on Marie Antoinette (she had been attacked by mobs long before her execution). Burke here sketched a philosophy of social protection, arguing that one function of traditions like chivalry is precisely to protect weaker people (notably women) from attack, ridicule and humiliation. Chivalry is symbolic of the victory of civilisation over brute force. This is an important example of his attempts to ensure that manners and emotions – what he called 'moral certainty' to distinguish it from rational certainty – were brought back into political thought.

Many of Burke's ideas were anticipated by the authors of the *Federalist Papers*. For instance, James Madison, in no.49 (written in 1788), argued that regular democratic appeals to the people would 'deprive the government of that veneration which time bestows on everything, and without which perhaps the wisest and freest governments would not possess the requisite stability

… A reverence for the laws would be sufficiently inculcated by the voice of enlightened reason. But a nation of philosophers is as little to be expected as the philosophical race of kings wished for by Plato.' Madison certainly did not want America to set a revolutionary example.

> The danger of disturbing the public tranquillity by interesting too strongly the public passions is a still more serious objection against a frequent reference of constitutional questions to the decision of the whole society. Notwithstanding the success which has attended the revisions of our established forms of government and which does so much honor to the virtue and intelligence of the people of America, it must be confessed that the experiments are of too ticklish a nature to be unnecessarily multiplied.

John Adams also replied, at somewhat shorter length than Burke, to Richard Price with a letter that included the famous line 'I know not what to make of a republic of thirty million atheists.' He deeply opposed the creation of a legislature of a single chamber, worried about the lack of balance in the institutional structures, and was appalled if not surprised by the bloodshed. He blamed the more radical of *les philosophes*, particularly Rousseau.

The other important immediate reaction came from Joseph de Maistre, who extended ideas of Enlightenment conservatism to connect them more strongly with an older reactionary tradition. The Burkean criticisms of contractarian theory were based on the observation that several types of human behaviour, especially custom and habit, were essentially uncalculating; de Maistre followed this line of reasoning to delineate many other deeply irrational types of political behaviour, including sacrifice. He also took the Burkean idea (following Montesquieu) that culture influences political institutions, and argued beyond it that actually the real 'constitution' of a nation was to be found not in its institutions but its culture – the habits, norms and behaviour that people follow uncomprehendingly. Any written political constitution would either have to respect these, or be irrelevant and ignored.

On the other hand, he admired sovereignty, and thought the exercise of power was vital to prevent anarchy. For this reason, he was dismissive of most of the actors in the French Revolution, who at various times had power within their grasp and failed to deploy it – everyone from Louis XVI to the Girondins were guilty. On the other hand, the Jacobins, whatever their faults (a long list, as far as de Maistre was concerned), at least did something with their power, and while establishing a rough and ready type of order at home also won wars abroad. To that extent, de Maistre admired them, all the while condemning them for their Godlessness and bloodthirstiness.[17]

Counter-reaction: Wollstonecraft, Paine and Godwin

Burke's rapidly-written and intemperate attack on the Revolution received answers in kind almost immediately. Indeed, if the French Revolution spawned, as an unintended consequence, the greatest work of conservative philosophy ever written, the *Reflections* also provoked at least three major radical texts as unintended consequences of its own. Mary Wollstonecraft's *A Vindication of the Rights of Men* appeared within a month of the *Reflections*, attacking Burke's vision of a world governed by tradition as completely inappropriate for an advanced world of commerce in which men were entitled to consideration on their own terms as rational creatures. She turned the tables on Burke by exposing the patronising senti-mentality of the defence of Marie Antoinette – Wollstonecraft was not at all sympathetic to the queen, whom she found vulgar, and whose scheming undermined Louis' precarious position as the Revolution unfolded. She accused Burke, bluntly, of fawning to the riches and the glory of the French royal family, of a 'contempt for the poor' and of 'contemptible hard-hearted sophistry, in the specious form of humility.'

She developed her ideas further in *A Vindication of the Rights of Woman* (1792), where she moved on from Burke to the resolutely sexist, now deceased, Rousseau; this is a work of great importance and originality too, but beyond the scope of this survey. However, it is worth noting that after the massacres which Burke had anticipated, Wollstonecraft did return to the subject of the Revolution, with her *Historical and Moral View of the French Revolution* (1794) in which she tried to separate the high ideals of the Revolution from their flawed implementation, and argued that the Terror was connected much more with the monarchy than the ideals of Enlightenment; the revolutionaries suffered from the failures of the French national character as much as the defeated royalists.

The first part of Thomas Paine's great work *The Rights of Man* appeared in February 1791, and was soon translated into French. The second part appeared in 1792, and is supposed to have sold nearly a million and a half copies, an incredible number for these times. Paine felt the heat – he was forced to flee to France, and was found guilty of seditious libel in Britain shortly afterwards. The first part of the book is a direct reply to Burke, its opening lines making the ironic point that he should not have lectured the French about their politics if he was serious about the importance of distinct cultures.

Among the incivilities by which nations or individuals provoke and irritate each other, Mr Burke's pamphlet on the French Revolution is an extraordinary instance. Neither the People of

France, nor the National Assembly, were troubling themselves about the affairs of England, or the English Parliament; and why Mr Burke should commence an unprovoked attack upon them, both in parliament and in public, is a conduct that cannot be pardoned on the score of manners, nor justified on that of policy.

Burke had extolled a neutered version of the Glorious Revolution, but Paine replied that the French Revolution was in the tradition of the far more important American Revolution. Indeed, although Burke was moved by the shedding of blood, more blood was spilt in America than France (Paine wrote before the Terror). In the second part of the book, he set out a positive set of proposals to reform British politics, including progressive taxation, and maintained that war could be abolished by compact between America, France and a Britain reformed along the lines Paine suggested.

Having fled to France, Paine was initially welcomed. The Assembly made him a citizen (joining an elite group which included Bentham, Priestley, George Washington, Hamilton and Madison), and he was elected as a deputy. However, in *The Rights of Man* Paine had called for Louis to be given a pension and allowed to leave the political stage, though he was naturally in favour of the republic. This moderate position put him in the Girondin camp, and he soon found himself awaiting execution. This he avoided apparently by pure chance, and managed to hang on until the fall of Robespierre. He seems to have blamed his period in prison on the machinations of George Washington; he harangued the latter, to whom he had dedicated the first part of *The Rights of Man*, with a long published letter in 1795, ending with the scathing comment:

And as to you, Sir, treacherous in private friendship (for so you have been to me, and that in the day of danger) and a hypocrite

in public life, the world will be puzzled to decide whether you
are an apostate or an impostor; whether you have abandoned
good principles, or whether you ever had any.[18]

William Godwin (later to become Wollstonecraft's husband)
had helped with the publication of *The Rights of Man*, but knew
that Paine was no philosopher. With that in mind, he conceived
his *Enquiry Concerning Political Justice* (1793) which dealt with the
Revolutionary arguments against a more rarefied background of
an abstract discussion of truth and reason, blending Lockean
empiricism with utilitarianism. Effectively, he found that *all*
government was bad, founded on opinion and valued by people
only in so far as they were weak and ignorant. Evil was basically
ignorance, and the cause was faulty education, perpetuated by
tyranny and greed. There was no place in a moral code for
subjective ideas: one should save the theologian and poet
Fénelon from a fire before one saved one's mother, because
Fénelon was of more use to mankind. On the other hand, he
strongly rejected Rousseau's argument that society was a moral
individual with a general will as an 'unintelligible chimera'.
Monarchy was no doubt the worst system, and no system that
incorporated a hereditary element was acceptable; Burkean
'tradition' was meaningless, and certainly not a factor in determining systemic legitimacy. Even Godwin's defence of representative republican democracy was negative: it might prevent
some evils but the truth of a political matter cannot be resolved
by a vote. Furthermore, a public vote can be subverted, but a
secret ballot facilitated hypocrisy, a particular bugbear of the
Enlightenment. Communication was the essence of liberty.
Government merely perpetuated the evils that it claimed to
remove. In the end, Godwin, who started out close to Paine,
developed one of the earliest recognisably anarchist political
theories.[19]

The French Revolution and the Enlightenment

The effect of the Revolution was to split the Enlightenment legacy into two, the moderate and the radical. The early phases of the Revolution were relatively benign, and although blood was shed, the world was hardly turned upside down. The French and American Revolutions were different in many ways but arguably in the same tradition, stemming from the Glorious Revolution of 1688, the measured arguments of Locke and Montesquieu, the scepticism and anti-clericalism of Voltaire and Diderot.

But the Terror polarised opinion. The Revolutionaries themselves consciously disconnected themselves from their moderate forebears. Robespierre tried to implement Rousseau's ideas, such as that of a secular religion to support civic society, while Voltaire and other *philosophes* fell out of favour – the bust of Helvétius which had pride of place in the Jacobin Club was removed on Robespierre's orders in 1792. Furthermore, the French had based much of their admiration of America, and much of the rationale for their own actions, on the obviously false idea that the American Republic was a completely new beginning for mankind. In fact, the Americans remained steeped in the English tradition, and many saw themselves as reinstating that tradition against an English government that had turned its back on it. Elsewhere, the Terror reduced the ground available to moderate Enlightened figures – it seemed one had to be a radical, and accept the bloodshed as the affordable price of liberty, or oppose all progress.

Only in America, well away from the carnage, could an Enlightenment of sorts carry on, although a conservative and neutered Enlightenment which repudiated the French upheaval. Indeed, the French Revolution remained popular there for some years, the excesses of the Terror put down to the iniquities of European monarchy and the evils of Catholicism, although sympathy waned eventually. America had had its own conflict along the same lines, as a radical constitution in Pennsylvania, admired by *les philosophes* and criticised by John Adams, had forced apart moderates and radicals, somewhat impeding the revolutionary effort in that state. However, neither the imposition of that constitution in 1776, nor its repeal in 1790, had been accompanied by great violence on the part of the victors, and so broad unity was preserved.[20]

7

Nature, reason and science

There has been much talk in the previous two chapters about nature: human nature, the state of nature, natural law. Indeed, it has been said that nature was 'the key Enlightenment concept'.[1] So it is not surprising that there was a great deal of investigation of nature that could either be scientific or theological – the book of nature could be read directly, or by contemplation of its creator. This chapter and the next will look in particular at developments in mankind's understanding of nature during the Enlightenment.

In general science advanced and religion declined, or, rather, scientific, critical and experimental thinking spread beyond a tiny intellectual clique, becoming a major influence, including on religion itself. It was increasingly understood that the world about us (both natural and supernatural) could be understood by using our reason. Indeed, the Enlightenment thinkers conceived of what we would now call science as continuous with philosophy (in English it was called 'natural philosophy'), although as Jonathan Israel has argued they were also conscious that the investigation of nature was going through a revolutionary period kick-started by Descartes.[2] Reason and experiment were not such common practices that their limitations became obvious. Even highly reactionary groups such as the Jesuits and the Jansenists found they made more progress when they armed themselves with the logical weapons of their enemies.

Scientific and mathematical progress was steady rather than impressive. The seventeenth century had been fertile if chaotic, with important contributions made by Kepler, Galileo, Descartes, Hooke, Boyle, van Leeuwenhoek, Swammerdam, Huygens, Stensen and Harvey to name but a few. The nineteenth century was the period where science really took off and became accepted as the most reliable source of knowledge. The Enlightenment, in contrast, was a period of consolidation where something approaching scientific method began to appear, and methodical analysis, investigation and experiment became prominent. A steady stream of results followed, but Newton, whose formative thought preceded the Enlightenment, looms largest.

His influence was powerful, but Enlightened scepticism would not allow wholly uncritical acceptance. I have already mentioned Pierre Bayle who challenged everyone and everything including Newton, but the French in general were very slow in discarding Cartesian mechanics for Newton's, while David Gregory (1659–1708), Euler and Chester Moor Hall (1703–71) challenged his theory of the limits of optical instruments. With a broader satirical brush, Swift's *Gulliver's Travels* contains a hilarious episode (book III, chapter five) in which members of the Academy of Lagado, situated in the clouds, tell us about their crazy scientific investigations (for example, extracting sunbeams from cucumbers, producing food from human excrement and investigating whether blind people could learn to feel colours) all of which appear to be genuine, and which Swift noted upon his own visit to the Royal Society in 1710.

These seem crazy now, but at the time there appeared to be no limits to the possibilities of man's understanding of the natural world. The pioneering work of Descartes and Newton into the understanding of motion was largely responsible for that confidence. Yet while Newton showed what reason could achieve when applied to discovery about the natural world, the fate of Descartes' theories already hinted at some of its limits.

Descartes, Newton and the fundamental laws of motion

In the years building up to the Enlightenment, a series of observations had been made of the heavens that had gradually undermined the adaptation of Ptolemaic astronomy intended to be consistent with the Bible that was promulgated by the Catholic Church. Copernicus, Tycho Brahe, Kepler and Galileo had all either shown the theory to be in error, or had produced alternatives which were better at explaining the observations. Galileo, the last of these men, was brought before the Inquisition, but treated leniently because of his age; he was forced to deny his own ideas, and sentenced to house arrest. It is safe to say that in 1642, the year of Galileo's death and Isaac Newton's birth, astronomy, physics and mechanics were in crisis.

Descartes' influence was important at this time. He was not an empirical scientist as we would recognise, but developed a theoretical system alongside (and as a corollary to) his philosophical work. The theory of *vortices*, influential for decades, was derived from pure thought, and although it required the existence of God to work, the Church always opposed it and suppressed it where it could. Although its creation precedes our era, it remained, thanks to a most un-Enlightened intellectual nationalism, a fixture in France at least until Voltaire began to popularise Newtonian thought in French in 1738.

The Cartesian system was based on four conceptual assumptions and one physical one. The concepts were: (i) the universe must be infinite, as the idea of a limitation to space is contradictory; (ii) it is always conceivable that a piece of matter could be divided, and so atoms, primitive 'units' of matter, cannot exist; (iii) there is no such thing as a vacuum, and therefore space must be filled with matter; and (iv) at Creation, God must have set the universe of matter in motion, because otherwise there would be no change. The physical assumption is now known as the principle of the conservation of momentum, implying that the total quantities of matter and motion remain constant in the universe. Because there is no vacuum, every time some matter moves, it has to be replaced at the same point in space by another piece of matter. These constantly moving particles collect into vortices, which rotate and exert pressure outwards. Fiery matter congregates in the middle, forming a star, while heavier particles revolve around. Planets, comets and other bodies are formed when stars accrete too much material and the vortex collapses.

The theory of vortices, by describing how planets orbit stars, supported the heretical theory of Copernicus, but there were many details that still needed working out, such as a precise explanation of Kepler's observations that planets orbited the sun on elliptical orbits. Many astronomers managed to work out that the sun's attraction operated on an inverse square law whereby the attraction diminished by the square of the distance of the planet from the sun, but the mathematics of such a system were impossible to work out before the invention of the calculus by Newton and Leibniz (see below), which allowed scientists to express the relations between constantly changing quantities such as the distance between an object and the sun, or the velocity of an object as it orbited.

Newton's intellectual domination of the age stemmed from his creation of a theory, backed by rigorous mathematics, to explain celestial, and indeed all, motion. The publication of his great work, the *Philosophiae Naturalis Principia Mathematica* (1687) helped start the Enlightenment, and remained influential throughout it, even on people who never read or could read it. It set out the three laws of motion on which were based the physics of centuries hence. The first law is that an object will continue moving at a constant velocity unless and until a net force is applied to it. The second, that the rate of change of momentum of an object (momentum being the product of its mass and velocity) is proportional to, and in the same direction as, the net force applied. When the mass of the object is constant, this law boils down to the famous formula $F = ma$ – force equals mass times acceleration – so the larger the mass of an object, the greater the force needed to get it to accelerate or decelerate at a given rate. The third law, that every force is paired with an equal and opposite force, can be used to derive the Cartesian principle of conservation of momentum.

Part of Newton's originality came from his refinements of scientific method. Whereas Descartes had tried to derive laws of nature from metaphysical principles and *a priori* ideas, Newton preferred the combination of analysis and synthesis, inducing laws governing reality, and then deducing their consequences. This method of induction and deduction was not original to Newton (it was advocated by Bacon for example), but was improved by him in two key ways. First he stressed that induced laws needed strong and frequent confirmation by experimental or observational evidence, and second he insisted that the experiments go beyond the original inductive evidence. He formulated a three-stage process for the advancement of science: first, a system of mathematically-specified definitions, axioms and theorems should be created; this axiom system should then be given an interpretation in terms of observable aspects of the real world; finally, the deductive consequences of the axiom system should be compared to experimental evidence, using the interpretation developed in the previous stage. This highly successful method strongly influenced all philosophers of the Enlightenment, including Locke, Leibniz and Kant.

The laws of motion set out above, or rather their precise mathematical expression (i.e. the axiom system), were shown by Newton to entail Kepler's observations of elliptical planet orbits, the inverse square law of attraction and many other observations. Particularly important was the computation by Sir Edmond

Halley, using Newton's theory, that the comet of 1682 would return in 1758; it did, a few days late, having been delayed by a slightly stronger effect than expected on the comet by the planet Jupiter. The fertility of Newton's laws was also vindicated by their use in the discovery of Uranus in 1781 by William Herschel.

The attraction of one body to another was neither the centrifugal/centripetal force that Descartes suggested in his vortex theory, nor magnetism, another popular choice among physicists and astronomers, but rather a universal force operating between any pair of bodies: gravity. The universality of gravity helped unify all sorts of calculations – the description of the attraction of two planets was in terms identical to the description of the attraction of two feathers, or indeed of a planet and a feather. Newton did not go into detail about what gravity was, other than setting out its properties as an attractor obeying the inverse square law and its sufficiency with respect to the prediction of the motion of the planets, and this rather English refusal to speculate metaphysically was another factor in the slow acceptance of Newtonian mechanics in France.

Institutions

Scientific development was aided by new institutional forms for storing and transmitting knowledge. The Royal Society, founded in 1660, was centrally involved in the publication of Newton's *Principia* (although in the event its finances were not up to the task),[3] and was a very important conduit for the new sciences. The Enlightenment was a sociable age, and the trend toward urbanisation that marked the century fostered innovation by bringing together scientists and patrons in societies where they could both discuss their work, and also form institutional relationships to regulate, judge and referee scientific progress. Most of the major academies of importance had already appeared by the beginning of our era, and are more properly part of the story of the seventeenth century, but their existence was extremely important – none more so than the Royal Society. The Académie des Sciences in France followed in 1666 and the Academy of Sciences in Berlin in 1700. All were devoted not only to the pursuit of science, but to publication and dissemination too. In America, scientists reported to the Royal Society until its own academies appeared; the American Philosophical Society Held at Philadelphia for Promoting Useful Knowledge, founded in 1768 as a merger of two smaller groups, and whose first president was Benjamin Franklin, was the most important society of the immediate pre- and post-revolutionary period.

The transient nature of institutions in an age of temperamental kings was demonstrated by the Florentine Accademia del Cimento, set up in 1657 by two of the Medici family with scientific interests and two of Galileo's students; Medici politics led to it closing down after ten years, but it had already promoted some advanced science. It may be that the longevity of the British, French and German efforts were down to their growing organically out of decades of informal meetings among scientists which the societies in question simply formalised; the Italians had many more formal learned societies, but few lasted longer than a few years.

However, this was not necessarily a problem. Much of the transmission of ideas happened away from the major metropolitan centres as provincial scientific academies proliferated, to some extent stepping into the breach as universities tended to keep to a traditional, classical curriculum of study and research. Places such as Bologna, Copenhagen, Dublin and Uppsala could support academies, private societies flourished alongside them, and journals sprang up to spread ideas further. It was in the Enlightenment that contributing to specialised periodicals became the chief outlet for scientific research.[4]

The sciences

The excitement that Newton generated, the new institutional support and improvements in the precision and theoretical value of scientific instruments meant that science made impressive progress during the century, even though it cannot be called a golden age. In optics, the nature of light had been a locus of theory and experiment for some time, and once more Newton led the way, demonstrating that white light was a mixture of light of all other colours by splitting a ray of sunlight into its component spectrum, and recombining it. His *Opticks*, however, was his last scientific publication (1704, twenty-three years before he died). He was President of the Royal Society, but moved from research to administration, amateur theology and even alchemy.[5]

The investigation of electricity began seriously in the 1720s when Stephen Gray (1666–1736) discovered that it could be transmitted over distance, while Charles-François Dufay (1698–1739) discovered that electrified bodies would either attract or repel each other. The first capacitor, the so-called Leiden Jar, was invented by Pieter van Musschenbroek in 1745 to 'store' static electricity, making possible a greater range of experiments. By 1750, Benjamin Franklin had been able to use a Leiden Jar to show that lightning was static electricity, and Franklin, Joseph Priestley, Henry Cavendish and Charles Coulomb were pioneers in the quantitative analysis of electricity, showing that its attractive and repulsive forces varied, like gravity, according to an inverse square law (Coulomb also showed that magnetic attraction varied in the same way).

In 1780 in Italy, Luigi Galvani showed that applying an electrical charge to a frog's spinal cord caused its legs to twitch (these experiments helped suggest the idea of *Frankenstein* to Mary Shelley). Galvani misinterpreted the experiment, believing that the frog's nerves contained a subtle fluid generating and carrying the electrical force around its body, which Alessandro Volta correctly realised that the frog was simply conducting electricity. There was a bitter dispute between the two, but the experimental method was by now so deeply ingrained in the Enlightenment consciousness that the question was finally settled, in Volta's favour, by a device he rigged up replacing the frog with a piece of wet card. The result of his experiments was the voltaic pile, which, by producing a consistent flow of electricity, was the forerunner of the electric battery. Electricity also became something of an aristocratic plaything – some considered it great sport to give servants (or in America, slaves) electric shocks.[6]

Chemistry was another important product of the Enlightenment, although once more its foundation was a series of relatively uncoordinated experiments performed in the seventeenth century by scientists such as Galileo, Robert Hooke and Robert Boyle. It was defined as the resolution of compounds into their elements, and the combination of those elements into compounds by Georg Stahl in 1723. Stahl was most interested in the nature of combustion, and postulated that all combustible materials included a substance called phlogiston as a component. Though this hypothesis was eventually shown to be false, it was extremely important in eighteenth century chemistry as it brought coherence to the study of combustion, and linked it with related topics such as respiration and calcination of metals.

Joseph Black's and Henry Cavendish's experiments in the 1750s and 1760s revealed that air was not a single substance, but a combination, one of whose components was combustible, possibly the phlogiston chemists had been seeking. Joseph Priestley found about ten components of air in the 1770s, using sealed containers which enabled him to introduce quantification, for instance discovering that the volume of air decreases by twenty per cent during respiration. One of these components, which he called 'dephlogisticated air', seemed to have links with water – exploding a mixture of inflammable and dephlogisticated air left drops of water as residue.

Antoine-Laurent Lavoisier was able to go even further than Priestley in quantification and precision. His theory of oxygen, that the combustible element in air was a constituent of all acids, was originally intended to supplement the phlogiston theory. But when he reproduced the experiments of Cavendish and Priestley, he was able to show not only that water appeared when air was ignited, but also that water itself broke down under some conditions, into the oxygen principle and a water principle (hydrogen). Hydrogen and oxygen explained many other phenomena, especially the reactions of acids on metals, without the need to postulate phlogiston.

The 1780s were very fruitful years for chemical theory, as Lavoisier's ideas spread around the scientific community. Lavoisier and his colleagues began to recast chemistry into modern terms, changing the original alchemical names of compounds into ones that were more descriptive in the new theoretical context. So *aqua fortis* became nitric acid, for instance. His *Elementary Treatise on Chemistry* (1789) was very influential as a textbook, soon translated into English. But the elaboration of the new theory had to be performed by others – Lavoisier was guillotined at the height of the Terror.

The Enlightenment was also an important moment for the study of the Earth. At the beginning of the period, scientists were starting to appreciate how fossilised and petrified bodies were challenging the Biblical account of a Creation datable to a few thousand years ago (the date of 4004 BC was a conclusion drawn by James Ussher in 1650), and many thinkers, inevitably including Descartes, had theories about the formation and constitution of the Earth that contradicted received views. Several important Enlightenment figures found evidence for a longer timescale. Halley looked at the level of salt in the oceans, Buffon considered changes in animal species, Johann Lehmann

(1719–67) examined stratification in rocks. Abraham Werner in the 1770s first comprehended that the Earth might be more than a million years old (although the geological timescale of billions of years was still beyond scientists' imaginations). The Lisbon Earthquake was studied in detail, not least by Kant, as a natural phenomenon rather than an act of God. The Rev. John Michell's *Conjectures Concerning the Cause of Observations Upon the Phaenomena of Earthquakes* (1760) was the first to explain them in terms of wave motion through the earth.

The Enlightenment prized understanding, and an important method for promoting this was classification. The Swedish biologist Carolus Linnaeus created an influential system, still in use today, naming animals after their genus and species. He made his discriminations on the basis of structures such as organs, teeth, fins, beaks and so on, which turned out to be pretty good guides to what are now considered to be the central classificatory aspects of species DNA. In France, Buffon gained great celebrity with his comprehensive *Natural History*, which dropped Linnaeus' assumption that species structure was fixed, and cited evidence from fossils, commonality of structure across species and organs that seemed to have lost their use (such as the appendix in humans), to argue that species could change through time, and even disappear. He even touched upon the great controversy of whether apes and humans might have a common ancestor.

Biology made much progress, particularly as life forms were generally more amenable to primitive experimentation than large land masses. Stephen Hales' *Vegetable Staticks* (1727) was a remarkable work which detailed a series of experiments showing how water passed through plants, how light might be involved in their growth, and how leaves expand, and are analogous to animal lungs. Hales' work was isolated from the botanical mainstream, but was part of a broader materialist programme that hypothesised people, animals and plants as functioning like machines; Hales himself studied blood pressure alongside sap pressure. Descartes had essayed the possibility that animals were 'mere' machines, although he believed people were genuinely animated by mentality, while Julien Offray de la Mettrie explored the physiological, psychological and philosophical implications of thinking that a human being might also be a purely physical system. His *Man a Machine* (1747) was a great success, influential on Diderot and d'Alembert. La Mettrie himself explored materialist philosophy perhaps too far; not only did he believe that goodness consisted in the pleasure of the senses and that virtue is self-love, but he pursued his version of virtues so far that he died.

In medicine, the Cartesian mechanistic view of matter was influential in suggesting that the body was a self-contained mechanism that could go wrong in the same way as a clock or a machine. The ancient theory of humours (that health depended on the correct balance between blood, phlegm, black bile and yellow bile) had led to a medicine whose chief tool was draining – altering the balance using laxatives, emetics, leeches and so on – but Cartesianism led to an interest in physical structure in isolation, and an increase in *post mortem* studies and dissection. The zoologist John Hunter (1728–93) studied virtually every type of animal, and first applied scientific principles to surgery.

Experimentation brought results, perhaps none more impressive than William Withering's discovery of *digitalis* as a means to slow the heartbeat in 1785, after analysing all the ingredients of an efficacious folk remedy. Experiments on inoculation – a Turkish practice brought to the West by Lady Mary Wortley Montagu in 1718 – began in earnest in the Enlightenment, and after a few experiments on criminals, two British princesses were inoculated against smallpox. Catherine the Great was so keen on inoculation that she whisked Thomas Dimsdale (1712–1800), a doctor from Hertford, at great expense, to Russia to inoculate her and her son, the Grand Duke Paul, making Dimsdale so rich he gave up medicine and opened a bank (the lancets used to inoculate Catherine are on display in London's Hunterian Museum). Nevertheless, progress was slow, and it took a while before a more thorough analysis of the phenomena enabled the breakthrough of the great pioneer Edward Jenner (1749–1823), shortly after our period.

Changing nature: the roots of the agricultural and industrial revolutions

The experimental method and the increasingly systematic investigation of the environment brought forth fruit in a series of solid methods for not merely harnessing the forces of nature, but improving them and tailoring them for man's purposes. The Enlightenment laid the foundation for not only the political revolutions but also revolutions in agricultural and industrial production that were certainly more gradual as processes, but were equally far-reaching in their effects. During the Enlightenment, the wealthiest countries, such as England, had just about reached the *per capita* level of income of third century Rome;[7] the technology of the age (only partially informed by pure science) underpinned the rapid growth of the next two centuries.

Although some improvement in agriculture followed political changes, such as the enclosure of previously communally-farmed land, it was partly down to changes in farming techniques developed through the experimental investigation of nature. Prominent among these was the use of crop rotation to reduce or eliminate the need for fallow. Single-crop agriculture denudes the soil of important nutrients and encourages the build-up of crop-specific pests and diseases, so in medieval times fields would be left fallow (i.e. uncultivated) for one year out of every two or three in order to allow the soil to replenish. This was obviously wasteful. A number of pioneers in North-Western Europe were able to discover sequences of different crops to be grown on the same land in different years, so that each crop would either replenish the soil, or alternatively be grazed by animals which would manure the land (the scientific principles behind this remained unclear until the nineteenth century). An important populariser of crop rotation was the 2nd Viscount Townshend (1674–1738), who for his pains will forever be known in history not as a statesman and distinguished President of the Council, but as 'Turnip Townshend'. His preferred rotation was wheat in the first year, then barley, then turnips, and finally clover for grazing.

The discoveries and explorations of the Enlightenment and previous eras led to the spreading of new foodstuffs which helped improve nutrition. The value of turnips and other root crops in not only providing food but also improving the soil was increasingly recognised, and the practice spread. New crops were introduced from the New World, especially maize and potatoes. Potatoes were the subject of a great deal of strangely irrational prejudice particularly in France, but Adam Smith waxed lyrical about them and their effects all the same, if not in the most PC of terms.

> The chairmen, porters, and coalheavers in London, and those unfortunate women who live by prostitution, the strongest men and the most beautiful women perhaps in the British dominions, are said to be the greatest part of them from the lowest rank of people in Ireland, who are generally fed with this root. No food can offer a more decisive proof of its nourishing quality, or of its being peculiarly suitable to the health of the human constitution.[8]

The key industrial technologies developed slowly during the course of the century, driven by economic requirements rather than scientific curiosity; this may help explain why many of the key discoveries were made in England and Scotland where commerce was less of a dirty word. Enlightenment scientists rarely managed to harness their skill for technological development, and expertise was spread less through scientific journals than social gatherings in organisations peopled by bluff English entrepreneurs, of which Birmingham's Lunar Society was the archetype.[9]

Three sets of innovations were particularly valuable. The first was in the field of metallurgy, specifically iron production. Abraham Darby's success in smelting iron using coke rather than charcoal (1709) is a case in point; he had experimented for a long time on the process before he achieved success (so can be seen as using something not unlike the scientific method), but the importance is not so much in the discovery as the economic importance of liberating the production of iron from the need for timber – iron production was halted more often by shortages of timber than by shortages of ore. By the end of the era much greater quantities of iron could be produced, nearer the places where it was needed, and, thanks to further processes such as puddling, discovered by Henry Cort in 1784, it was in much purer form.

The second set of innovations revolved around the harnessing of power, particularly steam, which as Karl Marx pointed out made industry mobile, taking it away from the rural water-wheels and bringing it into the city. The Newcomen engine of 1705 was able to use steam power to drive a piston to pump water, while Watt developed a series of engines that were general in purpose and improved the efficiency of steam by an order of magnitude. In a third wave, technology in the textile industry was driven by the need for machines to process cotton. Cotton was easier to grow than other textiles, and also very comfortable and durable, but harder to work with, needing complex, labour-intensive processing, so the men who developed ways of mechanising textile production helped create the giant profits of the cotton industry. John Kay's flying shuttle (1733), James Hargreaves' spinning jenny (1764), Arkwright's water frame (1769) and Samuel Crompton's mule (1779) all increased productivity many-fold by mechanising some of the processes involved in spinning and weaving.

Mathematics and logic

The mathematicians of the Enlightenment, like the scientists, achieved somewhat less than their colleagues of the seventeenth and nineteenth centuries. Once more, much important work was done by Newton in the 1660s and 1670s, although only published in the 1680s and 1690s. His contribution in mathematics as in physics was immense. For instance, he produced the remarkable result that some infinite series of algebraic terms could be seen as equivalent to finite series, which allowed him to take mathematics on to new, conceptually difficult, territory. The binomial theorem, which described the full (and finite) expansion of the expression $(x + y)^n$ for integer values of n (so, $(x + y)^2 = x^2 + 2xy + y^2$ and so on for $n = 3, 4, 5$ etc.) was well-known at the time, but his work on infinite series allowed Newton to generalise it for fractional and negative values of n – an important and unintuitive result.

His main contribution was in calculus, the mathematics of change, and as such essential to describe the physics of motion. Calculus gives us two operations, *differentiation*, which gives the rate of change at a particular point, and the inverse operation *integration*. If we have a formula for the position of a body at any particular time, differentiating the formula gives us the velocity of the body at any particular time, and differentiating again gives the acceleration. Similarly, integrating acceleration gives us velocity, and integrating again gives us distance travelled.

Calculus involves working with infinitesimally small quantities, and so requires quite a conceptual leap. Normally, to discover the velocity of something, you see how far it has travelled over a particular time, so that the velocity is taken over a section of road, rather than at a particular point. Newton's method, exploiting his work with infinite series, was to look first at the velocity over, say, 100m, then over 50m, then over 25m, and continually over smaller and smaller stretches. These velocities will form an infinite series, and he showed that if there are no sudden breaks or discontinuities, the velocity values will converge to a limit as the stretches of road get closer to a length of 0. He was then able to define the velocity at an infinitesimal point as that limit.

Calculus is now uncontroversial, but it had to withstand a philosophical onslaught in the sceptical Enlightenment. In particular, Berkeley launched an attack in 1734, arguing against Newton that the calculus was founded on error, and against Halley that it was less certain than religious doctrine, because of the incoherence of the idea of the limit of the sequence of velocities. Each item in the sequence would be calculated by the formula $\delta x / \delta t$, where δx is the increasingly tiny change in distance travelled, and δt is the increasingly tiny change in the time taken. Newton argued that the limit, with δx and δt constantly decreasing, was the velocity at the point. But Berkeley noted that at the limit, the change in distance = the change in time = 0, so that the velocity at any point was 0 divided by 0, which is meaningless (in Berkeley's words, 'neither finite quantities, nor quantities infinitely small, nor yet nothing. May we not call them ghosts of departed quantities?'). He had researched the topic and unlike many critics, understood the maths (and also satirised Newton's somewhat opaque descriptions); it took a geometric representation of Newton's theory by Colin Maclaurin in 1742 to settle the argument in Newton's favour. Though incorrect in criticising Newton's discoveries,

Berkeley was absolutely right to point out the lack of theoretical rigour in this field, and indeed the appropriately rigorous mathematical concepts did not appear until the nineteenth century.

Newton discovered calculus first. This was undisputed. Leibniz published it first. This was also undisputed. But Leibniz reacted angrily to the almost certainly false accusation (not made by Newton) that he had seen Newton's results in manuscript, and there was a bitter wrangle between their two sets of supporters that lasted until after both were dead. The upshot was that diplomatic mathematical relations between Britain and Europe were severed for some time, and the British fell behind, unable to capitalise on Newton's impetus.

Leibniz was an authentic mathematical genius, though self-taught, which perhaps explains why many of his results are rediscoveries. Many of his greatest innovations were clever notations which simplified the representation of many complex ideas, which is one reason why British mathematicians, who generally clove to Newton's more cumbersome notation, lagged after the deaths of French-born but British-based Abraham de Moivre (1667–1754), who made important discoveries in probability and trigonometry, and Maclaurin (1698–1746). Unlike the prickly Newton, Leibniz was a social animal who fostered an interested community of mathematicians in Europe, of which perhaps the most prominent members were the Bernoulli brothers, Jacob and Johann who continued Leibniz' work on infinite series, geometry and calculus, while the British tradition of mathematics more or less died out. Thomas Bayes worked in obscurity on probability theory, but Bayes' Theorem, which enables conditional probabilities to be assigned *after* an event has taken place (e.g. the probability of a diagnosis being correct given certain observations of symptoms), is now central to the intellectual foundations of statistics and large-scale computational analysis of data.

The greatest mathematician of the Enlightenment was Leonhard Euler, whose output was extraordinary – publication of his complete works began in 1907, and at the time of writing (2009) has yet to be completed. The number of theorems, equations and formulae named after him is enormous. He was one of the few people who worked at the academies sponsored by both Catherine the Great and Frederick the Great, as well as having a post early in his career in the St Petersburg Academy founded by the Empress Catherine, widow of Peter the Great (Catherine died in 1727, on the day that Euler arrived in Russia). His productivity is all the more amazing as he was blind for the last seventeen years of his life, not that this stopped the flow of results. He worked in most fields of mathematics, making important discoveries in the analytic geometry of surfaces and the theory of differential equations, but his main contributions were twofold. First, he generalised calculus and turned it into the branch of mathematics now known as 'analysis', the study of infinite processes and their limits. And second, his creation of fertile notation outdoes even that of Leibniz. Many of the notations we use nowadays date back to Euler; he either named or popularised π, e (for the base of the natural logarithm) and i (for $\sqrt{-1}$) and gave us the useful notations $f(x)$ (for a general function of x) and Σ (to indicate a general sum of terms).[10]

Enlightenment learning always aspired to social usefulness, and Euler, together with his sometime friend and co-editor of the *Encyclopédie* d'Alembert, led the way in applying higher mathematics to the problems of real society. Probability theory was invoked to study topics such as life expectancy, annuity rates and the success of inoculations. The campaign for inoculation against smallpox (see above) was analysed in some detail by several important mathematicians, including Daniel Bernoulli (son of Johann) and d'Alembert. D'Alembert calculated that inoculation led to an increase in the mean length of life, and in doing so discovered some interesting statistics: the 'probable life' of an infant was eight years (i.e. half the children of the time died at or before the age of eight), while the 'mean life' (i.e. average life span) was twenty-six.

France was one of the leading mathematical nations at the time of the Revolution, and many mathematicians threw themselves into the struggle. A new decimal measurement system was created which we still use today; Joseph-Louis Lagrange and Condorcet sat on the Committee of Weights and Measures; Condorcet died shortly before his planned execution. Mathematician and pioneer of military engineering Lazare Carnot (1753–1823) narrowly escaped death, but instead was deported (in fact, he was exiled by both the Revolutionary and the restored monarchical governments). Gaspard Monge (1746–1818) was a keen revolutionary, and steered a precarious course between extremist groups; he greatly facilitated the growth of mathematics in revolutionary France by setting up and teaching at the *École Polytechnique*.

Surprisingly, for an age that worshipped reason, there was very little new work in logic. Leibniz had a keen interest, but did most of his intriguing yet flawed work prior to our period. He criticised Locke for ignoring logic, and tried to design a logical language for helping people think and deduce clearly. He hoped that such a language would enable science to be given a firm methodological foundation, but unfortunately he left little room to express the all-important observations which act as the seed to rigorous reasoning. His view of the importance of formalising reasoning is a characteristically modern view which was an Enlightenment innovation.

Kant also took an interest in logic, and as we have seen wrote about pure reason, practical reason and analytic and *a priori* statements; his lectures on logic were collected posthumously into a book.[11] However, he was much more concerned with deep transcendental philosophy, and his studies of logic were strangely superficial. He did use his logical theories to expose St Anselm's proof of the existence of God. Anselm's proof, or the *ontological proof* (which had been recently championed by Descartes), argued that God is greater than anything that can be conceived. If He does not exist, then it is possible to conceive of something greater – namely something exactly like God who does exist. Because of the contradiction, it is impossible that He should not exist. Kant's refutation (in the *Critique of Pure Reason*) was that existence is not an attribute like 'tallness' that can be applied to God, and so it cannot be a necessary part of His definition. Existence is not part of the concept of anything – rather to say something exists is to state that there is a real object which falls under a concept. There is no difference in principle between the concepts of 'horse' and 'unicorn'; it is only that there happen to be existing objects that are horses, and none that are unicorns. Similarly, the pure concept of God cannot include within itself the notion of existence (as the ontological argument claims); it is a separate question as to whether there is an object that corresponds to the concept of God.

8
Religion in the age of reason

God and reason were destined to collide in the Enlightenment. Many spent their time constructing and evaluating critiques of Christianity, which despite religious schism and the rise of science was still the main intellectual framework. Of course, Christianity varied from country to country, and different sects were dominant to different degrees in different places, so the critiques and counter arguments also differed. Hostile critics included Spinoza and Hobbes in the seventeenth century, and Gibbon, who placed much of the blame for the decline and fall of the Roman Empire on the corrupting, intolerant and irrational nature of the Christianity it adopted.[1] Nevertheless, Christians found argument useful and reason enticing.

God and miracles in a scientific age

Enlightenment discoveries of regularities underlying physical reality were often seen as threatening to Christianity, but equally they could be exploited by Christians. The so-called *argument from design* stated that natural things' wonderful adaptation to their environments could not have happened haphazardly, and therefore must be the work of a designer. Although unconvincing in detail (the argument says little about the goodness, unity or perfection of God, so that for all its force it does not rule out the possibility that the world is a discarded prototype developed by a committee of demons), it gained force from scientific discoveries, and was a key weapon in the fight against creeping atheism. The most famous version, due to William Paley which appeared shortly after our era in 1802, is a powerful analogy with the discovery of a watch on a deserted beach. Even though there is no other supporting evidence, we must postulate the existence of a designer of the watch.

Science itself, however, produced the most convincing design arguments. Although Newtonian physics actually caused religion serious problems that it has not yet overcome, Newton was a convinced believer. If all motion in the world can be reduced to a small number of extremely simple principles, that is surely a better design argument than Paley's analogy, more fundamental and not resting on an analogy. As Newton put it in the *Opticks*, 'whence is it that nature does nothing in vain, and whence arises all that order and beauty which we see in the world?' Linnaeus too found evidence of design in his classification of animals and plants. He believed that the number and structure of species were fixed, and that therefore his classification system was correct if and only if it mapped onto God's construction of the animal and plant kingdoms. The fact that the principles of speciation were so clear, marked and understandable itself argued for a designer.

On top of this, Newton's physics still left space for God not merely as the divine watchmaker, but intervening constantly to keep things moving, and as such He was much more present than the God of the Cartesian physicists of vortex theory, whose mechanistic philosophy left no role for God after creation. The Newtonians laid great stress on the mysteries of creation and the impossibility of man ever achieving complete understanding.

If the world were designed on principles ordained by God, science and religion must be reconciled to some extent. However, there is an obvious problem in the case of miracles, which are events that apparently *contravene* nature's, and therefore, as Spinoza pointed out, God's order. In that case, miracles actually cast doubt upon God's existence. There are only two alternatives. We must *either* deny that miracles happen, which undermines much of the letter, and indeed the spirit in many versions, of the Christian faith, *or* accept that apparent miracles are consistent with the natural order, in which case their miraculous appearance is down to human ignorance (and certainly tells us nothing about God one way or the other). Much latitudinarian or freethinking religious argument followed this pattern, either acknowledging, with Newton, that the order of nature provided evidence of God's existence that did not therefore require miracles, or pointing out that the ability to produce miracles showed only that the perpetrator was power-ful, not that he was God. Hume's sceptical epistemological version of the argument was that miracles, by definition singular events, will necessarily be supported by less evidence than the natural laws with which they are inconsistent, and so, whether they happen or not, it can never be rational to believe them, even when one is the direct witness.[2] Gibbon pointed out that if the Bible were to be believed (he did not think it was), then the witnesses of most miracles were singularly unimpressed by them.

> When the law was given in thunder from Mount Sinai, when the tides of the ocean and the course of the planets were suspended for the convenience of the Israelites, and when temporal rewards and punishments were the immediate conse-quences of their piety or disobedience, they perpetually relapsed into rebellion against the visible majesty of their Divine King, placed the idols of the nations in the sanctuary of Jehovah, and imitated every fantastic ceremony that was practised in the tents of the Arabs, or in the cities of Phoenicia ... The contemporaries of Moses and Joshua had beheld with careless indifference the most amazing miracles.[3]

A reasonable God

The questions about miracles and design raised further questions about the nature of God, what type of a designer He was, and what His attitude towards His designs would be. In particular, is He a reasonable God, could human reason be used to try to understand the world's mysteries? Different churches and sects began to arise depending on how far parallels between God's and man's reason were pushed. In the Protestant world, religious thinkers were able to use the new Enlightened attitudes both to investigate their own churches, and to distance themselves from the Catholics, who were much less likely to question received wisdom.

These internal critiques were often sparked off by a typical Enlightenment scepticism about the claimed infallibility of revealed religion. Critics divided between those who thought that exposing problems would let Christianity put its house in order, and those who wished to reshape the Christian faith permanently. Many followed the methods of Bayle, showing that Christian tenets were inconsistent and therefore unsound. The debate was least shrill, and perhaps therefore most profound, in England, where Locke, Anthony Collins and Shaftesbury among many others gradually sketched out ways in which God was restrained by reason.

By denying innate ideas, Locke by definition ruled out that the idea of God appeared naturally in our heads. Nevertheless, he argued that it was certain that God existed, because it would not be possible to make sense of our own existence and relation to the world otherwise. Reason was the most important faculty for understanding the world, which was not to say that revelation was impossible. If the revelation came from God, then of course it could be taken at face value, but if it was relayed by another person, it had to be judged by reason. The revelation may go beyond reason – reason does not, after all, tell us everything – but it could not be contrary to reason, and so our critical faculties remain important. Samuel Clarke used the Boyle Lectures – founded by a legacy in the scientist's will to defend the truths of Christianity – in 1704 and 1705 to set out a basic Christian position consistent with Enlightenment principles as they were coalescing about the ideas of Newton and Locke, following Locke in most essentials, and arguing that Jesus' doctrines were above all reasonable, and would be agreed to by any reasonable person. As the Enlightenment matured, even very devout people preferred to be swayed by reason: Boswell significantly expresses his approval of Johnson's theological arguments about the nature of Christ's sufferings with the words '[h]e presented this solemn subject in a new light to me, and rendered much more rational and clear the doctrine of what our Saviour has done for us.'[4]

A common attitude stemming from the reasonable, balanced and moderate Enlightenment exemplified by Clarke was a deep suspicion of what was called 'enthusiasm', the loud, excited religiosity that could result in speaking in tongues, evangelical joy and other unseemly outbursts. When prejudice and superstition were taken as a ground for certainty and intolerance, the result was deeply distasteful, primitive and open to satire and ridicule, as Shaftesbury argued in *Characteristicks of Men, Manners, Opinions, Times, Etc.* 'There are many panics in mankind besides merely that of fear. And thus is religion also panic; when enthusiasm of any kind gets up, as oft, on melancholy occasions, it will.' Religious enthusiasm was especially hard to damp down or laugh out of polite society in America, where the frontier and the large distances between people made it possible for enthusiastic groups such as the Separate Baptists to thrive away from the strait-laced establishment in New England. Charismatic thinkers like Jonathan Edwards led a religious 'awakening', a backlash against Clarkean reasonableness, in the 1740s and 1750s.[5]

There was a bewildering variety of Christian sects which in many places managed to co-exist without fatal social fracture; Voltaire's *English Letters* described many of these in England and praised their reciprocal tolerance. Least prepared to compromise were the Calvinists, who believed that man was totally depraved, i.e. irrevocably fallen because of original sin, and that God had given or withheld His divine grace to each individual according to a humanly unfathomable decision made at the beginning of time. Some thought that was too stern an action for a charitable God, while more worldly types worried that if one's behaviour had no effect on whether one went to heaven or hell people would not be deterred from crime or immorality. Those who basically agreed with most Calvinist doctrine but denied predestination were called Arminians. The Arians were unwilling or unable to grasp the complexities of the doctrine of the Trinity, and argued that Christ was different from His Father. Socinians went further, and thought that Jesus was a man, though one on a divinely-inspired mission.

Very influential, because most reasonable in Enlightenment terms, were the Latitudinarians, who conformed to Church of England practice in religious observance while also believing that the finer details of doctrine were not particularly relevant. God, they reasoned, was interested in the goodness of the soul, and neither could nor would judge a man on his precise theological beliefs, knowing as He did that most men had not had the benefit of a theological education or philosophical sophistication. John Tillotson brought latitudinarianism to the see of Canterbury during his period of office (1691–4).

The most important intellectual and theological development of the early Enlightenment was deism, the view (sometimes seen as characteristically English, although it has been convincingly argued that it was drawn from a matrix including ideas from across Europe[6]) that God was totally reasonable. The deists lined up alongside anticlerical critics to argue that dogmatism and unintellectual love of tradition and authority were responsible for error; that priests fostered mystery and deception to preserve their worldly position; and that religious enthusiasm was superstitious and wrong, although best combated with mockery and not imprisonment. John Toland's *Christianity Not Mysterious* (1696) was a typical book title.

Deism ascribed to God the same humanitarian ethical outlook that the *philosophes* largely shared. If reason led us to tolerance towards those in religious error, love of humanity and a focus on the real moral content of religion rather than the accidents of practice and ritual, then surely God Himself should have the same views (only more so), because surely He was hardly likely to be irrational. God was manifest through His creation, and so it made sense to the deists to pay attention to that creation. Why should God make the world as a vale of tears? Surely a reasonable deity (and if God wasn't reasonable, what hope was there?) would create an arena for human happiness. Material well-being in the here and now surely mattered, otherwise why would God create the here and now at all? The failures of human happiness on Earth were down to failures in society (including priestly deception) and government, not an oddly malicious God.

Furthermore, why should God give man reason, if reason were not a reliable method of getting moral instruction? Hence the deist argument for a reasonable morality turned out to be self-supporting – if reason were a bad guide, then why would God provide us with a capacity which would lead us into moral error? However, the God of deism was a somewhat more shadowy figure than more traditional ideas would have it; beyond His reason and humanitarianism, nothing is conveyed about God's nature (was He even a He?). Voltaire's *Philosophical Dictionary* contains numerous attacks on virtually every positive statement of 'traditional' religion, and the reader could be forgiven for thinking that his rapier wit had filleted virtually all the content of religious belief. Hume's *Dialogues Concerning Natural Religion* (published posthumously and anonymously in 1779), kicked back against deism with a series of powerful sceptical arguments that human reason is not capable of understanding the nature of the divine will.

In America, deism struggled against the Calvinist orthodoxy. Nevertheless, many American revolutionaries, including Jefferson, Franklin, Adams, Madison, and the Englishman Paine, subscribed to a number of deist principles, with the result that even now there is a separation of church and state (still being fought over in the courts, as religious campaigners try to get religious symbols adopted in state schools, for instance). In England, by contrast, it became part of the foundation of a great deal of profound moral thought, via such thinkers as Shaftesbury and Collins. But the Anglican church was not a particular enemy of free thought, neither was it involved in an oppressive coalition with government. As early as the Glorious Revolution, the English genius for compromise showed itself in the elevation of the latitudinarian Tillotson. For this reason, deism faded away while its tenets were frequently accepted by theologians and were relatively pervasive in the Anglican church and English society.

On the continent the Catholic Church often furnished common symbols, arguments and protocols for both the religious and political establishment, and so the anticlerical nature of deism was handy for fighting both sides in a united front. In Germany, Protestant dogma was redrafted in deist terms; academic arguments still rage about whether Kant was a deist,[7] although the *Critique of Pure Reason* was a leading cause of deism's decline.

The French deists were a stellar line-up, including Voltaire, Montesquieu, Bayle and even Rousseau – whose follower Robespierre devised a deist national religion for post-revolutionary France. Religion had already been under severe pressure in the run-up to the Revolution because of the Church's traditional avoidance of tax, its close association with the court and aristocracy, its opposition to many of the ideas of the freethinking *philosophes*, and its wealth. From quite early in its course the Revolution had put a stop to tithes, and had taken over many administrative functions in the teeth of opposition from the Pope, but Robespierre wanted to wipe traditional religion off the calendar and the map. Places named after saints were renamed (Robespierre's lieutenant Louis Saint-Just kept his own name), churches repurposed, gold seized and Sunday abolished. A new calendar was adopted on 24 October 1793, with twelve months, each of three weeks, each of ten days, each of ten hours, each of a hundred minutes, each of a hundred seconds (decimal time was inconvenient, and was phased out from 1795). Lagrange and Monge were among those who worked on the scheme. The new calendar was deemed to have begun (year I) when the Republic was declared (i.e. 1792). Hence, it was already year II. Robespierre hoped to introduce a new civic religion, along lines suggested by Rousseau, and he instituted the Cult of the Supreme Being in May 1794. It did not outlast his fall in July.[8]

The deists' God was an insubstantial being, but even so few would go so far as to deny His existence at all. Atheism remained a dirty word throughout the Enlightenment, not necessarily in intellectual circles, but in most others. Most populations remained staunchly religious, supporting monasteries, going on long pilgrimages and taking part in traditional religious ceremonies, even when modernising authorities tried to ban them. Religious authorities tended to be put under more pressure when they attempted to reform church practice in line with Enlightened criticism, than when they supported traditional practice.

The boldest of the atheistical thinkers was d'Holbach, who took a materialist line following la Mettrie that all motion was caused by matter, explained and described by Newton's laws. Locke's sensationalist psychology explained thought as a property of matter. Given all these premises, it is a small step to deny that there is soul or spirit, and following that, no need for God in the picture. God was a monster invented by the ignorant to explain forces that were not understood, with the unfortunate result of denying men the happiness they could have had upon this Earth for the sake of a lie about a world to come.

The Catholic Church

While the Protestant societies reacted in a sometimes bewildering number of ways to the clash between human reason and God, the Catholic Church, which had already faced a serious attack from the Reformation, was not prepared to indulge in speculation. If the *philosophes* needed an enemy to draw their fire, the Church was ready-made for the task. In an age during which authority came under serious sceptical attack, the Pope was the ultimate authority figure, *de facto* (though not yet officially) infallible. The quality of churchmen and statesmen elevated to the Holy See during the Enlightenment might well have been at one of its lowest points, and the Vatican was haemorrhaging political power almost by the day, but the Papacy carried on trying to preserve the illusion of power legitimised by religious and moral authority. However, it was always easy for the *philosophes* – some, like Voltaire, almost acting as campaigning investigative journalists – to find evidence of scandal, of luxurious monasteries, fornicating priests and, far worse, atrocities committed in the name of God.

The fiction of Papal infallibility always compromised the ability of the Catholic Church to prosecute its worldly requirements, and the dissonance between its temporal wealth and its philosophy of spiritual poverty made an easy target for critics. The extravagant monasteries being built particularly in the first half of the eighteenth century (see chapter nine) could hardly be missed by locals in towns like Melk or St Gallen. In the *Philosophical Dictionary*, Voltaire imagined a dialogue between a Papist and the treasurer of the court in which he lived.

> THE PAPIST: And what do you say, sir, of original sin, which [the Unitarians in our court] deny? Aren't you completely scandalized when they assert that the *Pentateuch* doesn't say a word about it, that the Bishop of Hippo, Saint Augustine, was the first who positively taught this dogma, although it was clearly indicated by Saint Paul?
>
> THE TREASURER: Upon my word, it isn't my fault if the *Pentateuch* doesn't speak of it. Why don't you add a little reference to original sin to the *Old Testament*, since you have added to it, it is said, so many other things? I understand nothing of these subtleties. My business is to pay your wages regularly when I have money.

In France in particular, this perception was corrosive, as the clergy (the second estate) was complicit in the failure to accommodate the growing democratic forces. Towards 1789, the higher echelons of the Church were receiving more people of noble birth, who were not very inclined to visit the remote abbeys and dioceses over which they had nominal control. Another threatening effect of the Enlightenment was the decline in religious belief – not among the people, as we have noted, but rather among the educated clergy themselves. Several important prelates would in private admit not only to doubts, but actually to not believing at all. The result was that the Church, tainted by association with the late king, accelerated the secularism of the French revolutionary government (which it in turn attempted to export to neighbouring countries both Catholic and Protestant, without noticeable success).

The Papacy was anyway suffering from a problem of its status. The political order of Europe had been determined in large degree by the Treaty of Westphalia of 1648, which brought the Thirty Years War to a close and which set out the new map of Europe as nation states. This settlement was achieved without consulting the Papacy, and it in effect assumed a political system with the nation as the largest unit. Furthermore, from Hobbes onwards, as we have seen in chapter six, much political thought was devoted to determining the legitimacy or otherwise of the state and the ruler – the state was the pre-eminent unit of politics in theory and in fact. The Papacy, as a supra-national entity with authority across the borders of the Vatican State territories and over the Catholic kings, was anomalous and not welcomed by those whose authority over their own states was diminished by it. The Papacy had little temporal power, and was therefore dependent on the support of Catholic rulers, but they were not often inclined to support the Pope against another of their number.

The Society of Jesus

One of the most powerful orders within the Catholic Church was the Society of Jesus, known as the Jesuits, founded in the sixteenth century. Fiercely loyal to Catholic interpretations of doctrine, they were a proselytising order deeply opposed to the spread of Protestantism, which trained generations of children with rigorous education, and sent missionaries all over the world. They were also close to the seats of power, supplying the confessors to many Catholic rulers during the early Enlightenment period.

The Jesuits were the Church's attack dogs in the Enlightenment, and consequently were themselves regarded with suspicion by progressive thinkers. The first serious strike against them was landed by Pombal, King José of Portugal's minister responsible for rebuilding the capital after the earthquake. After a plot against the king's life in 1758 by a group of disaffected and reactionary nobles, Pombal took the opportunity to expel the Jesuits from Portugal; the enfeebled Pope Benedict XIV's support was no help. Expulsion had a number of advantages for Pombal; in particular, as well as freeing up public debate it gave him control of education and allowed him to expropriate church lands.

A similar tangled dispute, this time involving the bankruptcy of a Jesuit missionary in Martinique, led to their expulsion from France in 1764. The Enlightened Spanish king Charles III followed suit in 1767, and a number of other Catholic territories also found it convenient to get rid of a powerful and reactionary body. In the end, to preserve the unity of the Catholic community of nations Pope Clement XIV found himself forced to suppress the Society of Jesus – though without admitting the justice of the many charges against it – in 1773. Only Catholic countries took notice of the brief, and the Jesuits continued in various non-Catholic nations (notably Russia, which governed parts of Catholic Poland), until the suppression was rescinded in 1814. Enlightened despots, such as Catherine and Frederick the Great, were ironically important in keeping the Society going, by enforcing toleration within their domains.

The suppression of the Jesuits, however temporary, was hailed as a great triumph for the Enlightenment parties (for example by d'Alembert), which had actually played a very small direct role. The order's strong connection to the Papacy was, like the Papacy's temporal power, increasingly anachronistic in a nationalistic and secular age. Its wealth, power and secrecy lent themselves to conspiracy theories, and their instinctive reaction offended the most progressive thinkers (many of whom had received a Jesuit education).

Man and nature: a summary

More than anyone, Rousseau brought the idea of nature to the fore, arguing in his major works that 'natural' man was free, virtuous and happy, while 'civilised' man was fettered, devious and unfulfilled. The constraints of 'artificial' society necessarily take away the freedoms with which man is born. The worship of nature even affected the future of science. Robespierre suppressed the august Académie des Sciences, partly because it was culturally conservative, and partly because, in its focus on physics, mechanics and mathematics, it was not 'natural' enough. The National Convention expanded the Jardin des Plantes at the Académie's expense.

The most complex dialectic between nature and artificiality came in the attempt to understand mankind. Human nature was seen as an important invariant to be uncovered and, particularly in Rousseau's case, revered; the nature of man in his social context was generally studied less (Montesquieu being an exception here), while women were usually seen as less interesting (or more decadent, and therefore less natural) versions of men. Most were agreed that the advances of science, using deductive and experimental methods, could and should be replicated in the sciences of man. La Mettrie's materialism was influential, although few went with him so far as to think 'man a machine'. Buffon accepted most of la Mettrie's ideas, but still argued that the reasoning capacity of man differentiated him from the animals. The sceptical Hume argued, in his *Treatise of Human Nature*, that reason was rarely a motive for action, and claimed instead that the passions are what drive us. His historical writing was intended to show the lack of principled reason in human history, a theme taken up at the end of the Enlightenment by the proto-Romantic Johann Herder, who, building on Hume and Rousseau, argued in his *Outlines of a Philosophy of the History of Man* (1784–91) that history was neither stable nor conformed to lawlike behaviour. Human nature depended on national, personal and historical context – exactly the sort of anti-generalisation that would ultimately undo the Enlightenment's universalising cast of thought.

Understanding nature, and human nature, were one thing, but that understanding also had to be expressed. Indeed, it was soon discovered that modes of expression themselves could be more or less faithful to nature, and as theories of nature changed, so did the expressive possibilities. This led to a flourishing of, and theorising about, the arts, which I will examine in the next chapter.

9

The arts

If nature was a key concept of the Enlightenment, the aim of art, it was generally agreed, was to reflect nature, and therefore to be 'true'. Artistic progress during the period was uneven, with some forms (the novel, and most types of music) reaching new standards, while others sublimated the urge for individual expression to the need to conform to civilised standards. To complicate matters 'nature' meant different things to different people, and as definitions of and attitudes towards nature changed over time, so artistic values fluctuated in response.

There were, broadly, two main artistic movements in the century, both expressing new understandings of truth to nature. Evolving from the seventeenth century baroque movement, which had taken art in a somewhat populist direction heightening direct emotional content, *rococo* was a witty response to the overblown pomposity of the great rulers at the beginning of the eighteenth century, most notably Louis XIV. Louis' palace at Versailles is an extraordinary creation of decoration and splendour. Rococo mixed a love of glitziness with Enlightened scepticism about whether such art could have any deeper meaning, and was a civilised type of purposeless decoration. Following the logic of the psychology of the age, pleasure was its aim.

But rococo got out of hand too, glitz completely overwhelmed expression (even now, 'rococo' is usually a term of abuse) and came to be seen as 'unnatural'. Consequently, in the second half of the century art became suffused with a new social conscience, a republican sternness paralleling the move towards revolution and the *philosophes'* debates about virtue.

Classical models were back in fashion, reflecting the importance of reason and civilisation. Reason was a tool to understand nature, and man was a reasonable animal. Therefore his environment had to be shown to be reasonable; the *neo-classical* was born.

Very broadly speaking, the artistic story of the eighteenth century is the birth of rococo out of the baroque, followed by the ultimate triumph of the neo-classical, all a dialectic on the meaning of the word 'nature'. The art of the Enlightenment has seemed to other ages relatively sterile, eschewing psychological investigation for other, perhaps less compelling, imperatives – in the case of rococo, pleasure, in the case of neo-classicism, edifying instruction. The search for truth and likeness to nature tended – on the Enlightenment understanding of 'nature' – to rule out many of the engrossing mysteries that appeal to modern tastes.

That is not to say that the reasonable metropolitan veneer excised emotion from Enlightenment art. Some, Rousseau among them, argued that the need to repress it demonstrated the existence and importance of deep emotion dwelling under the civilised surface, and therefore preferred expression to repression. Emotionalism was a constant undercurrent of Enlightenment art, although artists were no more impressed by ritual, dogma and revealed truth than they were by conformity. Nevertheless, some were drawn to mysticism. Emanuel Swedenborg (1688–1772) was a respected scientist who, after studying the relations between matter and spirit and the finite and infinite, began a new career at the age of fifty-six as an interpreter of religious experience; Swedenborgian writings were influential on a number of artists for several decades, beginning notably with William Blake. Another path for those drawn to emotionalism was evangelism,[1] which was particularly popular in America.

It was in music and the novel that emotion and the social niceties were most successfully assimilated. Bach, Handel and

Mozart added emotional depth to music both religious and secular in a spectacularly successful fashion without ever transgressing the bounds of taste, with Antonio Vivaldi (1678–1741), Georg Philipp Telemann (1681–1767) and Joseph Haydn not far behind. Meanwhile, many a middle-aged male novelist expressed his emotional side through representations, often in the first person, of young women in various predicaments – Antoine Prévost's *Manon Lescaut* (1731), Pierre de Marivaux's *Marianne* (1731–42), and Samuel Richardson's *Pamela* (1740). The contrary Enlightenment spirit tended to mock these works – Henry Fielding responded to *Pamela* with both *Shamela* and the adventures of Pamela's impossibly moral brother, *Joseph Andrews*, but with the enormous success of Goethe's *The Sorrows of Werther*, emotion escaped its restraint.

The Enlightenment aesthetic

During the Enlightenment art itself became the subject of deep and animated discussion, although, at least to begin with, this had little effect on artists' practice. Prompted partially by the archaeological excavations of Herculaneum near Pompeii, the relative merits of ancient art from Greece and Rome were debated. The excavations began in 1738 and were published in a series of works beginning in 1755, revealing the Romans to be nowhere near as austere in private as they were in their public art. Johann Joachim Winckelmann (1717–68), often called the father of art history, argued in *Reflections on the Imitation of Greek Works in Painting and Sculpture*, that the Romans had merely imitated the Greeks and that modern artists ought to do the same – a key moment in the shift from rococo to neo-classicism.

This change coincided with an expansion of the artist's audience as the richer bourgeois began to join royalty and the aristocracy as patrons – but crucially as patrons requiring instruction. The cultivation of taste spawned a small industry, with contributions by the elite *philosophes*, including Montesquieu, Voltaire and Hume. For those unfortunate enough to be resident in philistine England, the Grand Tour developed as a way of providing the children of the wealthy with a background of culture that would not be obtainable at Oxbridge. Taste became a standard with rules to follow, although the increasing individualism of the century meant that artistic 'genius', either as a practitioner or patron, might express itself in the artful neglect of certain aspects of the rules (the ultimate expression of this feeling during the Enlightenment came during the period of *Sturm und Drang*, for which see below).

It even seemed that one could 'program' an appreciation of the arts. Jonathan Richardson the Elder (1667–1745) popularised the idea, invented about a century earlier, of a classification scheme for paintings, giving marks for their various qualities: composition, colouring, handling, drawing, invention, expression, grace and greatness, advantage and pleasure. He advised would-be connoisseurs to carry around a pocket-book ready to judge these components of a painting's greatness. The notion of a simple scale for judging aesthetic merit spread to other arts – for example in Britain in 1776 the *Gentleman's Magazine* awarded marks to a series of composers, including Handel, Thomas Arne and William Boyce, using a similar 'checklist' schema.[2]

Meanwhile, interest in the technical aspects of creation of all kinds helped foster the development of a critical public able to analyse paintings. Diderot was a pioneer here both as the editor of the *Encyclopédie* (and author of its article on 'Art'), and later as a commentator on the biennial official exhibitions of l'Académie des Beaux-Arts in Paris between 1759 and 1779. William Hogarth's *Analysis of Beauty* anticipated Diderot by arguing that an understanding of the mechanics of painting was needed for proper appreciation, and that beauty itself consisted in the exploitation of 'a serpentine line'. Edmund Burke's *A Philosophical Inquiry into the Origin of our Ideas of the Sublime and the Beautiful* made a distinction between 'feminine' beauty, which gives us pleasure, and 'masculine' sublime, a quality of greatness (that sometimes inspires terror), which were mutually exclusive.

The psychological theories of Locke put sensation at the forefront, and further refinements of the sensationalist theory (for example by Joseph Addison) made vision the foremost type of perception. From there it was a short step to portraying the visual arts as a type of intellectual discourse capable of as much profundity as poetry. Gotthold Lessing (1729–81) argued against Winckelmann that great visual works (specifically the Laocoön sculpture now in the Vatican) had their own particular aesthetic connected to the nature of the medium; painting and sculpture were at their best portraying a single telling moment, either of revelation or of drama. Lessing's claim that 'it remains true that succession of time is the province of the poet just as space is that of the painter' was a dramatic revelation of the possibilities of the visual arts as distinct from the other arts, implicit but not expressed in the work of Locke.[3]

Visual arts

The influence of the rococo was particularly noticeable in painting, and the first half of the eighteenth century saw a flowering of light-hearted art, sometimes showing religious or mythological subjects, but without making too many demands on the viewer. Jean-Antoine Watteau was most able to remain decorative and even theatrical without straining either the viewer's intellect or credibility; underlying his work is a strong sense of meaninglessness and melancholy. His *Departure from the Island of*

Cythera (also called, confusingly, the *Embarkation*, though it clearly shows a series of couples at various stages of departure) manages to say much about the routine yet wonderful transports of love and the unfortunate need to return to 'normal' afterwards, without overloading the message with moral purpose. His *Mezzetin* sings plaintively to an apparently absent or uninterested lover; behind him a stone statue of a woman (Venus?) is unmoved. His *Pierrot* is an extraordinary work, reminiscent of nothing so much than the surrealism of Magritte, showing the clown with a long-suffering look, ignoring the group of people playing around his feet.

Rococo painting flowered briefly, before overwhelming itself with its own conventions. Giovanni Battista Tiepolo's set pieces with their stern queens and ladies, and François Boucher's fanciful scenes populated by large numbers of nude girls were popular, but increasingly critically reviled. In the work of the last great rococo painter, Jean-Honoré Fragonard (1732–1806), the people dwindle into nothing, surrounded by great swathes of intricately-rendered background.

Whatever this was, it was not truth, and thanks to the actual existence and splendid proportions of the classical ruins dotted around Europe, particularly Italy and Greece, ancient art was seen as more reliable by a culture becoming steadily more sober. Several artists began to paint serious scenes based on classical history and the Bible without exoticism or fantasy. Truth was found by the eye in combination with reason and the moral sense. Early exponents of the neo-classical style were Anton Mengs (1728–79) and Gavin Hamilton (1723–98), while Benjamin West (1738–1820) borrowed the style to illustrate modern Enlightened themes (such as his depiction of Benjamin Franklin's experiments with lightning, or the *Death of General Wolfe*). It is also unsurprising that sculpture received a boost from neo-classicism, although imaginative use of its tenets is rare (for instance Francis Harwood's (c1726–83) bust of a black

athlete in black stone now in the J. Paul Getty Museum in Los
Angeles). More usually, a sculpted portrait would place the
subject either nude or in classical garb, creating a sense of dignity
and permanence. In painting, the artifice of portraiture was
rejected in favour of the depiction of unvarnished truth;
documents would be readable on desks, wrinkles visible on
faces, tears and imperfections identifiable in clothing.

The outstanding representative of the tradition, dominating
late eighteenth century painting, was Jacques-Louis David, one
of the most politically-engaged artists in history, who wanted to
express Cato's ancient virtue in a modern idiom. His *Oath of the
Horatii* (1784) shows three brothers pledging their lives to
Rome, with the full support of their father. As the revolution
loomed, this stern self-sacrifice (with overtones of obedience to
Rousseau's general will), immaculately and excitingly painted,
was a sensation. David voted for the execution of Louis XVI in
the National Convention, and became the virtual dictator of
artistic standards under Robespierre's government. But the
descent into the Terror disillusioned him to the extent of
prompting the wonderful portrait of the assassinated revolutionary journalist Jean-Paul Marat. After the Enlightenment was well
and truly buried, David shifted his allegiance to Napoleon,
which resulted in brilliantly expressed hero-worship, most
notably *Napoleon Crossing the Alps*. One wonders whether David
knew in his heart of hearts that Napoleon was a solution to
nothing. His depictions of heroism, impressive as they are, are
eclipsed by Goya's nightmares in which reason fights to maintain
control and the appalling cost of violence and war (whether
moral or immoral) is made clear.

There were important works beyond the traditions of rococo
and neo-classicism during the century, and the visual arts flourished in pockets outside the major centres of Paris and Venice.
Dutch painting was unable to scale the heights of the magnificent seventeenth century, and the decline of art in Holland

tracked the decline in the political fortunes of the nation itself. On the other hand, Britain's artistic development, always somewhat aloof from the continent (ignoring the Renaissance, and instead owing much to Van Dyck's interpretations of Titian and Rubens), continued apace, pretty well unnoticed elsewhere.

Many of the most interesting works outside the mainstream were British, including the anatomically exact animals of George Stubbs (1724–1806) which echoed the new scientific descriptive realism of Buffon, or the weird nightmares of Henry Fuseli (1741–1825). William Hogarth's satires show the follies of hectic, chaotic Britain, and his multi-part narratives, circulated widely in engravings, give a series of entertaining maps of the road to ruin. Rococo traditions lived on in Britain, somewhat amended, with the 'fancy' picture, accessible, sentimental and idealised portraits of street urchins, market sellers, beggars and poor children, pioneered by French émigré Philip Mercier (c1689–1760), and practised by Sir Joshua Reynolds (1723–92) and Thomas Gainsborough (1727–88) among others.

Perhaps the greatest of British painters, unknown elsewhere, was Joseph Wright, who was born and spent most of his life in the unfashionable town of Derby. From this unpromising vantage point he was able to depict the beginning of the industrial revolution with unparalleled brilliance, providing an ironic commentary on 'Enlightenment' with chiaroscuro effects dramatising the action. His portraits give a valuable visual record of early industrialists such as Richard Arkwright and Jedediah Strutt (1726–97), and he also showed Arkwright's Mill in Cromford, Derbyshire blazing light into the surrounding countryside. His most extraordinary work is the *Experiment on a Bird With an Air Pump*, where a scientist demonstrates the new technology by sucking the air from a glass globe in which flutters a trapped dove; the dove will die to prove a scientific point. The spectators, a family, watch with various levels of engagement. A boy seems to want to be somewhere else, and two girls are horrified and tearful while their father explains the details of the experiment to them. Only a man on the right, staring abstractedly into empty space, seems to be thinking about the wider implications. As thinkers like Burke and William Blake began to associate the objectivism and cruelty of science with cruelty in the wider world,[4] the man had much to think about.[5]

Architecture

The development of architecture was influenced by history as well as philosophical and artistic developments. In the age of Kings, creativity centred on spectacular palaces with extravagant designs, as much status symbol as administrative convenience. The period also saw inspired religious architecture as theological hostilities ceased, including splendid churches and cathedrals throughout Europe and beyond, as European-style architecture began to spread overseas alongside its religion.

Many of these palaces and churches were conceived in the baroque style, following the masters of the seventeenth century of whom the greatest was Bernini. Taking its lead from the monumental architecture of Ancient Rome, baroque played and experimented with the forms, introducing curved exterior features, oval interior plans, domes and garish colour. In many parts of Europe baroque evolved into rococo (echoing developments in painting and sculpture) where no form was safe from being dramatically, often pointlessly, embellished. The pursuit of happiness became in architectural terms incredibly elaborated decoration, and the boundaries between architecture, sculpture and painting were broken down. Rococo architecture's epicentre was Germany and Austria (possibly an expression of relief and thanks after the repulsion of the invading Turkish army from Vienna in 1683), where its greatest exponents, the Asam brothers Cosmas Damian (1686–1739) and Egid Quirin (c1692–1750) created masterpieces such as St Johannes Nepomuk in Munich, and the interior of the Romanesque Dom at Freising. At its best, rococo architecture can be compared to the joyous music of Bach. At its worst, it is pointless and ludicrous in its quest to ensure every square inch is a riot of colour and twisted forms; the Churriguera family's frenzied splashing of paint and plaster in Spain even resulted in the coining of the architectural insult 'Churrigueresque'.

In the second half of the century, consonant with the change of artistic mood generally, social values began to predominate. Buildings became utilitarian in purpose with a spate of theatres, prisons and libraries, while the dominant style was neo-classical. Exuberance was out, restraint was in. The rebuilding of Lisbon after the earthquake transformed the city, as if the blow that event dealt to the ideas of optimism and providence had to be solemnised in stone. In America, Thomas Jefferson (a self-taught architect among his many other talents) developed his own orderly, proportionate aesthetic for the New World; following the Renaissance master Palladio (who had himself looked back to Roman antiquity), Jefferson not only designed several distinguished public buildings such as the Virginia Capitol and the University of Virginia, but also his lovely country retreat Monticello. Even nature itself was subject to planning and refinement by the great landscape gardeners of whom the greatest was Lancelot 'Capability' Brown (1716–83) whose work can still be seen today all over England, particularly at Vanbrugh's Blenheim Palace, Warwick Castle and Harewood House.

There was much interest in the constraints of form and function. One symbolic project was the rebuilding of the Hôtel Dieu, a hospital for the poor with a dreadful reputation for overcrowding and squalor near Nôtre Dame in Paris. When it burned down in 1772, the Enlightened Parisian conscience was engaged, and a theoretical debate ensued about the ideal structure of a hospital (as a result rebuilding was delayed for many years). Another debate was sparked by Jeremy Bentham's idea for the Panopticon, a jail in which every occupant can be viewed by the guards.

Contempt for medieval 'gothic' and other irrational urban forms inspired a movement towards planning orderly, reasonable layouts. Fires, such as the Great Fire of London in 1666, provided all too frequent opportunities – but ideas of 'reasonableness' evolved with the era. A typical early Enlightenment plan would leave a town more or less as was, strategically inserting dramatic features, especially the palaces and churches which flourished at the time, with new avenues to open up the view of them. 'Improvement' was conservative, incremental and often based on the personal requirements of the ruling classes. Even where restructuring was widespread the new plan would often be an attempt to showcase a particular building, as at Karlsruhe, Aranjuez, St Petersburg or the original Place de la Concorde in Paris. More ambitious plans later on would be self-consciously revolutionary, creating novel structures on regular, aesthetically-pleasing and 'rational' lines, as with Edinburgh, Bath (particularly after the death of planner John Wood the elder in 1754, after which his more adventurous son John took over) or Washington DC. Of course, as many of their cities were built from scratch, the colonial Americans could be more radical, and earlier cities, such as Philadelphia (1682) and New Orleans (1721), were planned in a more thoroughgoing way.

Architecture was also influenced by the spread of knowledge and history, and the greater understanding of other civilisations through time and space, which – rather as in our own day – produced an explosion of stylistic experimentation and a lack of unity. This was a period when the same man – the Scot Sir William Chambers – could adorn London with both neo-classical Somerset House, and the pagoda in Kew Gardens, an exercise in elaborate *Chinoiserie*.[6]

Music

The progress of music was a triumph of the Enlightenment period both in its early and late phases. An oft-noted quirk of history is that the two authentic geniuses of the early, or baroque, period were born within 130km of each other, within a month – and yet Georg Friedrich Händel and Johann Sebastian Bach not only never met, but were about as different as composers or personalities might be. Handel (he dropped the umlaut during his long residence in England) was a showman determined to become a celebrity – he succeeded – after resisting fierce familial pressure for him to abjure the arts and follow the law. He travelled, settled in many places, was almost as much impresario as composer, and socialised with princes and kings. Bach left Germany only once, was brought up in a musical family (and sired an even greater dynasty of his own), and was happy writing music to order for his patrons, minor German princelings.

Handel liked to give the public what (he believed) it wanted. In the early part of his career he travelled and studied widely in Italy, and became a supreme exponent of the mannered style of Italian opera, in which conventionally there were six principal characters who would sing arias in a fixed set of styles, leaving the stage when they had concluded. The arias themselves were inflexibly structured *da capo*; i.e. they began with an opening section, followed by a middle section, followed by a repeat of the opening. The repetition meant that action could not be advanced by the aria, so the opera resolved into a series of static vignettes. Some of Handel's most wonderful melodies are found in these works, which include masterpieces based on classical history and mythology, such as *Agrippina* (1709) and *Giulio Cesare* (1724).

Such a mannered style was unlikely to remain in fashion, and after a long period (1717–37) of attempting to keep the genre going with a series of unsuccessful operatic ventures in London, he developed a new style of dramatic oratorio in English. These were more serious, based on Biblical stories; the best known of all of them is the Christmas story, the *Messiah* (1742), but other masterpieces include *Saul* and *Israel in Egypt* (both 1739). In these, Handel switched from direct drama to a series of commentaries on the action through recitative (where the singer delivers a narrative using speech-like rhythms) and aria. The oratorio was not played out on stage, as in an opera, but performed by soloists who would not act, but would sing a particular 'part'. Large and impressive choruses would express the reactions of communities (such as the Israelites).

Whereas Handel developed his own ideas in dialogue with the reactions of the opera-going public, Bach was content to write the music that his masters' establishments required, and nurtured an intensely personal aesthetic within those limits. Like Handel, he is most lauded for vocal music in which he creates feeling and beauty in equal measure, usually in a religious context. Unsurprisingly given his Lutheran background, he wrote only occasionally for Latin texts, although his *Magnificat* is extraordinary, and his B Minor Mass, designed for so many musicians and singers that it would have been unperformable at the time, is the apogee of his art. His small church cantatas, intended as part of a church service, would consist of about half a dozen vocal pieces, some for solo voice, some for chorus, all accompanied by an orchestra. The sung texts linked the theme of the service as a whole. These cantatas, when related to a narrative, were like mini-oratorios, and indeed one of Bach's most famous works, the *Christmas Oratorio*, is a linked series of six cantatas, each reflecting on the events of a single day of the season. In his final post at Leipzig, Bach was required to write large-scale choral works, and here came his supreme creations, the two great Passions (*St John Passion* and *St Matthew Passion*) where the story of Christ's death as told in the two Gospels was relayed using a more dramatic technique. Hence, although Handel was essentially dramatic and Bach reflective, at the end of their careers they both pursued more thoughtful, reserved analysis of usually Biblical events with music. The Enlightenment artist was rarely content to observe – criticism, commentary and analysis were also important.

It was a staple of the Enlightenment that music, like the other arts, should reflect nature, but here as elsewhere the nature of nature was a matter of dispute. When the French composer Jean-Philippe Rameau (1683–1754) set out his theory of harmony in a series of books and pamphlets from the 1720s onwards, and explored it more practically with a series of splendid operas begun when the composer was already fifty years old, he argued that sound is a facet of nature, created in nature, and that harmony is a special property of sound reflecting important aspects of nature. Consequently, harmony is the primary source of musical expression. Rousseau certainly agreed that music's goal was to reflect nature, but *contra* Rameau he maintained that this must be *human* nature, and that therefore language in musical expression was the most important, because most expressive of human nature. Hence melody, supporting the vocal line, was supreme. Rameau argued that music was universal, while for Rousseau, music was related to culture, and so ideals could vary. This issue was debated through the middle of the century, with *Encyclopédistes* Diderot and d'Alembert becoming involved, and Rousseau's influence increased alongside the success of Rameau's operas.[7]

The baroque style of the early part of the century began to look over-elaborate, and later composers such as Domenico Scarlatti (1685–1757) and Bach's son Carl Philipp Emanuel simplified and clarified, eschewing complexity for elegance, rather as had happened in the visual arts. Baroque complexity tended to reduce expressivity – the difficulties of balancing different lines of melody ruled out shifts in mood. In the following classical period, clarity allowed the composer to vary expression and mood throughout a piece. An orchestral work by J.S. Bach, for all its brilliance in exploring contrapuntal dynamics, producing beauty from complex juxtaposition of different strands of melody, sounds relatively flat compared to even an early work by Joseph Haydn because the later composer differentiates between the orchestral sections to allow deeper expression. As C.P.E. Bach put it, 'a composer cannot move unless he himself be moved'. The classical work is more emotionally involving, less academic.

Haydn's genius was first revealed in his pioneering string quartets, where the two violins, viola and cello supported each other to create and manipulate mood. His range of expression, encompassing and transcending the ideas of both Rameau and Rousseau, rendered their arguments over music and nature redundant. He played a decisive role in the development of the symphony, and his oratorios, notably *The Creation* (1798), were worthy successors to Handel's in their exploration of the text. One reason for this (beyond Haydn's genius) was his collaboration with his librettist, diplomat and patron of music Baron Gottfried van Swieten (1733–1803). Van Swieten was an enthusiast for what he called 'ancient' music – i.e. the music of Handel and Bach – and was extremely important for transmitting the ideas of the early Enlightenment to the later composers.

The second half of the Enlightenment was also vital for the development of the opera, largely thanks to impetus provided by Christoph Gluck. Opera was a social occasion in the eighteenth century, more like a modern night club than the reverent performances we are used to today. The opera was a good place to go out 'on the pull', and the audience would not typically be expected actually to listen to the whole thing. Star power was important, and a mid-century opera would generally consist of recitative to move the action along, interspersed with the star singers declaiming their arias centre stage. In so far as it was concerned with the performance at all, the audience wanted to see the singer, not hear the music. Its musical possibilities were diminishing all the time, and Handel was the last great exponent of opera in this form.

Gluck set out to change this, in particular with his *Orfeo ed Euridice* (1762), where recitative and aria were mixed up, musical form chosen on the logical basis of what was artistically required at the time. He did not park the story while the prima donnas strutted their stuff. The result was controversial both with performers and audiences, but the model eventually won out thanks to the second musical genius of the age, Mozart.

Mozart extended the classical style further by reintroducing baroque complexities suitably tamed and subordinate to the main purpose of a piece, as for example in his 29th Symphony (1774) which uses counterpoint in its main theme without letting his formal brilliance obscure the emotional expression. As with Haydn, his understanding of the early Enlightenment was aided by an association with Baron van Swieten (whose generosity included arranging Mozart's funeral and helping care for his young children after his untimely death). His string quartets and quintets are masterpieces of the art extending Haydn's use of musical form and instrumental function, while his piano concertos were essential for the development of that instrument. The piano quickly became dominant as a result; Diderot's interest in music, combined with his technician's fascination with the art of instrument manufacture, prompted him to create the suggestive image of the *philosophe* as both piano and pianist.[8]

Mozart's supreme achievement was in the opera where he produced both exceptional drama and comedy – some of his finest music is wrapped up in ludicrous farce, as with *Così fan Tutte* (1789) for instance. He adjusted style to situation, and paid great attention to the nuances of linguistic expression, for instance writing recitative for his Italian works because of the musical properties of that language, but using spoken words for operas in the more earthy German. He questioned the supremacy of the West over the East in a typically sceptical way in his *Die Entführung aus dem Serail* (1782), and showed little respect for nobility in *The Marriage of Figaro* (1786). The importance of one's own ideas – echoes of Kant's 'dare to know!' – as against the dead hand of tradition is an important theme in *Così* and *Idomeneo* (1781). His most enigmatic work is *The Magic Flute* (1791), given its premiere at the end of Mozart's life as the French Revolution was working itself out. 'Superstition will die, soon the wise will prevail' sing the messengers. Sarastro, the High Priest of Enlightenment, representative of reason, defeats the Queen of the Night. The work is strongly influenced by Mozart's interest in freemasonry which had the Rousseauvian aim of transcending individual religions and providing a universal morality for governing society based on a reasonable God, with somewhat odd mystical trappings.

Poetry and drama

The focus on nature had a curiously dampening effect on poetry. The 'nature' of the Enlightenment was not the mysterious and powerful nature of the Romantics which retains such an imaginative hold today, but the reasonable, ordered environment that the reasonable, orderly but otherwise unknowable deist deity would, it was assumed, have laid down, in accordance with the laws of Newton.

Poetry, which thrives on mystery, suffered. As a minor writer Antoine Houdar de la Motte (1672–1731) put it, 'the aim of speech being to make oneself understood, it seems unreasonable to submit to constraints which often defeat that end.'[9] Nicolas Boileau (1636–1711) set the neo-classical tone of French poetry in the early Enlightenment, and it didn't properly recover until the poetic triumphs of the nineteenth century. Boileau's work was civilised and regular, using the same Alexandrine metre, and although by 1688 his output had largely ceased, he was still active as a critic. He argued that literature should express a 'normal' view of the world which reflected its nature. Nature is both known and best expressed through reason; hence difficulty, obscurity and fantasy were equally inappropriate. In general, there were too many influential critics, like Boileau or Johnson as another instance, who, though not of the first rank, insisted in telling everyone else how to write.

Alexander Pope was perhaps the most characteristic poet of the Enlightenment era, and his work can easily be filleted to produce a soundbite commentary upon its thought.[10] The *Essay on Criticism* sets out his belief that the rules of poetry were contained in nature.

> Those RULES of old *discover'd*, not *devis'd*,
> Are Nature still, but *Nature Methodiz'd*;
> *Nature*, like *Liberty*, is but restrain'd
> By the same Laws which first *herself* ordain'd.

The ancients, particularly the Greeks, had originally discovered these laws, and so a study of their work was important (Pope produced an extraordinary translation of *The Iliad* which secured his financial independence). But equally, poetry was not a matter of mere rule-following, because irregularity was an essential part of the poetic experience (a thought he appropriately expressed by extending a heroic couplet to a triplet).

> In *Prospects*, thus, some *Objects* please our Eyes,
> Which *out of* Nature's *common Order* rise,
> The shapeless *Rock*, or hanging *Precipice*.

Wit, understood as appropriateness of thought reflecting nature, was the great poetic prize.

> True Wit is Nature to Advantage drest,
> What oft was Thought, but ne'er so well Exprest,

> Something, whose Truth convinc'd at Sight we find,
> That gives us back the image of our Mind.

Whatever the poet expresses, the reader should find in his mind, if repressed and ill-formed. It follows that the artist should try to discover the glories of God or metaphysics from studies closer to home – 'the proper study of Mankind is Man'.

There were exceptions, and the straitjacket of Enlightened poetical theory still allowed unusual work to emerge, grass growing between the cracks in the pavement. James Thomson's (1700–48) *The Seasons* is a set of four long poems describing with keen observation the annual cycles of nature clearly inspired by the sciences of the day. His description of a rainbow in *Spring* tips its hat, for example, to Newton's *Opticks*.

> Here, awful Newton, the dissolving clouds
> Form, fronting on the Sun, thy show'ry prism;
> And to the sage-instructed eye unfold
> The various twine of light, by thee disclos'd
> From the white mingling maze. Not so the boy;
> He wondering views the bright enchantment bend,
> Delightful o'er the radiant fields and runs
> To catch the falling glory.

Thomson also addresses evil, morality and the good life; unusually in his age he was able to use science to provide a spiritual sense of the goodness of the natural world, and its essential contribution to our emotional health. His work remained influential – as late as 1801, van Swieten used it as the basis for his libretto for Haydn's oratorio *The Seasons*.

Thomas Gray (1716–71) was also sensitive to the natural world, while placing human experience in its historical context – both the 'big events' of the history books, such as the grisly career of King Richard III, and the little ones that provide the continuity of life in a small community. His *Elegy in a Country*

Churchyard remains a favourite work in the English canon, and the way it places the exertions of the living in the wider cross-generational context of the lives, love and hopes of the dead lying in the churchyard is moving and thought-provoking. One unusual poet who kept to the Augustan style with impressive success was George Crabbe (1754–1832). He learned his trade in the eighteenth century, and produced one good poem, *The Village* in 1783, but for a period of twenty years or more he refused to publish, tearing up everything he wrote. His style remained constant while the poetic world changed, but the result, when he finally went back into print at the age of fifty-three, was a tremendous series of works, including *The Parish Register* (1807), *The Borough* (1810) and the magnificent *Tales* (1812), portraying individuals in mundane settings (often Crabbe's Suffolk) with brilliant psychological insight. *Peter Grimes*, a section of *The Borough*, is a penetrating story of insanity that remains his best-known work.

In France, André Chénier (1762–94) was an important precursor to the Romantic Movement, a sensitive poet whose enthusiasm for Revolution ended with his execution on Robespierre's orders, just three days before Robespierre's own beheading. A standard neo-classicist before the political upheavals, his series *Les Iambes*, smuggled out of prison, express the horror of his position and his appalled reaction to what he regarded as the betrayal of the Revolutionary ideals in the Terror.

Perhaps it was inevitable that the greatest poet of the Enlightenment was not of the major urban centres, although he was well-read in the literature and philosophy of the time. Robert Burns was an excise officer in Dumfries, but his *Poems, Chiefly in the Scottish Dialect* (1786) is a brilliant collection which he never again matched of vigorous, questing, satirical, warm, generous and sophisticated pieces. He was well aware of both the value and the foibles of his fellow men, and used the unfamiliar Scots dialect to create poetic effects that had been suppressed in worldlier, metropolitan English poetry. Not since Chaucer had poetry and satire been so expertly blended, or such great art distilled from the detail of daily life. The pressures of combining a career in poetry with ordinary life seem to have been too much for him, and he was still young when he succumbed to drink. His expression of the burgeoning democratic spirit was as resounding as, and more humane than, anything from Rousseau's pen.

> What though on hamely fare we dine,
> Wear hoddin grey,[11] and a' that;
> Gie fools their silks and knaves their wine,
> A man's a man for a' that:
> For a' that, and a' that,
> Their tinsel show, and a' that;
> The honest man, tho' e'er sae poor,
> Is king o' men for a' that!

The Enlightenment was not a great time for drama either, despite the popularity of the theatre. Both England and France were regressing after their greatest dramatists had left the stage. In England, 1688 was the heyday of Restoration comedy, heartless, cynical and hilarious farces which expressed nothing so much as the naughtiness pent-up during the Puritan interregnum. There was a second flowering of wit in the 1770s, which gave us Goldsmith's *She Stoops to Conquer* and Richard Sheridan's (1751–1816) *The Rivals* and *The School for Scandal*, but nothing much in between.

French drama was hardly more successful. The greatest of French tragedians was only forty-nine when our era begins, but Jean Racine had already renounced the theatre as a result of the unwarranted success of an inferior rival. The relatively minor successes of the early eighteenth century dramatists (such as Crébillon) came from exaggerating genre. Only by the end of the century did dramatists begin to write about contemporary issues rather than classical or Biblical themes. In performance, Shakespeare, Racine and Pierre Corneille (whose last work was written in 1674) remained more popular than living dramatists.

Drama was also the mainstay of Voltaire's very successful career, with twenty influential tragedies over a sixty year period. He followed the move away from classical models, often writing (as in his prose fiction) about the East and also setting works in Ancient Egypt and South America, but his work is too didactic and his characters too cardboard for the plays to impress now. Nevertheless, he was lauded to the skies. French comedy was somewhat more successful, flourishing in the new atmosphere of liberty. Marivaux's plays are sophisticated light romances based on the *commedia dell'arte*, where delightful young lovers get into and out of entanglements – one is reminded of some of the scenes of lovers in Watteau's paintings – and his exaggerated language led to the coining of the word *marivaudage*, or stylised love-making. *The Game of Love and Chance* (1730) is typical. Meanwhile Beaumarchais was writing in an earthier style, also using the *commedia*, creating a series of works of which two, *The Barber of Seville* and *The Marriage of Figaro*, remain well-known thanks to the operas of Rossini and Mozart based on them respectively. *Figaro* is the more radical work, banned for years, cleverly showing the lovers of *The Barber of Seville* married, but with the husband pursuing a pretty young girl. Figaro, the barber, is very lively and opinionated, and his fierce diatribes against the iniquities of the nobility give the play its bite (Mozart and his librettist Da Ponte toned down much of the satire in the opera, whose composition had been encouraged by Emperor Joseph II).

The novel

The new empirical Enlightened philosophy, particularly in its English incarnation, fostered a new type of lengthy narrative based around the experiences of a particular individual, coherently arranged and embedded in a recognisable and realistic picture of society.[12] The use of the protagonist's life story was central not only to the creation of a unified narrative, but also in the narrative development, as character drove, and was driven by, plot. The eighteenth century novel showed how people affected and were affected by events, exhibiting both social and psychological realism.

The novelists often worked by taking existing forms of genre writing and artfully fictionalising them, so that the reader (if he were extraordinarily naïve) would be unaware that he was reading a faked narrative. Daniel Defoe and Jonathan Swift subverted the tall travel story to produce *Robinson Crusoe* (1719) and *Gulliver's Travels* (1726) respectively (tales, probably apocryphal, abound of people who took Swift's giants, midgets and scientists in the clouds literally, such as an unidentified bishop who thought it was 'full of improbable lies, and, for his part … hardly believed a word of it'[13]). Defoe discovered the genre late in life, being nearly sixty when *Crusoe* appeared, but relished the narrative of struggle, following up with a series of fascinating works in which a leading character has to overcome a series of adverse events in an already difficult situation using only their wits, of which the finest is *Moll Flanders*, from which a remarkably lively sense of life in eighteenth century London can be derived. His innovation was to use original plots featuring unimportant people, in which the events unfold relatively haphazardly, as in real life – as Watt puts it, 'as defiant an assertion of the primacy of individual experience in the novel as Descartes' *cogito ergo sum* was in philosophy.'[14]

Samuel Richardson contrived a domestic art by making fiction from long series of letters portraying attempted seductions and other such social entanglements. He owed his fame to the aspiring middle classes and their domestic concerns, as he got the idea for the epistolary novel while composing a book of 172 model letters to guide the inexperienced correspondent. His protagonists had an even more limited view than Defoe's; whereas Crusoe, for instance, narrates his story with the advantage of hindsight, Pamela's letters were nearly contemporary with the events they supposedly narrated. Richardson was able to use the personal nature of the letter to make the small-scale action highly significant (the reader is, as it were, invited to luxuriate in the emotion, as if he were the actual recipient), and to string the stories out to colossal length, whether they be comic (*Pamela*, 1740) or tragic (*Clarissa*, 1747). It was his work, popular throughout Europe and America as well as in Britain, that really created the appetite for long, detailed narrative, although not all welcomed the development. Crèvecoeur's *Letters From an American Farmer* (1782) borrows and adapts the style in a late colonial context, and is able in passing to allow Farmer James' wife to voice a characteristically practical distrust of art. Men in England may live by writing, because 'they have no trees to cut down, no fences to make, no negroes to buy and to clothe.'[15] Reading long narrative, in Europe as well as America, was often seen as a pointless art best left to the women-folk.

Nothing was stable in the Enlightenment for long without challenge, and within a few months of the success of *Pamela* Henry Fielding was sending it up with *Joseph Andrews* (1742). Fielding himself had a splendid career as a parodist, with his own picaresque stories of decidedly contemporary and flawed people such as *Tom Jones* (1749). His comedy was as much of narration as plot – the expression of the action was as funny as the action itself. Lawrence Sterne, particularly in *Tristram Shandy* (1760–7), summed up the progress of the age with his playful-to-the-extreme narrative embodying facets of the novelists who preceded him, testing the reader's conventionality and hopping from topic to topic in homage to Locke's theory of association of ideas. After Sterne, exoticism of style was superseded by exoticism of content, as with the gothic novelists (see below), but the possibilities of expression created in their various ways by the great novelists of the time also allowed intimacy and emotion to emerge, for example in the work of Fanny Burney and ultimately Jane Austen.

In France, Voltaire pioneered the philosophic tale, generally short, written in more direct prose than the English were used to – even more direct than Swift, who seldom wasted a word. He exploited the same sort of fantastic juxtaposition as Swift, with tales of giants visiting Earth from Saturn and laughing at our puny wars and disputes (*Micromégas*, 1752), or noble savages visiting real society (*L'Ingénu*, 1767). In his greatest works (*Zadig*, 1747, *Candide*, 1759) he wallows in the injustice of life.

The use of characters from the East, a sort of fancy-dress Arabian Nights fairyland (the *One Thousand and One Nights* had been popularly translated by Antoine Galland in 1704–17), was found to be very useful as a means of exploring the foibles of Western society without risk of censorship; apparent criticism could be put down to the characters' foreignness. *Zadig* was preceded by Montesquieu's *Persian Letters* (1721), not strictly a novel but a clever dismemberment of French politics and society. Samuel Johnson was hardly likely to be censored in Britain, but his *Rasselas* (1759) copied the Voltairean model in a story of an Eastern potentate's pursuit of elusive happiness.

More exotic still were the works of the Marquis de Sade, whose novels *The 120 Days of Sodom* (unpublished until the twentieth century), *Justine* (1791) and *Aline and Valcour* (1795) explored his particular sexual obsessions, while still, in the Enlightenment tradition, genuinely attempting some social criticism alongside the libertinism (in and out of prison, de Sade played a small role as a revolutionary). A more popular example of free thought about sex and relationships is Choderlos de Laclos' *Les Liaisons Dangereuses* (1782), an epistolary novel in which a pair of libertines try to seduce a couple of innocents. It is Laclos' only novel, and it is not clear whether he was satirising *Ancien Régime* corruption or revelling in it – very possibly both.

Reasonable prose vs *Sturm und Drang*

The eighteenth century developed models of reasonable prose for the expression and expansion of careful argument, barbed comment and inspiring rhetoric. Voltaire, Diderot and Montesquieu in France, Addison, Steele and Johnson in England, Hume and Smith in Scotland, Franklin in America (where Addison and Montesquieu in translation were also popular) all produced civilised debate and narrative capable of engaging the best of minds in a publicly-accessible way.

Nevertheless, many pushed against the limits, and found them stifling, while for the general run of humanity reasonableness is an aspiration rather than an achievement. Franklin's *Autobiography* argues that real people are reasonable only superficially; his self-awareness provides the stuff of much comedy in this regard. In the wilderness, Crèvecoeur's Americans are formed by the rugged landscape, not civilisation. The nascent American culture was already being dragged away from humane scepticism towards a supposedly purer and certainly uncompromising expression, using Biblical language, of religious sensibilities, whose greatest exponent during the years of the Enlightenment was Jonathan Edwards. American writers were often pulled in that demotic direction – even Jefferson peppered the *Declaration of Independence* with apocalyptic words, most excised by Congress before publication. In England, in contrast, Addison and Steele set the tone of expression until William Blake, although the darker side of the mind was channelled through the invention of the genre of 'gothic'. Horace Walpole's *The Castle of Otranto* (1764), purporting to be a translation of a medieval Italian manuscript, was a weird, supernatural tale beginning with the bizarre crushing of a man on his wedding day by a giant helmet. William Beckford's *Vathek* (1782, composed in French), is a Faust-like tale set in Arabian Nights territory in direct imitation of Voltaire. Johnson paid the genre a back-handed compliment: it seemed 'remote from credibility', but he could understand its inharmonious mix of violence, gloom, ruggedness, plenty, gaiety and magnificence after exploring the Isle of Skye.[16] Jane Austen satirised it in her wonderful *Northanger Abbey*, the *Don Quixote* of its age.

In France, failed courtier Saint-Simon's (1675–1755) *Mémoires* recalled the last thirty years of the reign of Louis XIV with snobbery and rollicking inaccuracy, prizing valets' gossip over historical evidence, always pursuing petty vendettas and including himself in the action where possible, with original and clever turns of phrase – with some justice he has been compared to Marcel Proust. But the Frenchman who shook up Enlightened prose most effectively was Rousseau. His lyrical style, particularly in his descriptions of nature which reach forward to the Romantics, is very different from the drier stuff of *les philosophes*. His writings on art and music ensured he was influential in the arts beyond literature, and his novel *Emile* and his unreliable memoirs *The Confessions* are masterclasses in how a giant artistic ego should express itself. Meanwhile *La Nouvelle Héloïse* was a dramatic love story fashionably expressed via the letters of the principals (it started a French fashion for rustic and philosophical novels, all of which are now forgotten). His political writings with their recurring theme of 'civilisation' imprisoning and fettering 'natural' man, exploit the idea that reason is of only limited importance, and that the measured and restrained tones of eighteenth century France needed to be shaken up with violent rhetoric.

The artistic movement of the eighteenth century that most effectively departed from the Enlightenment models was the German *Sturm und Drang* (storm and stress, named after a play about the American Revolution by the now-forgotten Friedrich

Klinger, 1752–1831), which in the 1770s and 1780s championed individual expression over rationalised and 'civilised' discourse, and implied that being reasonable necessarily involved dangerous repression of deep feeling. Such 'ignoble' sentiments as greed or revenge were just as important as benevolence or sympathy. *Sturm und Drang* was detectable in music as an increase in emotion, especially with Haydn, the sons of J.S. Bach, and in Mozart's magnificent 25th Symphony (1773), one of only two that he wrote in a minor key. Mozart's father confiscated his money – melancholy pieces tended not to be successful in a generally optimistic age. The symphonies were not praised, and after all, as Gutman puts it, unlike Mozart 'successful *Stürmer und Dränger* had … comfortable private incomes.'[17] The visual arts were less susceptible to storm and stress, with Fuseli's work perhaps coming closest to its implicit tenets.

Sturm und Drang was felt most strongly in literature. Friedrich Schiller (1759–1805) and Johann von Herder were prominent, but the greatest of its exponents was Goethe, whose defection from the movement about 1776 robbed it of its motive force. His novel *The Sorrows of Young Werther* (1774), purporting to be the letters of a young man so lovestruck with a married woman that he finally kills himself, was an enormous success, making the young Goethe famous overnight. Goethe himself grew to loathe the work, and quit the *Sturm und Drang* style together with Schiller to develop a German style of classicism.

Nevertheless, the importance of the deeper, if less coherent, feelings which Goethe et al had been expressing was evinced by the large number of young men who copied Werther's suicide across Europe in a sort of mass hysteria. The hold of the Enlightenment was already slipping before the events of the French Revolution changed the dynamic forever. It could be criticised, and new generations would interpret its legacy in different ways; its influence in the succeeding centuries – including the twenty-first – is the topic of our final substantive chapter.

10
The Enlightenment's legacy

The trauma of the Revolution ended the positive period of development of Enlightenment thought and reaction set in. But light having arrived, it could not be banished so easily, and positive attitudes to reason, freedom, tolerance and democracy are woven through the subsequent history of Western thought. Sometimes it has been an influence, sometimes a horrible warning against hubris; like most other great intellectual movements, the Enlightenment has veered in and out of fashion.

In general, those in the Enlightenment tradition have focused on the use of reason (particularly science) to improve human existence, and on tolerance to secure freedom, while complaining against parochialism, rigid hierarchies, intolerance and superstition (including most forms of organised religion). They have aspired to improve the material lot of humankind, leaving individuals to sort out their own spiritual needs. Those in the opposite camp extol diversity, individual expression, individual as opposed to socially-determined standards, small cultures and communities as opposed to 'the brotherhood of man.' They complain of conformity, the inhumanity of 'rational' and bureaucratic solutions to problems, and the marginalisation of people who do not accept so-called 'improvements' to their lives.

These two types of thinker have absorbed the Enlightenment tradition, although they have reacted to it differently, and are recognisable at various times in the two centuries and more since the Revolution. And sitting across the debate is the view, applied by the Enlightened Edward Gibbon to the barbarians who brought down the Roman Empire, and by the critic of Enlightenment John Gray to al-Qaeda, that once Enlightenment has brought science and progress, the forces of destruction and darkness will merely adopt the tools of modernity to serve their own ends.[1] For European civilisation, Enlightenment might be simply an own goal.

In this final chapter, we will review a few of the arguments which have preserved the Enlightenment as a living idea. This can hardly be a complete intellectual history of the last two hundred years, but we gather together some discrete episodes relevant to the Enlightenment's legacy in our general under-standing of culture, the special case of the continuing struggle over religion and secularisation, the limits to reason and its application to the world, and our understanding of human motivation.

The Counter-Enlightenment

The eighteenth century intellectual milieu was more complex and various than our strict focus on the Enlightenment would suggest, and it would be wrong to assume that there was no outright opposition to the basic currents of Enlightened thought at the same time. There were thinkers, writers, political figures and churchmen who were simply against the whole thing, and hated the hero-worship of figures like Voltaire. Such opposition, as we have seen in chapter eight, was particularly associated with Catholic and royalist authoritarians who thought of the Enlightenment as a dirty Protestant import. In France in partic-ular, Enlightened figures were constantly struggling with the Jesuits, and their dour, puritanical rivals the Jansenists. This opposition saw proper and traditional religion as essential for keeping order, thought that the new middle classes needed to be kept in their place and their ideas and writings censored, and recommended that the seat of power should be genuinely powerful (rejecting the Montesquieu argument for separation of powers). Such oppositional figures occasionally triumphed, as in Portugal after the death of King José I (see chapter three), but they included few thinkers of note, and tended to overstate their cases. They blur into an angry noise.

More nuanced positions did emerge. A number of thinkers opposed the idea of a universal human nature. Even Rousseau was held by anti-Enlightenment types to have not gone far enough in his emphasis on the distortion of human feeling caused by universal human rights. The English dramatist and educator Hannah More (1745–1833) sneered upon the publication of Wollstonecraft's *Vindication of the Rights of Women* that children and babies would have rights next – and she was right, they did, courtesy of Thomas Spence's *The Rights of Infants* (1797). The particularists thought this was crazy – human diversity makes a mockery of attempts to produce universal standards of behaviour and treatment. Punishments and incentives that made sense applied to one person might well leave another absolutely cold.

A related thought was that as societies differed, people immersed in those societies would differ too. This thought had appealed to thinkers with impeccable Enlightenment credentials, such as Montesquieu, and some on the borderline, such as Giambattista Vico, Justus Möser and Burke. Isaiah Berlin, for example, takes Vico as a quintessential counter-Enlightenment thinker (his work was not widely read until well after the Enlightenment had ended, and so he was not influential in its decline) for his focus on the uniqueness of cultures and the impossibility of an ideal society, although his theory of cycles of history and of the foundational cultural role of expressive activities hints at commonality at the core. Johann Herder was explicit in his insistence that one could not begin to understand a work of literature until one had been immersed in the author's context. Using a strategy that became common he borrowed an Enlightenment idea, the 'centre of gravity' from Newtonian physics, to negate Enlightened thinking – each culture has its own centre of gravity which we have to adopt before we can understand it. He became a strong German nationalist.

A third Counter-Enlightenment idea was that reason, far from being a good way to understand the world, was not an appropriate tool at all. Johann Georg Hamann (1730–88) borrowed liberally from Hume (he subscribed to Enlightenment values for a while, and was a friend of Kant) to argue that truth was always particular, and that all reason can do is to classify disparate things uselessly into patterns which themselves correspond to no reality. At most reason gives the skeleton, while poetry can describe the flesh; God speaks in poetry, not mathematics. William Blake was another early opponent of the inappropriate use of reason, famously caricaturing Newton as a materialist obsessed with his compass; his 'dark Satanic mills' referred not only to the mills of Arkwright and his fellow industrialists admiringly painted by Wright, but also to the implacable calculation methods of Newton and his kind. Reason was an illusion, tangling us in 'mind forg'd manacles.' Like Herder, Blake had a complex relationship with the Enlightenment, admiring at least some aspects of the revolutions in America and France. Many critics also consider Robert Burns as a proto-Romantic, and indeed he is a transitional figure. His *Verses Written on a Window of the Inn at Carron* (near Falkirk, where the Carron iron works had been operational since 1759) express a Blakean horror.

> We cam na here to view your warks,
> In hopes to be mair wise,
> But only, lest we gang to hell,
> It may be nae surprise.

A fourth reaction against the Enlightenment took the idea that each individual was ultimately responsible for his or her own moral behaviour and caricatured it as an extreme, violent individualism (of the kind we associate with Max Stirner and Friedrich Nietzsche), aiming to escape the overwhelming rules of reason and the weight of authority. Rousseau certainly moved in this direction as did de Sade in his erotic novels and some of the *Sturm und Drang* authors.

Enlightenment optimism was a target for attack, although often enough from within. Chapter three recalls the catastrophic events in Lisbon which led to Voltaire's pessimism and the writing of *Candide*; Montesquieu's and the Founding Fathers' doctrine of separation of powers was based on a political philosophy of distrust of faction; Adam Smith's free market was an economic system designed to work without excessive optimism in altruism. But still gloomier philosophies resulted when pessimism was allied to the Catholic idea of original sin. Joseph de Maistre had extremely dark views about the propensity of mankind for evil, and thought that idealism about human nature and society was a deep, indeed fundamental, error. As he wrote, 'all greatness, all power, all social order depends upon the executioner; he is the terror of human society and the tie that holds it together. Take away this incomprehensible force from the world, and at that very moment order is superseded by chaos, thrones fall, society disappears.'

Finally, we have already noted that Enlightenment was very much an elite occupation, and as the eighteenth century progressed, reaction set in against the aristocratic freethinkers as bourgeois classes profited from increased trade and became deeply concerned about 'the proprieties'. Whereas the intellectuals wanted freedom, the ordinary middle class wanted quite the opposite. Public bathing, drinking, sensibility and individual choices of religion were all seen as *de trop*, and while poets and painters were indulging themselves, the townsfolk began the long prudish march towards the Victorian era.[2]

The Romantics

Rousseau and Goethe were each schooled in Enlightenment, but neither felt that reason was sufficient for producing understanding of the drama and depth of people's lives. *Sturm und Drang* had already questioned order and sense; direct, sometimes violent emotion seemed a more 'human' quality, and calm deliberation appeared bloodless in comparison. A single tale of suffering should be of more import than a heap of statistics; rationality *in extremis* was a sign of too much detachment. Aesthetics began to trump other sources of value, and 'natural' aesthetics – untamed nature, Gothic architecture – replaced the love of order and classical values of the Enlightenment. The Romantic sensibility was being born. Goethe's titanic *Faust* was a poetic manifesto for the German Romantics, with Faust as a representative figure for the rationalists' *hubris*.

By the end of the Enlightenment, religious conflict had been dampened down by the focus on well-being and self-interest, and the demonising of superstition and enthusiasm. Memories of seventeenth century carnage were fading, and a complacent Europe looked back on several decades of (relative) calm and demanded excitement. Politeness became a constraint against man's deepest instincts. The Enlightenment, for the Romantics, denied nature; it explained everything, but provided no understanding. Rational civilisation had not lifted us out of the miserable pre-social-contract existence described by Hobbes, but rather had prevented us from realising our own destinies. It superseded passion, negated heroism, and tried to cajole us into a cold-blooded respect for all people, rather than allowing us to revel in the love of those to whom we feel most attached – friends, families, lovers and those with whom we share national loyalties. Romanticism was the background to the deep nationalisms of our modern era.

The poet Samuel Taylor Coleridge (1772–1834) was one of the people who made the journey away from Enlightenment.

He originally espoused Unitarianism and materialism, and tried to set up an ideal community in Pennsylvania in the 1790s (the proposed location switched to Wales, and then the ideal community, as ideal communities are wont to do, collapsed in rancorous argument before it had started). By the turn of the century he was upbraiding Locke and Newton, arguing that the materialist mind was passive, the political public space was corrosive and imagination and religion needed to be restored.[3]

The rise and fall of ideology: positivism, Marxism, neo-liberalism and the transvaluation of all values

The promise of an intellectual understanding of what seems to be human chaos has always been a goal of Western thought. Previous to the Enlightenment, the Christian idea that God had created the world with a structure and purpose in which mankind was unavoidably implicated led to a number of grand schemes, from the great chain of being to Dante's heaven, hell and purgatory in the *Divine Comedy*. Now that the claims of religion had been fundamentally and permanently undermined, the aspiration for understanding remained, but now human reason, not God's purposes, had to ground the effort.

The Enlightenment influenced many thinkers over the next couple of centuries who looked to science to provide under-standing of our environment and the ability to control it, and also to provide inspiration for the development of similarly rigorous and effective methods for understanding and predicting human behaviour, so-called social science (recall the dream that goes back as far as Hobbes to produce a reasoned derivation of the conditions of sovereignty along the lines of Euclid's deriva-tions of geometric truths).

In the nineteenth century, *positivism*, whose major theorist was Auguste Comte (1798–1857), took faith in science to the ultimate degree, adding it to Locke's empiricism to forge a view that all knowledge was ultimately rooted in experience, mediated by scientific method. The *ne plus ultra* of positivism was logical positivism, which declared that not only was all knowledge rooted in experience, but indeed all *meaning* was so rooted. Everything other than science – theology, metaphysics, ethics – was meaningless. Positivism remains influential, although few would make such bold claims nowadays. In general, most commentators, even those supportive of science's claims to truth, worry that positivism's privileging of science ignores many human concerns, which is particularly remiss given the roots of science in human interests.

Ironically, science itself has been the greatest threat to its own position as queen of inferential methods. Psychoanalytic theories, following Freud, undercut the role of rationality in ordinary life – backed up in more recent times by neuroscientists who have shown that the unconscious brain makes many important decisions before conscious reflection, and the role of reason is more often than not to provide a post hoc justification for action.

Meanwhile, the use of science to 'improve' society artificially is a very unfortunate offshoot of positivism. The 'science' of eugenics aimed to improve human heredity by inhibiting 'lower' types from breeding, and was an absolute disaster which involved removing children and sterilising parents from marginalised groups. At the same time many schemes have been hatched to try to change human thought itself in order to make the social order more 'rational' and human beings more controllable. Such ethically problematic ideas have led to suspicion and distrust of science, as voiced in works such as Aldous Huxley's *Brave New World*.[4]

Karl Marx (1818–83) was the most prominent of all thinkers who attempted to develop methods to construct new societies based on rational principles, to replace imperfect current societies. He was influenced by a number of post-Enlightenment thinkers, most notably Hegel, but the roots of his project can be found in Enlightened ideas about the human ability to drive progress. Optimism, reason and suspicion of authority were all aspects of Marx's as well as the Enlightenment's thought, and in that general sense Marxism is very much in the Enlightenment tradition.

Marx's debt to the Enlightenment is also evident in matters of detail. For instance, one can see the germ of his model of social progress in Rousseau. The ultimate ideal for both was a society without repression, where the whole people's interests were served, and seen to be served, by the state. A state was required, but there was always a danger that it would threaten popular sovereignty, and hence should, where possible, be kept small (hence Engels' notion of the 'withering away of the state'). As Marx put it, 'the aim of the proletarian movement – that is to say the abolition of social classes – once achieved, the power of the state, which now serves only to keep the vast majority of producers under the yoke of a small minority of exploiters, will vanish, and the functions of government become purely admin-istrative.' We can see here echoes of the Rousseauvian theory of the general will, as exploitation and faction are driven out of society to be replaced by a unified, coherent association 'in which the free development of each is the condition for the free development of all.'[5]

Following the Russian Revolution, it was discovered that Marx's analyses failed to apply (he had predicted revolution would arrive first in the industrialised world). The Leninist variation of Marxism supported the creation of a vanguard party of committed and theoretically-marshalled revolutionaries who would lead the proletariat towards a socialist society. In the short term at least, far from the state withering away, its influence would grow, as the 'dictatorship of the proletariat'. The interest of this for the Enlightenment is less to do with its contradiction of a key Marxian tenet, than the implication that political development and the economy could be driven and planned by a small number of technocrats. The economy of the Soviet Union was underpinned by plans and planners until it finally bankrupted itself in the 1980s.

The Fabian Society in Britain, formed in 1884, put forward a series of socialist reforms of society, eschewing revolution for a gradualist approach to developing social justice, but still with sympathy for the idea of planning. Its ethos was concerned with understanding society and its institutions in order to improve them, and optimistic about the possibility of using reason and science (including social science) to understand society, while also making the classic Enlightenment assumption that human nature can be characterised narrowly, and that therefore the idea of an improvement in society can be described easily. Condorcet's optimism about the future, undimmed even by the shadow of the guillotine, appears almost unchanged in the work of prominent Fabian H.G. Wells (1866–1946).

The other great ideology of the nineteenth and twentieth centuries, alongside Marxism, was liberalism, which we have already seen as a major driver of Enlightened thinking. The tradition of liberty that followed Locke reached an apogee in the work of John Stuart Mill (1806–73), who carried on the development of utilitarianism (producing a much more sophisticated version than Bentham's) and championed liberty as the most important social value. Continuing the Enlightenment theme of questioning the relation between the state and the individual, he argued that the latter should have complete freedom as long as no harm is caused to others; in particular, it is not the business of the state to save the individual from harm he causes himself. He was also a stout defender of free speech, pointed out that free exchange of ideas is much more productive of knowledge than restricted debate, and was wary of the 'tyranny of the majority' that a badly-organised democracy might produce.

An important variant of liberalism arose when championing liberty combined with Adam Smith's free market philosophy to produce what has been called *neo-liberalism*, closely associated with Friedrich Hayek (1899–1992). This variant of liberalism began with an epistemological humility not usually seen in Enlightened circles, with an argument that the world was too complex and dynamic for anyone to understand – hence the failure of planned economies – but that free, competitive markets would allocate resources optimally.

According to this view, markets were the only fair and sensible way to decide allocations. Hence the epistemological humility disappeared as soon as it appeared, with the claim that the market mechanism should be supreme. A common theme of the Enlightenment's legacy is a worry about tradition and culture as barriers to human progress, and neo-liberalism certainly shares that. There is some evidence that market forces can unsettle communities, remove the legitimacy from traditional institutions and create hardship for many individuals who find it difficult to adapt to fast-changing conditions. The neo-liberal rejects these complaints, arguing that this is how societies develop. Hayek also argued strongly that a free market will make government repression harder, and therefore economic liberty will promote the political liberty which commands support across the political spectrum.

While the conservative inclines to defend a particular established hierarchy and wishes authority to protect the status of those whom he values, the liberal feels that no respect for established values can justify the resort to privilege or monopoly or any other coercive power of the state in order to shelter such people against the forces of economic change. Though he is fully aware of the important role that cultural and intellectual elites have played in the evolution of civilization, he also believes that these elites have to prove themselves by their capacity to maintain their position under the same rules that apply to all others.[6]

Note the echo of the categorical imperative in that last sentence. The apparently simple privileging of the free market turns out to be a complex amalgam of scepticism and faith: scepticism in the ability of a person or group of persons to direct a society's affairs, and faith in the price mechanism to produce the best outcomes.

The cultural movement known as *modernism*, while making little contribution to human *knowledge*, was an important attempt to develop a cultural background for scientific, technical and industrial work, to expunge traditional, outdated and obstructive practices and norms and replace them with art and literature that celebrated progress, change and modernity, machines, movement, noise, mass production and abrupt, inorganic angles. Intellectualism and secularism combined with a total disregard of common taste to produce a fearsome body of literature, music and art that appalled popular opinion, but otherwise is hard to generalise about. A representative list would include Joyce's novels, particularly *Ulysses* and *Finnegan's Wake*, Picasso's cubist paintings, Ezra Pound's poetry, Le Corbusier's buildings, Schönberg's music, Dziga Vertov's films and the philosophy of Edmund Husserl and Antonio Gramsci.

The urge to drive people to modernity in the end was self-defeating. Planning economies proved hard, and the idea of scientifically-driven perfection soon disconnected itself from the people it was supposed to perfect. The aim of grounding moral and social thinking on a reasonable base was always risky. The moral or economic agent, freed from oppression by hierarchies, religion or social pressure, is supposed to be sovereign, but then that begs the question of how, in the absence of such authorities, we should judge between competing claims. The Enlightenment assumption is that reason can supply a general, basic method – but if we can't find it, or if we disagree on what it is, then society is without a way of resolving disputes.

One response to this, taken to the logical limit, is to follow the German philosopher Friedrich Nietzsche (1844–1900), who argued that in the absence of an agreed ground for reason and morality, there is little stopping an individual and sovereign moral agent replacing reason with his will to power, and interpreting and inverting values as he wishes (the so-called 'transvaluation of all values'). This irrationalism goes well beyond any Enlightened thinker, even Rousseau, and (when misrepresented by Nietzsche's sister) played an important part in the development of the Nazi ideology (so it is incorrect to lay the blame for the violent political conflict of the twentieth century solely on the Enlightenment – the Enlightenment programme of undermining the social foundations of moral values while treating the individual as sovereign has, since Nietzsche, been identified as the root problem with the Enlightenment's legacy by several thinkers in the twentieth and twenty-first centuries).

Theodor Adorno and Max Horkheimer

The most important critique of the Enlightenment in the twentieth century, Adorno and Horkheimer's *Dialectic of Enlightenment* of 1944, borrowed freely and not always consistently from Nietzsche, as well as Hegel's and Marx's writings on the dialectics of thought. Their basic criticism, that the Enlightenment already contained the elements of its own dissolution – a very Hegelian idea – has a ready plausibility, recalling for instance the Enlightenment scepticism that was devastating against religious mystery but which could be just as readily turned upon Newtonian physics, Lockean psychology or Leibnizian optimism. In Adorno and Horkheimer's language, the aim of Enlightenment was to rid mankind of myth, yet to do this it set up myths of its own, thereby failing in its own terms. So for example the attempt to rationalise everything resulted in an increase in irrationality, and the promotion of liberty produced greater compulsion. A particularly pernicious instance was the development of science into a species of rational and instrumental thinking used to control the world in the service of capitalism and meaningless consumerism. '[T]wentieth century factory space has been purchased by melting down all cultural values in a gigantic crucible.'

Adorno and Horkheimer took the Kantian idea that one should 'dare to know' – that one should seek the truth unaided, using only reason – and extended it as far as they could, claiming that the 'real' representative of Enlightenment morality was not Kant, but de Sade whose position they represent as not dissimilar to Nietzsche's extreme and sociopathic individualism. Reason, being ultimately scientific, is unable to support moral judgement: 'the totalitarian order gives full rein to calculation and abides by science as such. Its canon is its own brutal efficiency.' They found this efficiency in the frenetic sexual coupling in de Sade's *Juliette* (1797), in which a convent girl, seduced at thirteen, fornicates and murders her way through the book in search of enjoyment and excitement without concern for others. Industrially organised human activities 'have their exact counterpart in the sexual teams of *Juliette*, which employ every moment usefully, neglect no human orifice, and carry out every function.'

When relationships are reduced to such basic conjugations, 'liberation went further than its human progenitors had conceived. The unleashed market economy [i.e. the reduction of society to purely instrumental interactions] was both the actual form of reason and the power which destroyed reason.' Any type of worship, compassion or pity has to be rational, or is otherwise to be despised, as a surrender to emotion: enthusiasm is bad (a common Enlightenment sentiment). Emotion is demarcated 'from everything deserving of the title of knowledge or cognition. It limits cold reason in favor of immediate living, yet makes this no more than a principle inimical to thought.' Even family ties should logically be surrendered to the claims of the community.

> Even Kant himself made no exception in [compassion's] favor. According to him, it can be 'softheartedness' and without the 'dignity of virtue'. He does not see, however, that the principle of 'general benevolence toward the human race', by which ... he seeks to replace compassion, is subject to the same anathema of irrationality ...

This is the transvaluation of values once more, an extreme position and no doubt one that de Sade was keen to explore, but the complete separation of emotion and reason is not something that many Enlightenment thinkers were interested in, even if it was 'already implicit in the Cartesian separation of man into cognitive and extensive [material] substances'. Locke, for instance, aimed at producing a realistic psychology, while as we have already seen Hume was keen to stress that reason was not only not disconnected from the passions, but rather a slave to them. But Adorno and Horkheimer are less interested in the actual positions adopted in the Enlightenment (intellectual positions, I hasten to add, in the context of de Sade) than the extreme consequences of dogmatically unfolding the assumptions. 'Unlike its apologists, the black writers of the bourgeoisie have not tried to ward off the consequences of the Enlightenment by harmonizing theories ... Whereas the optimistic writers merely disavowed and denied in order to protect the indissoluble union of reason and crime, civil society and domination, the dark chroniclers mercilessly declared the shocking truth.' Nevertheless, to take a marginal figure like de Sade as representative of the Enlightenment is surely going too far.

Adorno and Horkheimer portrayed the Enlightenment as a giant ideological force and gave remarkably little guidance on how to resist it. By contrast, Kant in 'What is Enlightenment?'

wrote extensively on the individual's culpability in failing to Enlighten himself. For Adorno and Horkheimer the individual is a victim, whereas for Kant the individual sins through omission because though society is not Enlightened, the individual can still dare to know. The effect of *Dialectic of Enlightenment* is to remove agency from people, and put failure down to civilisation. Even if this socialisation of the problem is correct, Adorno and Horkheimer give us no method of addressing the issue. In fact, people may be much more sophisticated consumers of popular culture than they are given credit for, and spend hours watching valueless television not because they have no aesthetic values left, but rather because they agree with the critics who do not accept that aesthetic values are relevant to an evening relaxing in front of the television set.

A modern, more positive version of Adorno and Horkheimer's argument has been presented by Dan Hind, who argues that the division between the reason of the Enlightenment and the unreason of the counter-Enlightenment is less important than the distinction *within* the Enlightenment between those who use reason in good faith, and those who exploit reason and rational methods covertly to extend state and corporate power – in Nietzschean terms, reason, far from underpinning moral value, is all too often used as a tool of the will to power. He co-opts Kant's 'What is Enlightenment?' in service of his argument that we must ensure that reason is used to secure the ideals of the Enlightenment, the sovereignty of truth, sincere public debate and the open exchange of information.[7]

The 'Enlightenment project'

The age of ideology is closing: Marxism has barely survived the collapse of the Soviet Union while free market neo-liberalism has been severely strained by its failure to deliver benefits to all sections of society, by the disruptive effects it has had in certain contexts and by its complicity (via philosophies of deregulation and innovation of financial products) in the economic crisis that began with the failure of financial instruments linked to sub-prime mortgages in 2007. How does the Enlightenment feed into political discourse today?

The so-called 'Enlightenment project' is generally taken to be a proposal, less ambitious than the major ideologies, to apply reason to ethical and moral dilemmas. Characterisations differ, but the idea is that one can work out ethical problems by thinking about general principles and rights, and by downplaying local conditions and prejudices which are often if not always inimical to justice and fairness.

It is something of a misrepresentation to make this idea the mainstay of Enlightenment. It should be clear by now that several thinkers were properly sceptical about the capacity of human reason, including in their very different ways Locke, Bayle, Montesquieu, Hume and Smith. It is certainly true that some Enlightenment philosophers had great faith in reason, and the Enlightenment project takes its inspiration from Kant and the categorical imperative, but equally the rationalism that the project rests on is also present in non-Enlightened thinkers – Plato for one.

Jonathan Israel identifies the Enlightenment project as what he calls the 'radical core' of Enlightenment thought, located in a rough arc from Spinoza, through Bayle, to Diderot, which has bequeathed much of what is constitutive of modernity. In contrast, he argues, 'a consistent and coherent Enlightenment moral philosophy was never very strongly promoted, or adequately expounded, in the thought of many of those philosophers and scientists traditionally acknowledged as the principal heroes of the Enlightenment, most notably Locke, Newton, Hume, Voltaire, Montesquieu, and Kant.' For Israel, the Enlightenment project can be summarised as eight cardinal points.

1. Adoption of philosophical (mathematical-historical) reason as the only and exclusive criterion of what is true.
2. Rejection of all supernatural agency, magic, disembodied spirits, and divine providence.
3. Equality of all mankind (racial and sexual).
4. Secular 'universalism' in ethics anchored in equality and stressing equity, justice, and charity.
5. Comprehensive toleration and freedom of thought based on independent critical thinking.
6. Personal liberty of lifestyle and sexual conduct between consenting adults, safeguarding the dignity and freedom of the unmarried and homosexuals.
7. Freedom of expression, political criticism, and the press, in the public sphere.
8. Democratic republicanism as the most legitimate form of politics.[8]

This is a good summary of the Enlightenment's legacy, although it is clear that such a list was not universally held by Enlightened figures. The negative results of the French Revolution could be taken to vindicate those more moderate thinkers who warned of top-down attempts to impose order on unready societies. The advent of the radical Enlightenment had to wait for decades, even centuries, of economic, social and educative changes before this moral wish-list appeared plausible and practical. Even now it is controversial and divisive.

The major modern-day exponent of the Enlightenment project was John Rawls (1921–2002), whose *A Theory of Justice* incorporates a method for resolving ethical conflicts. His idea was that someone who is rational should support legislative institutions that allowed everyone to pursue their own ideas of the (morally) good life, because everyone benefits from such tolerance. We would still need methods to resolve disputes, and Rawls suggests that we can do this by thinking about what minimal institutions we should basically require. If we knew nothing about ourselves at all, then this would produce the fairest outcome (since we would not be tempted to load the system, e.g. in favour of men, or white people, or heterosexuals, or Christians, or Muslims, or college-educated people or whatever), so we should imagine what rational people would think if what Rawls calls a 'veil of ignorance' somehow prevented them from knowing about their own lives and characteristics (even gender). Such a thought experiment would allow us to pursue a just system rationally.

These ideas have been tremendously influential, and owe an important debt to Kant, but they have come under strong attack from those who maintain that the veil is an implausible and undesirable fiction, that various facts about us (gender, our status as parents, cultural identity) are so constitutive of our personal identity that it begs the question to suggest that we could hide it all behind a veil and still function rationally. Morality is not simply a set of rules that we may or may not follow, it is culturally embedded and impossible to separate out or even reconcile at the extreme point. Such critics have included Alisdair Macintyre, Bernard Williams and Annette Baier, although the most basic statement of this position was authored by a *bona fide* paid-up Enlightenment figure, David Hume (it is no coincidence that Baier writes supportively of Hume's work).[9] Rawlsians reply that this is simply to take the veil of ignorance too seriously – it is merely a device of representation to illustrate the broader point. Asking people to imagine a situation as if they were dispossessed of certain features is neither psychologically arduous nor meaningless. They don't have to shed those characteristics, merely to put themselves in that position for the short period in which they are considering questions about just political institutions.

A related criticism of Rawls comes from postmodernist theorists who refuse to accept any kind of overarching 'narrative' to history or society, and who consequently refuse to allow reason, science or secular tolerance any priority over alternative ways of thinking.[10] Postmodernists, together with feminists and communitarians, also reject what they argue to be an inadequate idea of what constitutes a person. The Enlightenment self was autonomous, able to operate alone and indeed even isolated in society, only able to gain an imperfect picture of the world and its fellow individuals via unreliable perception. It is no coincidence that *Robinson Crusoe* appeared at that time. The opposite view is that man – and woman – is a social animal, that group identity is much more important than Enlightened theorists gave credit for, that meaning is a communal creation, and that the self is socially constructed. Robinson Crusoe might well have been alone on his island, but had he not already been socialised he would not have been able to do any of the things he did.

Perhaps the most implacable foe of the Enlightenment project is John Gray, who argues that its self-negating character has led to a shattering of all the illusions it maintained. 'Contrary to the hopes which buoyed up Enlightenment thinkers throughout the modern period, we find at the close of the modern age a renaissance of particularisms, ethnic and religious.' The mistake Rawls makes, following on from the Enlightenment tradition, is to 'equate the moral point of view with that of impartiality … thereby [denying] moral standing to personal projects and attachments except in so far as they are compatible with impersonal standards of justice.'[11] Ironically it was thought by many Enlightenment figures that diversity would follow from tolerance, and that it was the unenlightened places where people were forced into cultural straitjackets, not the other way round.

Many commentators stress the positive gains from Enlightenment, notably the spread of tolerance and individual liberty. For instance, A.C. Grayling argues that the rights of liberty and conscience enjoyed in the West are important triumphs to be celebrated, and places Enlightened thinkers such as Locke, Montesquieu, Diderot and Voltaire in a longer context including Martin Luther, John Stuart Mill and American civil rights activists such as Rosa Parks. Israel also suggests that critics of the Enlightenment project such as Williams and Gray make the mistake of conflating the moderate and the radical Enlightenment, attacking the Enlightenment superstars (e.g. Kant) who did not actually contribute much to the radical 'Enlightenment project'.

This last is too complex an issue to unpick in this introductory volume, but the project's defenders would concur with Israel's conclusion that those like Baier or Williams who disparage Enlightenment for good liberal reasons nevertheless provide 'massive if spurious leverage for a wide range of social conservatives, nationalists, fundamentalists, anti-democrats, and adherents of Counter-Enlightenment ... The Postmodernist and Postcolonialist claim that "all values are equally valid" is thus a major threat to democratic, egalitarian values and individual liberty and ... [provides] a gigantic fig-leaf of wholly spurious moral justification to what amounts to systematic infringement of individual liberty, democratic integrity, and the basic equality of all men, tacitly endorsing the subordination and disadvantaging of long despised minorities, as well as of women and homosexuals.'[12]

Wars of religion

Enlightenment types have always found religion unsettling. Attitudes have not changed since the eighteenth century, when, as Henry May put it, 'to believers in progress, rationality, balance, order, and moderation, outbursts of religious emotion were (and are) alarming, disgusting, and inexplicable.' Enthusiasm is an affront. 'Contemporary critics [of the mid-eighteenth century upsurge in American religiosity] could not understand why this outburst of enthusiasm took place in the middle of an enlightened age.' Most thinkers in or close to the Enlightenment tradition assumed that economic progress, wealth, the spread of education and democracy, and the instrumental superiority of science as a way of understanding the world would gradually cause religion to wither and die.

To a large extent, this narrative does apply in a European context, where religious belief has waned, though certainly not disappeared, among the indigenous population – and moreover has waned faster in wealthier and more tolerant places. However, it is not universally true – the United States, one of the most advanced and liberal nations, remains one of the most religious. China wrestles with the problem of religion as it becomes ever-wealthier. Islam has been energised, and to some extent radicalised, by the encroachment of modernity, allowing a global vision to emerge thanks to the Internet and satellite television. Meanwhile charismatic religions such as Pentecostalism are growing fast in places as different as the United States, South America (where its growth is disconcerting the Catholic Church) and Africa. On the other hand, even if religion is here to stay it has to be admitted that in its own time Enlightenment was successful in helping remove the heat from the religious struggles that followed the Reformation.

In recent years, particularly following the appalling outrage at the World Trade Center in 2001, those of an atheistic bent have moved beyond tolerance to explicit retaliation. Richard Dawkins' bestseller *The God Delusion* opened up a major front against religion, arguing that science is clearly the better conceptual scheme, and that religions are all based on unfalsifiable fairy stories of no merit whatever. Religion explains nothing, holds progress back and trades on a supposed moral superiority over science, despite having caused more harm. Daniel Dennett has tried to explain religion in scientific terms, to show that ideas or intellectual processes have little to do with its spread. Sam Harris adds that faith is responsible for intolerance, homophobia, inter-communal violence, terror and despicable crimes such as honour killings, and that in the days of weapons of mass destruction, faith cannot be tolerated if that means reason taking a back seat. If you give the religious an inch, they take a mile.[13]

It might be pointed out against Dawkins that religious people rarely see their religion as a 'conceptual scheme'. It is usually something deeper and more meaningful to them than that. Dawkins' work resembles Adorno and Horkheimer's caricature of Kantian thinking: 'In the Enlightenment's interpretation, thinking is the creation of unified, scientific order, and the derivation of factual knowledge from principles, whether the latter are eluci-dated as arbitrarily postulated axioms, innate ideas, or higher abstractions.' This, the Christian is likely to respond, is a very etiolated view of religious faith. Archbishop Rowan Williams has argued that the word 'reason' was hijacked by Enlightenment thinkers who made a fetish out of it. It used to mean being in tune with one's times and with the cosmos. Enlightened reason, that which tells you whether or not an argument is true, is only a small part of thought, and the danger he highlights is that those who hold a wider set of values tend to be disregarded – adding that notions of inferiority based on 'lack of reason' were also used to support European imperialism. Williams also notes that Enlightened thinkers, though they generally condemned slavery, did not do a great deal about it; William Wilberforce, who was instrumental in its abolition, was an evangelical who believed 'rational Christianity' to be merely 'nominal Christianity'. In short, Williams argues that reason cannot give us all the answers about how to create a moral and humane world, and religion has an important role to play. Other philosophers, such as Annette Baier and Bernard Williams, have made similar arguments in a secular context, while still others, for instance Mary Midgley, have made the analogous point that reason and science function as something like a faith alongside other faiths.

Benjamin Kaplan's longer historical perspective maintains that religious toleration can be detected across Europe not only in the Enlightenment, but even in the war-ravaged seventeenth century, and to assume that 'religion cannot play a prominent role in politics or public life without leading, in a diverse society, to conflict,' and that 'societies whose laws, customs, institutions, and values are shaped by religion will feel obliged to persecute heretics and wage holy war against infidels' is not only historically inaccurate, but also 'tempts us to fear and condemn religion in general'.

Some have argued that Enlightenment attitudes are responsible for the cleft between the Western and Islamic worlds. The Egyptian novelist Alaa al Aswany recently wrote that Western-trained Egyptian intellectuals were taught that 'progress' and 'the West' were virtually synonymous, and that they all revered the great Western values of democracy, freedom, justice, hard work, and equality, while being ignorant of Egypt's heritage and contemptuous of its traditions, which they felt pulled it towards Backwardness. The Enlightenment demonised Islam as devoid of reason despite the fact that many vital mathematical and scientific results (and much ancient philosophy) were discovered or preserved by Islam during Europe's long dark age. There are plenty of anti-Islamic passages in Enlightenment works. Gibbon wrote of how the effete Romans, who despised death, were finished by the enthusiastic Moors, who welcomed it, while Beaumarchais, in the original *Marriage of Figaro*, describes the fraught relationship between East and West through the mouth of Figaro.

I sketched a comedy about harem life; being a Spanish writer, I assumed I could be irreverent towards Mohammed without any scruples; but at once an Envoy from somewhere complained that my verses offended the Sublime Porte, Persia, a part of India, all Egypt, the kingdoms of Barca, Tripoli, Tunis, Algiers and Morocco; and there was my comedy burned, to please some Mohammedan princes not one of whom I suppose knows how to read, and who keep cursing away at us all as 'Christian dogs' – not being able to degrade the human spirit, they take revenge by abusing it.

Enlightenment was not inimical to religion as long as it was sober and reasonable, but twenty-first century arguments are polarising, turning the inheritors of Enlightenment thought against religion and removing the middle ground. Even so, in their hostility Dawkins, Dennett and Harris are in the tradition of Voltaire, who needed no goading to attack clerics, and Thomas Paine, whose *Age of Reason* sets out to destroy Christianity and replace it with a deist alternative.[14]

Motivation and Enlightened self-interest

One of the most important effects of Enlightenment theorising was a new set of attitudes to honour, nobility, self-interest and trade. As Roy Porter points out, both the Graeco-Roman and Judeo-Christian traditions of European thought had demonised love of wealth (without conspicuously affecting the number of people who either were rich or wanted to be). Money was vulgar, greed a sin, prices and wages often more or less fixed, and profiting from shortages unethical. Several Enlightenment thinkers countered these ideas, particularly from the English or Scottish traditions, most notably Adam Smith of course, but also Defoe, Mandeville, Addison and Hume. The Enlightenment encouraged each individual to be the measure of his or her life and rejected transgenerational notions such as original sin. Eventually it became extremely hard to see why someone would *not* act in his or her self-interest.

This shift was criticised by many thinkers during and immediately after the Enlightenment, most pithily by Hegel who argued that, although people are of course motivated by their interests as animals are, they are distinct from animals in their need for *recognition*, an acceptance by others that they are beings worthy of dignity. History could be understood in terms of striving for recognition, and the significance of the French Revolution was that it wiped away divisions in society between slaves and masters – in the post-Revolutionary world, everyone could be recognised. The Rights of Man were not there to allow people a private space in which they could conduct their lives according to their own ideas of what was good, as Locke and the Founding Fathers believed. Rather, rights conferred recognition of a person's worth.

In the late 1980s, as communism went bankrupt and the democratic powers were able to crush a well-armed dictator in the Gulf War of 1990 with superior technology paid for by superior financial and political systems, the evolving geopolitics was dubbed a 'New World Order' in which the United Nations would be able to play a rationalising part in international politics, unhindered by the stresses of the Cold War. In the midst of this euphoria, political scientist Francis Fukuyama developed his thesis that liberal democracy had triumphed, and we had finally reached the Enlightenment dream of the perfect system married to Hegelian recognition, the end of history.

Fukuyama was not of course saying that nothing more would ever happen. His idea was that liberal capitalist democracy supplied *both* the material wants *and* the need for recognition that motivated people. This is a very powerful idea, because it is clear that life in a liberal capitalist democracy is happier, freer and more prosperous than under alternative systems. Only there can one complain about the government (a) without fear of arrest and persecution, and (b) in a centrally heated lecture hall. Why would anyone want to live anywhere else? A pluralism of

values, in which liberal democracy competed against alternatives, seems irrelevant after liberalism's triumph.

Of course, the years following publication of *The End of
History* have been unkind to Fukuyama. Enlightened values do
not seem to be universally held. Many people and cultures have
shown themselves extremely reluctant to enjoy their benefits.
Opposition to globalisation comes in many shapes and sizes,
while events in Rwanda, Somalia, Yugoslavia, Congo, Liberia,
Sierra Leone and Iraq have shown how determined people with
machetes, roadside bombs or AK-47s can face down the might
of the United Nations with impunity, at least in the short term.
Meanwhile, capitalism is having problems of its own, as it has
morphed from Smith's combination of work ethic, civic responsibility, tolerance and willingness to trade and exchange, to a
rampant consumerism that creates unpleasant inequalities and –
more importantly – seems to be unsustainable with regard to the
environment. The effects of climate change are potentially
devastating, and it is devilishly hard to see how it can be tackled
effectively in a democratic system which punishes politicians for
slowing growth. Fukuyama's worry that 'we risk becoming
secure and self-absorbed last men, devoid of ... striving for
higher goals in our pursuit of private comforts' seems unlikely to
transpire at this particular juncture of history.

It is therefore unsurprising that doubts about Fukuyama's
thesis have emerged. In one of the more trenchant, Samuel P.
Huntington argued that so deeply are values embedded in
cultures that it will not be possible to avoid clashes between
entire civilisations, and the purpose of international politics can
only be to manage, not resolve. Walter Russell Mead brought
Fukuyama thesis and Huntington antithesis together to conclude
that a global world system rooted in the moderate Anglo-
American Enlightenment does indeed exist, but that it does not
imply stasis. In the first place, many people will struggle against
it and refuse to accept it, though they will use the benefits of

capitalism to attack it, while secondly human nature is to strive, innovate and change. Capitalist liberal democracy fits human nature very well, but by fostering change, not stasis. A simpler hypothesis than Mead's, however, is that liberal capitalist democracy remains one value set among many, and the idea that people choose values in accord with their self-interests, goals and aspirations is not borne out by the evidence.[15]

Behavioural economics and neuroeconomics

The field of economics, in large part a creation of Enlightenment theorists of whom the most prominent was Adam Smith, has for a long time been the final redoubt of those who believe in the essential rationality of humankind. However, even here ideas about rational motivation are being challenged.

It has always been a caricature of Enlightened thought that reason carries all before it. Certainly there were Enlightened thinkers who believed that, but there were others, such as Diderot and la Mettrie whose materialism and fatalism forced them into difficult corners with regard to psychological motivation, while Hume and Rousseau went the whole way and argued for two-way interaction between reason and what were known as the passions. Work in social science is coming to similar conclusions about the importance of emotion in shaping action, and the subordinate role of reason in comparison.

The newish fields of *behavioural economics* and *neuroeconomics*, which use the insights respectively of behavioural psychology and neuropsychology (particularly via fMRI scanning) are challenging some assumptions of the dismal science, such as selfishness and rationality (not, it should be pointed out, automatic assumptions of Adam Smith). Human behaviour is more altruistic than typically thought, with a lot more trust and cooperation than can be rationally explained. People have either innate or highly socialised instincts for fairness and justice, and together try to cope with the uncertainties and risks prevalent in economic life. None of this undermines traditional views of economists, but the application of many economic tools (e.g. game theory) will need to be rethought. The award of a Nobel Memorial Prize in Economic Sciences to Daniel Kahneman for his creation of prospect theory, an alternative to standard utility theory, is a sign that complexity of motivation and the importance of trust and cooperation has been taken on board by the discipline.[16]

Last technological word: the World Wide Web

To finish our survey of the Enlightenment's legacy, we will review one of the most influential developments of the late twentieth century, a boon to intellectuals and anti-intellectuals alike: the World Wide Web. This is a classic offshoot of the Enlightenment project in two ways. Firstly, its governing ideology of allowing anyone to say anything and link to anyone is classically liberal and tolerant. There is no central editor to censor content, or to determine what should be linked to. The links on the Web do form coherent maps of connected content, but organising principles (such as Google's PageRank algorithm) are based on statistics of use, not fiat from on high. Secondly, the engineering principles of the Web require that information should flow freely. The decentralisation of the Web is not merely an ideological whim, but essential to the engineering, in that centralised structures do not scale. A centralised version of the Web (if it was centralised, it could hardly be called a Web) might work with small quantities of content, but would seize up irrevocably if it grew – and the point of the Web is that it should be able to grow without limit. As the Web is a space designed to let information flow, to create opportunities for cooperation and collaboration, we can say that the Web is a liberal artefact that necessarily embodies Enlightenment ideals. Indeed, it is extraordinary reading Diderot's article in *L'Encyclopédie* on '*Encyclopédie*' to note how much of the ideology of the Web is already present in that archetypal Enlightenment work. Furthermore the Web has helped implement the international perspective Diderot sought, transcending national boundaries.

There is opposition to the Web from many sources (most of which, it is fair to say, are more than happy to use it as a tool for organisation, communication and dissemination). Many illiberal governments restrict their citizens' use of the Web, often using adaptations of firewall technology to create what is in effect a giant intranet within their borders. The Web has also been seen as an agent of globalisation, with its slick websites and mass appeal, which has destroyed the anarchistic potential of the Internet and normalised the online world. Marketing has replaced democracy. In these discourses, neologisms such as 'cyberhegemony' and 'cyberdependency' abound. The new development of user creation of content called Web 2.0, which turns the Web into more of a two-way conversation, has silenced many of these critics.

For the Web to be a contributor to global well-being its developers have to pick their way through a number of tricky debates such as this; it is essential that the Web does not become a global monoculture, while also avoiding the alternative of decomposing into several cultish mini-webs with little or no connectivity in between. The balance of respect for others' points of view and proper defence of one's own has always been a difficult one to strike in any sphere of human activity. At the moment, the Web surprises us with the fruitfulness of its connectivity. It is important that this is retained. The free movement of information is extremely important, but this impinges on other values we hold dear, such as our privacy. We also need to understand the way that the Web is used in developing nations in order to ensure that it can serve as wide a set of peoples as possible. The United Nations Working Group on Internet Governance's 2005 report made a number of recommendations for including more stakeholders in Internet governance, which might change the liberalism of the Web as repressive states such as Saudi Arabia and China become more involved. Nevertheless, for the moment the World Wide Web remains the most visible and tangible, though virtual, manifestation of the Enlightenment project.[17]

Conclusions: the Enlightenment Today

The Enlightenment is still an issue of burning concern. What should our verdict be?

For myself, I have to assert that reason and tolerance have quite clearly made the world a better place. Areas which did not host the Enlightened movement seem to be less free, more dangerous, more discontented and poorer, by and large, than North-Western Europe and the United States. Many of the Enlightenment's most trenchant critics in the West criticise from comfortable posts in prestigious universities in agreeable cities whose free intellectual culture has been shaped precisely by the *philosophes* they oppose. Others dissent with a freedom which, were they in charge, they would deny their opponents.

That is not to say that reason and tolerance are the answers to everything. There are other sources of value, and the Enlightenment tradition has also been responsible for great damage to alternative ways of life and views of the good. At worst, rationality can become a coarse instrumentalism where monetary value and scientific progress trump the beauty of a forest, or the obligations and relationships within families, or the silence of a wilderness. Science and technology solve problems, but cause them as well.

Moving from the legacy of the Enlightenment to its achievements, we find – as with any other era in history – they are patchy. Surprisingly, it was not a golden age for either science or mathematics. Progress was made and there were great figures, but historians of those disciplines rightly get more excited by the century before and the century after. Neither was it a great period for the visual arts – eighteenth century names do not feature on lists of the greatest painters. But the novel, especially in English, was a democratic and artistic triumph of form, and no other period has produced four musical geniuses of the stature of Bach, Handel, Haydn and the incomparable Mozart.

Politically, the Enlightenment was a time of undoubted progress. Warfare remained common, but justice and religious freedom spread slowly across the continent. Populations grew healthier and richer, especially towards the end of the century. The revolutions in England and America were lasting settle-ments. The French Revolution remains a matter of fierce debate. In my view the bloodshed, followed by Napoleonic imperialism and reaction, mean that its gains were dubious, although so badly-run was the nation prior to 1789 that it is hard to resist the conclusion that something had to give.

The question of the Enlightenment's legacy, and its real meaning, is vigorously debated today. Was it the moderate, sceptical, tolerant Enlightenment of Locke, Voltaire, Hume and Montesquieu? Or is it better represented by democrats and radicals like Diderot, Condorcet and above all Rousseau? The answer I would give, as is probably clear by now, is 'both'. There are continuities between the two positions, and they had and have common enemies. But equally they do diverge, forced apart by the brutal events of 1793 and 1794 in Paris.

There is much to be said for each of the two sub-traditions. The moderates caused little harm, and were responsible for a number of incremental improvements in political and social life. They overthrew British misrule in America in 1776, and played their part in 1789. But equally their moderation can appear weak, not least in their dealings with the slave-based economy. The radicals were destructive and dangerous – Rousseau's writings are like a naked flame – but it is hard to deny that it was they who refused to compromise over the freedoms and rights we value most today. They also, with the excitement they generated, did most to export Enlightenment values out of the middle class; the moderates rarely had much faith in democracy and the lower orders. Still, the Enlightenment figure with by far the greatest global influence today is a moderate, Adam Smith.

Those are my views. They were probably clear anyway from the tone of this book, but if you took them for gospel, you would not be a worthy successor to the Enlightenment. The debate is still live, and I hope you will be itching to join it.

Notes

Chapter 1

1. See also Bayle's argument that tradition is a very bad guide to truth, excerpted in Isaac Kramnick (ed.), *The Portable Enlightenment Reader*, New York: Penguin, 1995 (hereinafter referred to as 'Kramnick').
2. Cf. Bayle in Kramnick.
3. Isaiah Berlin, *Four Essays on Liberty*, London: Oxford University Press, 1969.
4. Joseph Priestley, 'An Essay on the First Principles of Government', quoted in Roy Porter, *Enlightenment: Britain and the Creation of the Modern World*, Allen Lane, London, 2000, 397.
5. James Boswell, *The Journal of a Tour to the Hebrides*, Edinburgh: Canongate Classics, 1996, 188.
6. Philippe Roger, *The American Enemy: The History of French Anti-Americanism*, Chicago: University of Chicago Press, 2005, especially 1–29.
7. Jonathan I. Israel, *Enlightenment Contested: Philosophy, Modernity, and the Emancipation of Man 1670–1752*, Oxford: Oxford University Press, 2006.
8. Conor Cruise O'Brien, *The Long Affair: Thomas Jefferson and the French Revolution 1785–1800*, London: Pimlico, 1998, 12–13.
9. David Hume, *A Treatise on Human Nature*, Oxford: Clarendon Press, 1978, 415 (II.III.III), and Jean-Jacques Rousseau, 'A discourse on the origin of inequality', in *The Social Contract and Discourses*, G.D.H. Cole (trans.), London: J.M. Dent, 1973, 31–126, at 61.

10. For a fuller account of racist attitudes lurking in the Enlightenment, see Richard H. Popkin, 'The philosophical bases of modern racism', in Richard H. Popkin, *The High Road to Pyrrhonism* (Richard A. Watson & James E. Force, eds.), Indianapolis: Hackett Publishing Company, 1993, 79–102.

11. Gibbon, *The Decline and Fall of the Roman Empire*, vol. iv, 19 (chapter 37).

12. Henry E. May, *The Enlightenment in America*, New York: Oxford University Press, 1976, xviii.

13. Leonard Krieger, *Kings and Philosophers 1689–1789*, New York: W.W. Norton & Company, 1970, 175.

14. Jenny Uglow, *The Lunar Men: Five Friends Whose Curiosity Changed the World*, London: Faber & Faber, 2002.

15. Gertrude Himmelfarb, *The Roads to Modernity: The British, French and American Enlightenments*, London: Vintage, 2008.

16. The classic text on this topic is Jürgen Habermas, *The Structural Transformation of the Public Sphere*, Thomas Burger & Frederick Lawrence (trans.), Cambridge: Polity Press, 1989. See also Richard Sennett, *The Fall of Public Man*, London: Penguin, 2002, 1–122.

17 Gibbon, *The Decline and Fall of the Roman Empire*, vol. iii, 79 (chapter 27).

18. For the arguments in this section, see Richard Yeo, 'Encyclopaedism and Enlightenment', in Martin Fitzpatrick, Peter Jones, Christa Knellwolf & Ian McCalman (eds.), *The Enlightenment World*, London: Routledge, 2007, 350–365 and Israel, *Enlightenment Contested*, 840–862. Robespierre is quoted in Habermas, *The Structural Transformation of the Public Sphere*, 69.

Chapter 2

1. Leonard Krieger, *Kings and Philosophers 1689–1789*, New York: W.W. Norton & Company, 1970; Gertrude Himmelfarb, *The Roads to Modernity: The British, French and American Enlightenments*, London: Vintage, 2008; Norman Hampson, *The Enlightenment: An*

Evaluation of its Assumptions, Attitudes and Values, London: Penguin, 1968; Roy Porter, *Enlightenment: Britain and the Creation of the Modern World*, Allen Lane, London, 2000; Christopher Hill, *The Intellectual Origins of the English Revolution*, Oxford: Clarendon Press, 1965; Theodor W. Adorno & Max Horkheimer, *Dialectic of Enlightenment*, London: Verso, 1997, 3ff; Maurice Cranston, *Philosophers and Pamphleteers: Political Theorists of the Enlightenment*, Oxford: Oxford University Press, 1986; Jonathan I. Israel, *Radical Enlightenment: Philosophy and the Making of Modernity 1650–1750*, Oxford: Oxford University Press, 2002.

2. John Lynch, *Simón Bolívar: A Life*, New Haven: Yale University Press, 2006.

3. Hampson, *The Enlightenment*, 128. See also Henry E. May, *The Enlightenment in America*, New York: Oxford University Press, 1976, for a fourfold division of the Enlightenment along similar lines: the moderate Enlightenment, the skeptical Enlightenment, the revolutionary Enlightenment and the didactic Enlightenment (a final process, taking place in the early nineteenth century, when thinkers tried to preserve the essential discoveries of the Enlightenment in the face of widespread disillusionment about it).

4. Israel, *Radical Enlightenment*.

Chapter 3

1. Jonathan I. Israel, *Enlightenment Contested: Philosophy, Modernity, and the Emancipation of Man 1670–1752*, Oxford: Oxford University Press, 2006, 863–866.

2. Norman Hampson, *The Enlightenment: An Evaluation of its Assumptions, Attitudes and Values*, London: Penguin, 1968, 128–129, and Roger Pearson, 'Introduction' in Voltaire, *Candide and Other Stories*, Oxford: Oxford University Press, 1990, vii-xxxix, at vii.

3. Henry E. May, *The Enlightenment in America*, New York: Oxford University Press, 1976, 33.

4. Gertrude Himmelfarb argues that Britain was the primary locus of Enlightenment, and wishes to 'restore it … to the British' (*The Roads to Modernity: The British, French and American Enlightenments*, London: Vintage, 2008, 3). She believes the French Enlightenment was characterised by an 'ideology of reason', while the more moderate British were less concerned with reason than virtue – in particular the social virtues (compassion, benevolence and sympathy) – and supported reason only to the extent that it helped society by promulgating virtue.

5. The ideal of Inigo Jones (1573–1652).

6. Leonard Krieger, *Kings and Philosophers 1689–1789*, New York: W.W. Norton & Company, 1970, 176; Israel, *Enlightenment Contested*, 11.

7. Himmelfarb (*The Roads to Modernity*) characterises the American Enlightenment as qualitatively different from those of Britain and France. The American Enlightenment on her account was political (rather than ideological or sociological), and concerned with liberty (as opposed to reason or virtue).

8. May, *The Enlightenment in America*, 133–149 for scepticism in Virginia and South Carolina, 118–122 for reactions to European sceptics, 54–65 for the Massachusetts establishment.

9. Arthur Herman, *The Scottish Enlightenment: The Scots' Invention of the Modern World*, London: Fourth Estate, 2001, especially 15–63 for the roots of Enlightenment.

10. Jonathan I. Israel, *Radical Enlightenment: Philosophy and the Making of Modernity 1650–1750*, Oxford: Oxford University Press, 2002, for Spinoza's influence, and Hugh Dunthorne, 'The Dutch Republic: "that mother nation of liberty"' in Martin Fitzpatrick, Peter Jones, Christa Knellwolf & Ian McCalman (eds.), *The Enlightenment World*, London: Routledge, 2007, 87–103.

11. Geoffrey Brereton, *A Short History of French Literature*, Harmondsworth: Penguin, 1954, 202.

12. This account of the Lisbon Earthquake is heavily indebted to

Nicholas Shrady, *The Last Day: Wrath, Ruin and Reason in the Great Lisbon Earthquake of 1755*, New York: Viking, 2008.

Chapter 4

1. John Henry, *Knowledge is Power: How Magic, the Government and an Apocalyptic Vision Inspired Francis Bacon to Create Modern Science*, Duxford: Icon Books, 2002.
2. A poll in 2005 held by the Royal Society in the United Kingdom found that Newton had made a bigger overall contribution to science, and a bigger contribution to humankind, than Einstein. *Newton Beats Einstein in Polls of Scientists and the Public*, Royal Society press release, November 23, 2005, http://royalsociety.org/news.asp?id=3880.
3. For a good discussion of Bayle, see Richard H. Popkin, *The History of Scepticism From Savonarola to Bayle*, Revised and Expanded Edition, New York: Oxford University Press, 2003, 283–301, or 'The high road to Pyrrhonism', in Richard H. Popkin, *The High Road to Pyrrhonism* (Richard A. Watson & James E. Force, eds.), Indianapolis: Hackett Publishing Company, 1993, 11–37, at 25–37.

Chapter 5

1. Voltaire, 'The ingenu', in *Candide and Other Stories*, Roger Pearson (trans.), Oxford: Oxford University Press, 1990, 203–274, at 272. 'Micromégas', in *Candide and Other Stories*, 101–121.
2. David Hume, *A Treatise on Human Nature*, Oxford: Clarendon Press, 1978, 93 (I.III.VI).
3. John Locke, *An Essay Concerning Human Understanding*, II.i.2.
4. Richard H. Popkin, 'Randall and British empiricism', in Richard H. Popkin, *The High Road to Pyrrhonism* (Richard A. Watson & James E. Force, eds.), Indianapolis: Hackett Publishing Company,

1993, 39–53, at 52–53. The whole of this essay questions many assumptions usually made about 'the British empiricist tradition' and usefully unpicks the relationship most historians of ideas believe held between Locke, Berkeley and Hume.

5. Hume, *A Treatise on Human Nature*, 180 (I.IV.I). For an account of Hume's scepticism and the reaction to it, see Richard H. Popkin, 'Skepticism and anti-skepticism in the latter part of the eighteenth century', in Popkin, *The High Road to Pyrrhonism*, 55–77, and 'David Hume: his Pyrrhonism and his critique of Pyrrhonism', *The High Road to Pyrrhonism*, 103–132.

6. Bertrand Russell, *A History of Western Philosophy*, London: George Allen & Unwin, 1946.

7. Henry F. May, *The Enlightenment in America*, New York: Oxford University Press, 1976, 62–65.

8. Darrin M. McMahon, 'Pursuing an Enlightened gospel: happiness from deism to materialism to atheism', in Martin Fitzpatrick, Peter Jones, Christa Knellwolf & Ian McCalman (eds.), *The Enlightenment World*, Abingdon: Routledge, 2007, 164–176.

9. Roy Porter, *Enlightenment: Britain and the Creation of the Modern World*, Allen Lane, London, 2000, 383–396.

10. E.g. Richard Layard, *Happiness: Lessons From a New Science*, London: Allen Lane, 2005.

11. Arthur Herman, *The Scottish Enlightenment: The Scots' Invention of the Modern World*, London: Fourth Estate, 2001, 63–81.

12. One reason for this might be that in the years preceding the Enlightenment, reason and love were seen as antagonistic. As one of many examples, see Jean-Baptiste Lully's opera *Armide* (1686), which contains several set-pieces showing how reason and love were opposed, particularly the 4th act duet between the Danish Knight and Ubalde, and again the 5th act duet between Armide and Renaud. Lully was a celebrity in France, as befitted Louis XIV's favourite composer.

13. Porter, *Enlightenment*, 339–363.

14. May, *The Enlightenment in America*, 32–34, 74.

Chapter 6

1. Benjamin J. Kaplan, *Divided By Faith: Religious Conflict and the Practice of Toleration in Early Modern Europe*, Cambridge MA: Bellknap Press, 2007, argues that this picture is too sharp, and shows that tolerance and intolerance co-existed well before the Thirty Years' War and well into the Enlightenment period. He gives a full picture of the ways in which diverse religious communities found ways of living together. He argues that much liberal tolerance theory is a *post hoc* rationalisation of actual practice, which is surely the case. However, he implausibly underestimates the power of ideas to change practice.

2. In the *Persian Letters*, letter 83.

3. Aristotle, *Politics*, III.7. Each type of government has a 'good' type (monarchy, aristocracy or constitutional government) and a 'bad' type (tyranny, oligarchy or democracy). Note Aristotle's understanding of democracy as a bad type of government.

4. Quotes and references from Merrill D. Peterson (ed.), *The Portable Thomas Jefferson*, Harmondsworth: Penguin, 1977. Letter to Roger C. Weightman, June 24, 1826, 584–585, 'A summary view of the rights of British America', 1–21, 'The declaration of independence', 236–241. The version in Peterson contrasts Jefferson's original text (available in Kramnick) with the amended version; this quote is taken from the amended version, but is very little altered from Jefferson's original.

5. Samuel Scheffler (ed.), *Consequentialism and its Critics*, Oxford: Oxford University Press, 1988; Stephen Darwall (ed.), *Consequentialism*, Oxford: Blackwell Publishing, 2003. The former collects twentieth century papers, while the latter also includes primary sources from Bentham and John Stuart Mill.

6. For papers on Enlightenment conservatism, see Jerry Z. Muller (ed.), *Conservatism: An Anthology of Social and Political Thought from David Hume to the Present*, Princeton: Princeton University Press, 1997, 32–77. As well as the *Reflections*, Burke is quoted from the

following pieces in Isaac Kramnick (ed.), *The Portable Edmund Burke*, New York: Penguin, 1999: 'Observations on a late publication entitled "The present state of the nation"', 246–254; 'Letter to William Burgh, Esq.', 534–536; 'Vindication of natural society', 29–63 (for the Preface of the 'Vindication', see Muller, *Conservatism*, 66–69); and 'Speech on Mr Fox's East India Bill', 363–378. For commentary on the *Reflections*, see Conor Cruise O'Brien, 'Introduction' in Edmund Burke, *Reflections on the Revolution in France*, London: Penguin, 1968, 9–76, and Frances Ferguson, 'Burke and the response to the Enlightenment', in Martin Fitzpatrick, Peter Jones, Christa Knellwolf & Ian McCalman (eds.), *The Enlightenment World*, Abingdon: Routledge, 2007, 610–620. For John Adams, see Henry F. May, *The Enlightenment in America*, New York: Oxford University Press, 1976, 279–283. For Johnson, see Nicholas Hudson, 'The nature of Johnson's conservatism', *English Literary History*, 64(4), 1997, 925–943. For the philosophy of sceptical conservatism in general, see Kieron O'Hara, *After Blair: Conservatism Beyond Thatcher*, Cambridge: Icon Books, 2005.

7. Albert Camus, *The Rebel*, Anthony Bower (trans.), Harmondsworth: Penguin, 1962, 85.

8. Jean-Jacques Rousseau, 'The social contract', in *The Social Contract and Discourses*, G.D.H. Cole (trans.), London: J.M. Dent, 1973, 179–309, at 181 (Book I, Chapter 1). The correct translation of the famous opening is 'man *was* born free', as an anonymous reviewer of a draft of this book pointed out. As the editors of the Everyman edition argue, 'either translation fits Rousseau's general meaning, which is both historical and moral' (349). Later quotes in this section from 'The social contract' Book I, Chapters 6, 7 and 8.

9. John Locke, *Two Treatises of Government*, London, J.M. Dent, 1924, II.82, 156–157.

10. Edward Gibbon, *The Decline and Fall of the Roman Empire*, London: Everyman, 1910, first quote from vol. iv, 20, the second from vol. iv, 7 (both chapter 37). There are copious examples in *Decline and*

Fall of detaching the gendering of attitudes and styles from actual gender; unmanly men are bad, manly women are fine. For instance, in chapter 36, Gibbon sympathises with the intrepid Emperor Majorian who couldn't find enough 'manly' Italian youths to allow him to assemble a 'Roman' army, and instead 'like the weakest of his predecessors, was reduced to the disgraceful expedient of substituting barbarian auxiliaries in the place of his unwarlike subjects.' Chapter 32 includes a bizarre attack on the eunuch Eutropius, 'the first of his artificial sex who dared to assume the character of a Roman magistrate and general.' On the other hand, in his discussion of the pregnancy of Honoria, sister of Valentinian, in chapter 35 he attacks the sexual double standard with twenty-first century gusto, while in chapter 44 he argues strongly against unfair treatment of women in family law.

11. Lucy Peltz, '"A revolution in female manners": women, politics and reputation in the late eighteenth century', in Elizabeth Eger & Lucy Peltz (eds.), *Brilliant Women: Eighteenth-Century Bluestockings*, London: National Portrait Gallery Publications, 2008, 94–125.

12. Norman Hampson, *The Enlightenment: An Evaluation of its Assumptions, Attitudes and Values*, London: Penguin, 1968, 81.

13. Richard H. Popkin, 'The philosophical bases of modern racism', in Richard H. Popkin, *The High Road to Pyrrhonism* (Richard A. Watson & James E. Force, eds.), Indianapolis: Hackett Publishing Company, 1993, 79–102, at 84–90. For Hume, see 'Of national characters', in *Essays Moral, Political and Literary*, Indianapolis: Liberty Fund, 1985, 197–215, at n.10, and 'Of the populousness of ancient nations', in *Essays Moral, Political and Literary*, 377–464, at 383–386.

14. May, *The Enlightenment in America*, 70–71, and 99–100.

15. May, *The Enlightenment in America*, 95–101; John Dunn, *Setting the People Free: The Story of Democracy*, London: Atlantic Books, 2005, 71–84.

16. Dunn, *Setting the People Free*, 102–111.

17. The pieces mentioned in this section are Burke, *Reflections*, 128, James Madison, Alexander Hamilton & John Jay, *The Federalist Papers*, London: Penguin, 1987, Joseph de Maistre, *Considerations on France*, Richard A. Lebrun (trans.), Cambridge: Cambridge University Press, 1994, first published in 1797 (see also the 'Introduction' by Isaiah Berlin) and de Maistre, 'Essay on the generative principle of political constitutions and of other human institutions', in Muller, *Conservatism*, 136–145. See also the introduction to this essay by Muller, at 134–136. The essay was first written in 1815. For a selection of passages from Burke, see Russell Kirk, *The Portable Conservative Reader*, New York: Viking Penguin, 1982, 3–48.

18. Quotes from Thomas Paine, 'The rights of man', in *The Thomas Paine Reader*, London: Penguin, 1987, 201–364, at 20, and 'Letter to George Washington', in *The Thomas Paine Reader*, 490–502, at 502.

19. Cf. e.g. Peter Marshall, *Demanding the Impossible: A History of Anarchism*, London: Fontana, 1993, 191–219, Roy Porter, *Enlightenment: Britain and the Creation of the Modern World*, London: Allen Lane, 2000, 455–459.

20. May, *The Enlightenment in America*, 178–179, 192–202.

Chapter 7

1. Roy Porter, *Enlightenment: Britain and the Creation of the Modern World*, London: Penguin, 2000, 295.

2. Jonathan I. Israel, *Enlightenment Contested: Philosophy, Modernity, and the Emancipation of Man 1670–1752*, Oxford: Oxford University Press, 2006, 6–7.

3. For the story of the somewhat childish arguments that delayed the publication of the *Principia*, see Colin A. Ronan, *The Cambridge Illustrated History of the World's Science*, Cambridge: Cambridge University Press, 1983, 347–348. Clearly reason wasn't the only thing driving Enlightenment luminaries such as Newton and Hooke. Halley comes out of the mess pretty well.

4. See Steven Shapin, *A Social History of Truth: Civility and Science in Seventeenth-Century England*, Chicago: University of Chicago Press, 1994; Ronan, *The Cambridge Illustrated History of the World's Science*, 373–374; Henry E. May, *The Enlightenment in America*, New York: Oxford University Press, 1976, 34; Luciano Boschiero, *Experiment and Natural Philosophy in Seventeenth-Century Tuscany*, Dordrecht: Springer, 2007.

5. B.J.T. Dobbs, *The Foundations of Newton's Alchemy, or the Hunting of the Greene Lyon*, Cambridge: Cambridge University Press, 1975. Joseph Priestley was another Enlightened scientist who explored the prophetic books, but by his time the practice was becoming rare. See Porter, *Enlightenment*, 414.

6. May, *The Enlightenment in America*, 136, and 375n.6.

7. William J. Baumol, *The Free-Market Innovation Machine: Analyzing the Growth Miracle of Capitalism*, Princeton: Princeton University Press, 2002, 20.

8. Adam Smith, *An Inquiry into the Nature and Causes of the Wealth of Nations*, Book One, XI, Part I.

9. Jenny Uglow, *The Lunar Men: Five Friends Whose Curiosity Changed the World*, London: Faber & Faber, 2002.

10. Cf. http://www.leonhard-euler.ch/ and Emil A. Fellman, *Leonhard Euler*, Basel: Birkhäuser-Verlag, 2007, or Carl B. Boyer, *A History of Mathematics*, Princeton: Princeton University Press, 1968, 481–507.

11. Immanuel Kant, *Lectures on Logic*, Cambridge: Cambridge University Press, 1992. This contains a number of writings on logic; for the lectures published as *Logik* see 521–642.

Chapter 8

1. Edward Gibbon, *The Decline and Fall of the Roman Empire*, London: Everyman, 1910, chapters 15, 16, 20, 21 and 28 in particular, though see throughout that work for several effective side-swipes, as well as a broad-brush picture of the deleterious effects of Christianity.

2. David Hume, *An Enquiry Concerning Human Understanding*, Oxford: Oxford University Press, 2000, 83–99.

3. Gibbon, *The Decline and Fall of the Roman Empire*, vol. i, 433–434 (chapter 15).

4. James Boswell, *The Journal of a Tour to the Hebrides*, Edinburgh: Canongate Classics, 1996, 218. But for a satirical version of a clergyman using reason, see Henry Fielding's *Joseph Andrews*, where Parson Adams uses reason to comfort Joseph in affliction 'calculated for the Instruction and Improvement of the Reader'. Henry Fielding, 'Joseph Andrews', in *Joseph Andrews & Shamela*, Oxford: Oxford University Press, 1999, 1–303, at 230–232 (Book III, Chapter XI).

5. Henry F. May, *The Enlightenment in America*, New York: Oxford University Press, 1976, 42–65.

6. Jonathan I. Israel, *Radical Enlightenment: Philosophy and the Making of Modernity 1650–1750*, Oxford: Oxford University Press, 2001, 599–609.

7. Christopher McCammon, 'Overcoming deism: hope incarnate in Kant's rational religion', in Chris L. Firestone & Stephen R. Palmquist (eds.), *Kant and the New Philosophy of Religion*, Bloomington, IN: Indiana University Press, 2006, 79–89; Alan Wood, 'Kant's deism', in Philip J. Rossi & Michael Wreen (eds.), *Kant's Philosophy of Religion Reconsidered*, Bloomington, IN: Indiana University Press, 1991, 1–21; Onora O'Neill, *Kant on Reason and Religion*, The Tanner Lectures on Human Values delivered at Harvard University, 1996, http://www.tannerlectures.utah.edu/lectures/documents/onei1197.pdf.

8. For more on this extraordinary episode and the religiosity that accompanied the Revolution, see Michael Burleigh, *Earthly Powers*, London: HarperCollins, 2005, 67–111. Albert Camus penetratingly describes the route from Rousseau's *Social Contract* to the Terror, focusing on Saint-Just and the religion of virtue, in *The Rebel*, (Anthony Bower, trans.), Harmondsworth: Penguin, 1962, 82–102. The still evocative names of the months were:

Vendémiaire, Brumaire, Frimaire, Nivôse, Pluviôse, Ventôse, Germinal, Floréal, Prairial, Messidor, Thermidor and Fructidor.

Chapter 9

1. Cf, Leonard Krieger, *Kings and Philosophers 1689–1789*, New York: W.W. Norton & Company Inc, 1970, 147–150.
2. Susan Sloman, catalogue note in Karen Hearn (ed.), *Van Dyck and Britain*, London: Tate Publishing, 2009, 210.
3. For works mentioned in this section, see the following excerpts in Charles Harrison, Paul Wood & Jason Gaiger (eds.), *Art in Theory 1648–1815: An Anthology of Changing Ideas*, Malden MA: Blackwell Publishing, 2000; Jonathan Richardson, *Essay on the Theory of Painting* and *The Science of the Connoisseur*, 326–334; Denis Diderot, 'Art', 581–587, and also examples of his critical commentaries at 602–626; William Hogarth, *The Analysis of Beauty*, 491–501; Edmund Burke, *A Philosophical Inquiry into the Origin of our Ideas of the Sublime and the Beautiful*, 516–526; Joseph Addison, *On the Pleasures of the Imagination*, 382–388; and Gotthold Lessing, 'Laocoön: an essay on the limits of painting and poetry', 477–486. Excerpts from Burke's *Enquiry* also appear in Kramnick.
4. Cf. e.g. Edmund Burke, 'A letter to a noble lord', in Isaac Kramnick (ed.), *The Portable Edmund Burke*, New York: Penguin, 1999, 213–229, at 226.
5. In this section, see Michael Levey, *From Rococo to Revolution: Major Trends in Eighteenth-Century Painting*, London: Thames & Hudson, 1966; for Watteau, 52–83; for neo-classicism, 164–199; and although Goya is beyond the scope of this book, Levey's survey explores the continuities of his work with David's at 200–234. For portraiture, see Malcolm Baker, 'The portrait after the antique', in *Citizens and Kings: Portraits in the Age of Revolution 1760–1830*, London: Royal Academy of Arts, 2007, 210–225; Robert Rosenblum, 'Portraiture: facts versus fiction', in *Citizens and Kings*,

14–24, at 22–24. For Dutch art, see R.H. Fuchs, *Dutch Painting*, London: Thames & Hudson, 1978, 143–147. For Van Dyck's influence on English art, see Susan Sloman, 'Van Dyck's Continuing Influence', in *Van Dyck and Britain*, 205–208. For Hogarth, see David Bindman, *Hogarth*, London: Thames & Hudson, 1981; David Bindman, *Hogarth and His Times*, London: British Museum Press, 1997; *William Hogarth (1697–1764): The Artist and the City*, Manchester: Whitworth Art Gallery, 1997. For the fancy picture, see Martin Postle, *Angels and Urchins: The Fancy Picture in Eighteenth-Century British Art*, London: Draig Publications, 1998. For Wright, see Jane Wallis, *Joseph Wright of Derby 1734–1797*, Derby: Derby Museum & Art Gallery, 1997.

6. This section is indebted to John Summerson, *The Architecture of the Eighteenth Century*, London: Thames & Hudson, 1986. For the episode of the Hôtel Dieu, 128–130. Kenneth Clark, *Civilisation*, London: Penguin, 1987, 157–158, links rococo architecture and Bach. See also Jeremy Bentham, 'Panopticon', in Jeremy Bentham, *The Panopticon Writings*, London: Verso, 1995, 29–95.

7. Cynthia Verba, 'Music and the Enlightenment', in Martin Fitzpatrick, Peter Jones, Christa Knellwolf & Ian McCalman (eds.), *The Enlightenment World*, Abingdon: Routledge, 2007, 307–322.

8. Robert W. Gutman, *Mozart: A Cultural Biography*, San Diego: Harcourt, 1999, 124–127.

9. Quoted in Geoffrey Brereton, *A Short History of French Literature*, Harmondsworth: Penguin, 1954, 200.

10. See for example an interesting review in R.W. Harris, *Reason and Nature in Eighteenth Century Thought*, London: Blandford Press, 1968, 195–227.

11. I.e. coarse homespun cloth.

12. Ian Watt, *The Rise of the Novel: Studies in Defoe, Richardson and Fielding*, London: Pimlico, 2000.

13. Mentioned in Michael Foot, 'Introduction', in Jonathan

Swift, *Gulliver's Travels*, Harmondsworth: Penguin, 1967, 7–29, at 10.

14. Watt, *The Rise of the Novel*, 15.

15. J. Hector St John de Crèvecoeur, *Letters From an American Farmer*, Oxford: Oxford University Press, 1997, 21–22.

16. Samuel Johnson, *A Journey to the Western Isles of Scotland*, Edinburgh: Canongate Classics, 1996, 67.

17. Gutman, *Mozart*, 318–331, quote from 329.

Chapter 10

1. Cf. Roy Porter, *Enlightenment: Britain and the Creation of the Modern World*, Allen Lane, London, 2000, 424–427, and John Gray, *Al Qaeda and What It Means To Be Modern*, London: Faber & Faber, 2003.

2. For the issues raised in this section, see Darrin M. McMahon, *Enemies of the Enlightenment: The French Counter-Enlightenment and the Making of Modernity*, New York: Oxford University Press, 2001. For the quote from More, see Porter, *Enlightenment*, 467. For Vico, see Isaiah Berlin, 'The Counter-Enlightenment', in *Against the Current: Essays in the History of Ideas*, London: Pimlico, 1999, 1–25, at 4–6; 'Vico's concept of knowledge', in *Against the Current*, 111–119; 'Vico and the ideal of the Enlightenment', in *Against the Current*, 120–129. For Hamann, see Berlin, 'The Counter-Enlightenment', 6–10. De Maistre is quoted in Isaiah Berlin, 'Introduction' in Joseph de Maistre, *Considerations on France*, Cambridge: Cambridge University Press, 1994, xxviii-xxix. For middle class prudishness, see Ben Wilson, *Decency and Disorder: The Age of Cant 1789–1837*, London: Faber & Faber, 2007.

3. Cf. Porter, *Enlightenment*, 461–463.

4. See Jürgen Habermas, *Knowledge and Human Interests*, Jeremy J. Shapiro (trans.), Cambridge: Polity Press, 1987, which discusses positivism in particular at 71–90. The classic logical positivist

229 **Notes**

text, brilliantly written and monumentally implausible, is A.J. Ayer, *Language, Truth and Logic*, London: Penguin, 2001. For neuroscientific discoveries, see Chris Frith, *Making Up the Mind: How the Brain Creates Our Mental World*, Malden MA: Blackwell, 2007. For social engineering, see Rebecca Lemov, *World as Laboratory: Experiments With Mice, Mazes and Men*, New York: Hill & Wang, 2005.

5. Karl Marx, *The First International and After*, Harmondsworth: Penguin, 1974, 314, *The Revolutions of 1848*, Harmondsworth: Penguin, 87.

6. F.A. Hayek, *The Constitution of Liberty*, London: Routledge & Kegan Paul, 1960, 402–403.

7. For this section, the main reference is Theodor W. Adorno & Max Horkheimer, *Dialectic of Enlightenment*, John Cumming (trans.), London: Verso, 1997, quotes taken from xv–xvi and 86–118. Adorno and Horkheimer quote Kant from his *Observations on the Feeling of the Beautiful and Sublime*. See also Dan Hind, *The Threat to Reason: How the Enlightenment Was Hijacked and How We Can Reclaim It*, Cambridge: Verso, 2007. Useful commentaries on Adorno and Horkheimer to which I am indebted are Howard Williams, 'An Enlightenment critique of the *Dialectic of Enlightenment*', in Martin Fitzpatrick, Peter Jones, Christa Knellwolf & Ian McCalman (eds.), *The Enlightenment World*, Abingdon: Routledge, 2007, 635–647, and Lawrence E. Cahoone, *The Dilemma of Modernity: Philosophy, Culture and Anti-Culture*, Albany: State University of New York Press, 1988, 181–193.

8. Jonathan I. Israel, *Enlightenment Contested: Philosophy, Modernity, and the Emancipation of Man 1670–1752*, Oxford: Oxford University Press, 2006, 866. Quote in previous paragraph, 868.

9. Alisdair Macintyre, *After Virtue: A Study in Moral Theory*, London: Gerald Duckworth & Co Ltd, 1981; Bernard Williams, *Ethics and the Limits of Philosophy*, Cambridge MA: Harvard University Press,

1985; Annette C. Baier, *Moral Prejudices: Essays on Ethics*, Cambridge MA: Harvard University Press, 1994; *The Commons of the Mind*, Chicago: Open Court, 1997. For Hume, see 'Of moral prejudices', in *Essays Moral, Political and Literary*, Revised Edition, Indianapolis: Liberty Fund, 1987, 538–544, and Baier's endorsement, *Moral Prejudices*, 51–94.

10. Jean-François Lyotard, *The Postmodern Condition: A Report on Knowledge*, Geoff Bennington & Brian Massumi (trans.), Manchester: Manchester University Press, 1984.

11. John Gray, *Enlightenment's Wake: Politics and Culture at the Close of the Modern Age*, London: Routledge, 1995, 145, and 4–5.

12. A.C. Grayling, *Towards the Light: The Story of the Struggles for Liberty and Rights That Made the Modern West*, London: Bloomsbury, 2007, and Israel, *Enlightenment Contested*, 806–8 and 869.

13. Richard Dawkins, *The God Delusion*, London: Bantam Press, 2006; Daniel C. Dennett, *Breaking the Spell: Religion as a Natural Phenomenon*, London: Allen Lane, 2006; Sam Harris, *The End of Faith: Religion, Terror, and the Future of Reason*, London: Free Press, 2005. For energised Islam, see Olivier Roy, *Globalized Islam: The Search for a New Ummah*, New York: Columbia University Press, 2004. For the quote from May, see Henry F. May, *The Enlightenment in America*, New York: Oxford University Press, 1976, 42.

14. For the quote from Adorno & Horkheimer, *Dialectic of Enlightenment*, 81–82. For Wilberforce, Porter, *Enlightenment*, 469–470. Williams and Midgley appear in a symposium on reason in the *New Scientist*, a collection well worth reading and including contributions from Noam Chomsky, Roger Penrose and A.C. Grayling. See Rowan Williams, 'Reason stands against values and morals', *New Scientist*, July 26, 2008, 44–45, and Mary Midgley, 'Reason's just another faith', 50–51. Kaplan's historical perspective is in Benjamin J. Kaplan, *Divided By Faith: Religious Conflict and the Practice of Toleration in Early Modern Europe*, Cambridge MA: Bellknap Press, 2007, 358. On Islam, for a short polemic, see Ziauddin Sardar, 'The erasure of Islam', *The Philosophers' Magazine*,

3rd quarter, 2008, 77–79, and for Egyptian intellectuals, Alaa al Aswany, *The Yacoubian Building*, Humphrey Davies (trans.), London: HarperPerennial, 2007, 73. See also Thomas Paine, 'The age of reason part one', in Michael Foot & Isaac Kramnick (eds.), *The Thomas Paine Reader*, London: Penguin, 1987, 399–451. Beaumarchais is excerpted in Kramnick.

15. Francis Fukuyama, *The End of History and the Last Man*, London: Penguin, 1992 (quote from 328). See also Samuel P. Huntington, *The Clash of Civilizations and the Remaking of the World Order*, London: Simon & Schuster UK, 1997, and Walter Russell Mead, *God and Gold: Britain, America and the Making of the Modern World*, London: Atlantic Books, 2007. For changes to attitudes to trade, see Porter, *Enlightenment*, 384–385.

16. Daniel Kahneman & Amos Tversky, 'Prospect theory: an analysis of decision under risk', *Econometrica*, 47, 1979, 263–291, and see Pete Lunn, *Basic Instincts: Human Nature and the New Economics*, London: Marshall Cavendish Business, 2008.

17. See Tim Berners-Lee (1999), *Weaving the Web: The Past, Present and Future of the World Wide Web by its Inventor*, London: Texere Publishing, and Tim Berners-Lee, Wendy Hall, James A. Hendler, Kieron O'Hara, Nigel Shadbolt & Daniel J. Weitzner, 'A framework for Web Science', *Foundations and Trends in Web Science*, 1(1), 2006, 1–130, at 107–109, from which this section is adapted. For postmodern opposition to the Web, see David Resnick, 'Politics on the Internet: the normalization of cyberspace', in Chris Toulouse & Timothy W. Luke (eds.), *The Politics of Cyberspace*, New York: Routledge, 1998, 48–68, or William Dan Perdue, 'The new totalitarianism: cyber-hegemony and the global system', *International Roundtable on the Challenges of Globalization*, http://i-p-o.org/perdue.htm, 1999. For Web 2.0, see Don Tapscott & Anthony D. Williams, *Wikinomics: How Mass Collaboration Changes Everything*, London: Atlantic, 2007, and Charles Leadbeater, *We-Think: Mass Innovation, Not Mass Production*, London: Profile, 2008. For issues to do with equitable distribution of the benefits of the

Web, see Kieron O'Hara & David Stevens, *inequality.com: Power, Poverty and the Digital Divide*, Oxford: Oneworld, 2006, and the *Report of the Working Group on Internet Governance*, http://www.wgig.org/docs/WGIGREPORT.pdf, 2005, (available in a number of languages and formats from http://www.wgig.org/), and for privacy, Kieron O'Hara & Nigel Shadbolt, *The Spy in the Coffee Machine: The End of Privacy As We Know It*, Oxford: Oneworld, 2008.

Brief biographies of some figures mentioned in this guide

As an aid to continued study, here are brief details of some of those mentioned in this guide, including those who are considered part of the Enlightenment, those who lived through the period and engaged with Enlightenment, some of the more prominent inspirations for the Enlightenment and some contemporary and near-contemporary critics.

John **Adams**, 1735–1826, American statesman, President of the United States 1797–1801.

Joseph **Addison**, 1672–1719, English essayist, co-founder of *The Spectator* magazine.

Jean le Rond **d'Alembert**, 1717–83, French mathematician and philosopher, co-editor of the *Encyclopédie*.

Sir Richard **Arkwright**, 1732–92, English entrepreneur, inventor of the spinning frame.

Jane **Austen**, 1775–1817, English novelist, author of *Pride and Prejudice*.

Carl Philipp Emanuel **Bach**, 1714–88, German composer of several influential keyboard sonatas, son of J.S. Bach.

Johann Sebastian **Bach**, 1685–1750, German composer of the *St Matthew Passion*, father of C.P.E. Bach and several other major composers.

Francis **Bacon**, 1561–1626, English philosopher and statesman, author of *Novum Organum*.

Rev. Thomas **Bayes**, 1702–61, English mathematician, discoverer of Bayes' theorem relating the probabilities of random events.

Pierre **Bayle**, 1647–1706, French philosopher, author of *Historical and Critical Dictionary*.

Pierre-Augustin Caron de **Beaumarchais**, 1732–99, French dramatist and revolutionary, author of *The Marriage of Figaro*.

Cesare Bonesana, Marchese di **Beccaria**, 1738–94, Italian philosopher and penologist, author of *On Crimes and Punishments*.

Jeremy **Bentham**, 1748–1832, English philosopher, theorist of utilitarianism.

Bishop George **Berkeley**, 1685–1753, Irish philosopher, author of *Three Dialogues of Hylas and Philonous*.

Daniel **Bernoulli**, 1700–82, Dutch mathematician, pioneer of statistics and probability, son of Johann Bernoulli.

Jacob **Bernoulli**, 1654–1705, Swiss mathematician, pioneer of calculus and probability theory, brother of Johann Bernoulli.

Johann **Bernoulli**, 1667–1748, Swiss mathematician, pioneer of calculus, brother of Jacob Bernoulli, father of Daniel Bernoulli, tutor of Leonhard Euler.

Joseph **Black**, 1728–99, Scottish chemist, discoverer of carbon dioxide.

William **Blake**, 1757–1827, English poet, painter and printer, author of *Songs of Innocence and Experience*.

Henry St John, 1st Viscount **Bolingbroke**, 1678–1751, English philosopher, politician and Jacobite intriguer.

James **Boswell**, 1740–95, Scottish writer, lawyer and diarist, author of *The Life of Samuel Johnson*.

François **Boucher**, 1703–70, French artist, painter of numerous portraits of Mme de Pompadour.

Sir Robert **Boyle**, 1627–91, Irish physicist, discoverer of Boyle's Law connecting the pressure and volume of a gas in a closed system.

Georges-Louis Leclerc, Comte de **Buffon**, 1707–88, French naturalist, author of *Natural History, General and Particular*.

Edmund **Burke**, 1729–97, Irish politician and philosopher, author of *Reflections on the Revolution in France*.

Frances **Burney** (Fanny Burney), 1752–1840, English novelist, author of *Cecilia*.

Robert **Burns**, 1759–96, Scottish poet, author of *Poems, Chiefly in the Scottish Dialect*.

Catherine II (the Great), 1729–96, Tsarina of Russia from 1762.

Henry **Cavendish**, 1731–1810, French-born English chemist, discoverer of hydrogen.

Sir William **Chambers**, 1723–96, Swedish-born Scottish architect of Somerset House, London.

Anthony **Collins**, 1676–1729, English philosopher, author of *A Discourse of Freethinking*.

Marie Jean Antoine Nicolas de Caritat, Marquis de **Condorcet**, 1743–94, French philosopher and mathematician, author of *Outlines of an Historical View of the Progress of the Human Mind*.

Charles-Augustin de **Coulomb**, 1736–1806, French physicist, discoverer of Coulomb's Law of electrostatic force.

John Hector St John de **Crèvecoeur**, 1735–1813, French writer, author of *Letters From an American Farmer*.

Jacques-Louis **David**, 1748–1825, French artist, painter of *The Death of Marat*.

Daniel **Defoe**, c1660–1731, English writer, author of *Robinson Crusoe*.

René **Descartes**, 1596–1650, French philosopher and mathematician, author of *Meditations on First Philosophy*.

Denis **Diderot**, 1713–84, French writer, co-editor of the *Encyclopédie*.

Jonathan **Edwards**, 1703–58, American theologian, author of *Freedom of the Will*.

Leonhard **Euler**, 1707–83, Swiss mathematician, the pre-eminent mathematician of the age.

Henry **Fielding**, 1707–54, English writer, author of *Tom Jones*.

Bernard le Bovier de **Fontenelle**, 1657–1757, French writer, author of *Conversations on the Plurality of Worlds*.

Benjamin **Franklin**, 1706–90, American writer, scientist, politician, philosopher, inventor and printer.

Frederick II (the Great), 1712–86, King of Prussia from 1740.

Edward **Gibbon**, 1737–94, English historian, author of *The Decline and Fall of the Roman Empire*.

Christoph **Gluck**, 1714–87, Bavarian composer of *Orfeo ed Eurydice*.

William **Godwin**, 1736–1836, English philosopher and novelist, author of *An Enquiry Concerning Political Justice* and *Caleb Williams*, husband of Mary Wollstonecraft.

Johann Wolfgang von **Goethe**, 1749–1832, German writer, author of *Faust*.

Oliver **Goldsmith**, c1730–74, Irish poet, novelist and dramatist, author of *She Stoops to Conquer*.

Sir Edmond **Halley**, 1656–1742, English astronomer, applied Newtonian mechanics to the physics of celestial bodies.

Alexander **Hamilton**, 1755–1804, American statesman, co-author of the *Federalist Papers*.

Georg Friedrich **Händel**, 1685–1759, German composer of *The Messiah*.

Joseph **Haydn**, 1732–1809, Austrian composer of *The Creation*.

Claude-Adrien **Helvétius**, 1715–71, French philosopher, author of *On the Mind*.

Johann von **Herder**, 1744–1803, German poet and philosopher, author of *Outlines of a Philosophy of the History of Man*.

Thomas **Hobbes**, 1588–1679, English philosopher, author of *Leviathan*.

William **Hogarth**, 1697–1754, English artist and printmaker, painter of *The Rake's Progress*.

Paul-Henri Thiri, Baron **d'Holbach**, 1723–89, German-born French philosopher and salon host, author of *The System of Nature*.

Sir Robert **Hooke**, 1635–1703, English physicist, discoverer of Hooke's Law of elasticity.

John **Howard**, 1726–90, English prison reformer, author of *The State of the Prisons in England*.

David **Hume**, 1711–76, Scottish philosopher and historian, author of *A Treatise of Human Nature*.

Francis **Hutcheson**, 1694–1746, Ulster-born Scottish philosopher, author of *A System of Moral Philosophy*.

John **Jay**, 1745–1829, American statesman, co-author of the *Federalist Papers*.

Thomas **Jefferson**, 1743–1826, American statesman, philosopher and architect, President of the United States 1801–9, main author of the *Declaration of Independence*.

Dr Samuel **Johnson**, 1709–84, English writer and lexicographer, author of *Dictionary of the English Language*.

Joseph II, 1741–90, Holy Roman Emperor from 1765, son of Maria Theresa and brother of Marie Antoinette.

Immanuel **Kant**, 1724–1804, Prussian philosopher, author of *The Critique of Pure Reason*.

Pierre Ambroise François Choderlos de **Laclos**, 1741–1803, French novelist and soldier, author of *Les Liaisons Dangereuses*.

Joseph-Louis **Lagrange**, 1736–1813, Italian-born mathematician, extended Newton's theories of mechanics.

Antoine-Laurent **Lavoisier**, 1743–94, French chemist, known as the father of modern chemistry.

Gottfried **Leibniz**, 1646–1716, German philosopher and mathematician, author of *Monadology*.

Carolus **Linnaeus**, 1707–78, Swedish biologist, creator of the modern biological taxonomic system.

John **Locke**, 1632–1704, English philosopher, author of *An Essay Concerning Human Understanding*.

Louis XIV, 1638–1715, King of France from 1638, great-grandfather of Louis XV.

Louis XV, 1710–74, King of France from 1715, grandfather of Louis XVI.

Louis XVI, 1754–93, King of France from 1774–92, grandson of Louis XV, husband of Marie Antoinette.

Catherine **Macaulay** (née Sawbridge, Mrs Catherine Graham), 1731–91, English historian, author of *History of England from the Accession of James I to the Elevation of the House of Hanover*.

James **Madison**, 1751–1836, President of the United States 1809–17, co-author of the *Federalist Papers*.

Joseph-Marie, Comte **de Maistre**, 1753–1821, Savoyard philosopher and lawyer, author of *Considerations on France*.

Bernard **de Mandeville**, 1670–1733, Dutch satirist, author of *The Fable of the Bees*.

Maria Theresa, 1717–80, Holy Roman Empress from 1740, mother of Joseph II and Marie Antoinette.

Marie Antoinette, 1755–93, Queen of France, wife of Louis XVI, daughter of Maria Theresa, sister of Joseph II.

Julien Offray de **la Mettrie**, 1709–51, French philosopher, author of *Man a Machine*.

Charles-Louis de Secondat, Baron de la Brède et de **Montesquieu**, 1689–1755, French political philosopher, author of *The Spirit of the Laws*.

Wolfgang Amadeus **Mozart**, 1756–91, Austrian composer of *The Magic Flute*.

Sir Isaac **Newton**, 1643–1727, English physicist and mathematician, inventor of the calculus and the theory of gravity.

Thomas **Paine**, 1737–1809, English political philosopher and revolutionary, author of *The Rights of Man*.

Peter I (the Great), 1672–1725, Tsar of Russia from 1682.

Sebastião José de Carvalho e Melo, 1st Marquis of **Pombal**, 1699–1782, Portuguese statesman and administrator.

Alexander **Pope**, 1688–1744, English poet, author of *Essay on Man*.

Joseph **Priestley**, 1733–1804, English scientist and theologian, discoverer of oxygen.

Thomas **Reid**, 1710–96, Scottish philosopher, author of *Inquiry into the Human Mind on the Principles of Common Sense*.

Maximilien **Robespierre**, 1758–94, French revolutionary, President of the National Convention.

Jean-Jacques **Rousseau**, 1712–78, Swiss philosopher, novelist and composer, author of *The Social Contract*.

Donatien Alphonse François de Sade, Marquis **de Sade**, 1740–1814, French writer, author of *Justine*.

Anthony Ashley-Cooper, 3rd Earl of **Shaftesbury**, 1671–1713, English politician and philosopher, author of the *Characteristicks of Men, Manners, Opinions, Times, etc.*

Abbé Joseph **Sieyès**, 1748–1836, French clergyman, author of *What is the Third Estate?*

Adam **Smith**, 1723–90, Scottish economist and philosopher, author of *The Wealth of Nations*.

Baruch de **Spinoza**, 1632–77, Dutch philosopher, author of *Ethics*.

Sir Richard **Steele**, 1672–1729, Irish essayist, co-founder of *The Spectator* magazine.

Lawrence **Sterne**, 1713–68, Irish novelist, author of *Tristram Shandy*.

Jonathan **Swift**, 1667–1745, Irish writer and cleric, author of *Gulliver's Travels*.

Giovanni Battista **Tiepolo**, 1696–1770, Venetian artist, painter of frescoes.

John **Tillotson**, 1630–94, English churchman, Archbishop of Canterbury from 1691.

Giambattista **Vico**, 1668–1744, Italian historian, author of *The New Science*.

François-Marie Arouet (**Voltaire**), 1694–1778, French writer, author of *Candide*.

George **Washington**, 1732–99, American statesman, President of the United States 1789–97.

Jean-Antoine **Watteau**, 1684–1721, French painter of *Departure from the Island of Cythera*.

Mary **Wollstonecraft**, 1759–97, English writer and philosopher, author of *A Vindication of the Rights of Woman*.

Joseph **Wright**, 1734–97, English artist, painter of *Experiment on a Bird With an Air Pump*.

Further resources

I begin by suggesting a range of primary sources, followed by suggestions for further reading, viewing and listening grouped by chapter to allow the reader to follow up on particular points of interest.

Primary resources

Most of these works appear in a variety of editions. The editions listed here have been selected above the others for some reason or other – I may consider the introduction useful, the further reading comprehensive, the translation superior, the collection of shorter pieces valuable – but that is not to say that other editions should be avoided. The main thing is to read the original Enlightened thinkers in their own words.

Robert J. Allen (ed.), *Addison and Steele: Selections From* The Tatler *and* The Spectator, 2nd edition, Fort Worth: Holt, Rinehart and Winston, 1970.

James Boswell, *The Life of Johnson*, Harmondsworth: Penguin, 1979.

Edmund Burke, *Reflections on the Revolution in France*, London: Penguin, 1968.

Robert Burns, *Poetical Works of Robert Burns*, Edinburgh: Chambers, 1990.

George Crabbe, *Selected Poems*, London: Penguin, 1991.

J. Hector St John de Crèvecoeur, *Letters From an American Farmer*, Oxford: Oxford University Press, 1997.

Daniel Defoe, *Moll Flanders*, London: Penguin, 1989.

Daniel Defoe, *Robinson Crusoe*, London: Penguin, 1985.

Daniel Defoe, *A Tour Through the Whole Island of Great Britain*, London: Penguin, 1971.

Denis Diderot, *Jacques the Fatalist*, David Coward (trans.), Oxford: Oxford University Press, 1999.

Simon Eliot & Beverley Stern (eds.), *The Age of Enlightenment: An Anthology of Eighteenth-Century Texts*, 2 volumes, London: Ward Lock Educational, 1979.

Peter Fairclough (ed.), *Three Gothic Novels* (Walpole, *The Castle of Otranto*; Beckford, *Vathek*; M. Shelley, *Frankenstein*), London: Penguin, 1968.

Michael Foot & Isaac Kramnick (ed.), *The Thomas Paine Reader*, London: Penguin, 1987.

William Godwin, *Enquiry Concerning Political Justice*, London: Pelican, 1973.

Johann Wolfgang von Goethe, *Faust*, Walter Arndt (trans.), New York: W.W. Norton & Co Ltd, 1976. Includes immediate reaction and a selection of critical papers.

Charles Harrison, Paul Wood & Jason Gaiger (eds.), *Art in Theory 1648–1815: An Anthology of Changing Ideas*, Malden MA: Blackwell Publishing, 2000.

David Hume, *Dialogues Concerning Natural Religion*, New York: Hafner, 1948.

David Hume, *An Enquiry Concerning Human Understanding*, Oxford: Oxford University Press, 2007.

David Hume, *Essays Moral, Political and Literary*, Indianapolis: Liberty Fund, 1985.

David Hume, *A Treatise on Human Nature*, Oxford: Clarendon Press, 1978.

Immanuel Kant, *The Critique of Pure Reason*, Norman Kemp Smith (trans.), Basingstoke: Macmillan, 1929.

Isaac Kramnick (ed.), *The Portable Edmund Burke*, New York: Penguin, 1999.

Isaac Kramnick (ed.), *The Portable Enlightenment Reader*, New York: Penguin, 1995.

John Locke, *Two Treatises of Government*, London, J.M. Dent, 1924.

James Madison, Alexander Hamilton & John Jay, *The Federalist Papers*, London: Penguin, 1987.

Joseph de Maistre, *Considerations on France*, Richard A. Lebrun (trans.), Cambridge: Cambridge University Press, 1994.

Montesquieu, *Persian Letters*, C.J. Betts (trans.), London: Penguin, 2004.

Montesquieu, *The Spirit of the Laws*, Anne M. Cohler, Basia C. Miller & Harold S. Stone (trans.), Cambridge: Cambridge University Press, 1989.

Merrill D. Peterson (ed.), *The Portable Thomas Jefferson*, Harmondsworth: Penguin, 1977.

Alexander Pope, *Selected Poetry*, Oxford: Oxford University Press, 1994.

Maximilien Robespierre, *Virtue and Terror* (John Howe trans.), London: Verso, 2007, also called *Slavoj Žižek Presents Robespierre: Virtue and Terror*.

Jean-Jacques Rousseau, *The Social Contract and Discourses*, G.D.H. Cole (trans.), London: J.M. Dent, 1973.

Adam Smith, *The Wealth of Nations Books I-III*, London: Penguin, 1999.

Adam Smith, *The Wealth of Nations Books IV-V*, London: Penguin, 1999.

Laurence Sterne, *Tristram Shandy*, London: J.M. Dent, 1912.

Jonathan Swift, *Gulliver's Travels*, Harmondsworth: Penguin, 1967.

Voltaire, *Candide and Other Stories*, Roger Pearson (trans.), Oxford: Oxford University Press, 1990. There are better translations of *Candide*, but this is an exceptionally useful selection of Voltaire's novellas.

Voltaire, *Letters on England*, Leonard Tancock (trans.), London: Penguin, 2005.

Voltaire, *Philosophical Dictionary*, Theodore Besterman (trans.), Harmondsworth: Penguin, 1971.

Mary Wollstonecraft, *A Vindication of the Rights of Men; A Vindication of the Rights of Woman; An Historical and Moral View of the French Revolution*, Oxford: Oxford University Press, 1993.

Chapter 1

From Isaac Kramnick (ed.), *The Portable Enlightenment Reader*, New York: Penguin, 1995: Kant, 'What is Enlightenment?' D'Alembert, 'The human mind emerged from barbarism.' Diderot, '*Encyclopédie*.' Condorcet, 'The future progress of the human mind.' Bayle, 'On superstition and tolerance.' Locke, 'A letter concerning toleration.' In general, see the selections from pp.ix–xxvi and 1–38.

Kenneth Clark, *Civilisation*, Harmondsworth: Penguin, 1982.

Robert Darnton, *The Forbidden Best-Sellers of Pre-Revolutionary France*, New York: W.W. Norton & Company, 1996.

Martin Fitzpatrick, Peter Jones, Christa Knellwolf & Ian McCalman (eds.), *The Enlightenment World*, Abingdon: Routledge, 2007, chapters 11, 17, 21, 22, 23 & 33

Jürgen Habermas, *The Structural Transformation of the Public Sphere*, Thomas Burger & Frederick Lawrence (trans.), Cambridge: Polity Press, 1989.

Jonathan I. Israel, *Radical Enlightenment: Philosophy and the Making of Modernity 1650–1750*, Oxford: Oxford University Press, 2002.

Haydn Mason (ed.), *The Darnton Debate: Books and Revolution in the Eighteenth Century*, Oxford: The Voltaire Foundation, 1998.

Civilisation: A Personal View by Lord Clark: The Complete Series, BBC DVD, 2 Entertain Video. See episodes 9 & 10 for the Enlightenment.

Chapter 2

Tim Blanning, *The Pursuit of Glory: Europe 1648–1789*, London: Allen Lane, 2007.

Norman Hampson, *The Enlightenment: An Evaluation of its Assumptions, Attitudes and Values*, London: Penguin, 1968.

Civilisation: A Personal View by Lord Clark: The Complete Series, BBC DVD, 2 Entertain Video. See episode 8 for the seventeenth century precursors.

Chapter 3

Martin Fitzpatrick, Peter Jones, Christa Knellwolf & Ian McCalman (eds.), *The Enlightenment World*, Abingdon: Routledge, 2007, chapters 6, 7, 8, 9 & 34.

Arthur Herman, *The Scottish Enlightenment: The Scots' Invention of the Modern World*, London: Fourth Estate, 2001.

Gertrude Himmelfarb, *The Roads to Modernity: The British, French and American Enlightenments*, London: Vintage, 2008.

Henry E. May, *The Enlightenment in America*, New York: Oxford University Press, 1976.

Roy Porter, *Enlightenment: Britain and the Creation of the Modern World*, Allen Lane, London, 2000.

Nicholas Shrady, *The Last Day: Wrath, Ruin and Reason in the Great Lisbon Earthquake of 1755*, New York: Viking, 2008.

E.N. Williams, *The Ancien Régime in Europe: Government and Society in the Major States 1648–1789*, Harmondsworth: Penguin, 1970.

Chapter 4

From Kramnick: D'Alembert, 'The human mind emerged from barbarism.'

Gregory S. Kavka, *Hobbesian Moral and Political Theory*, Princeton: Princeton University Press, 1986.

Steve Pincus, *1688: The First Modern Revolution*. New Haven: Yale University Press, 2009.

Bernard Williams, *Descartes: The Project of Pure Enquiry*, London: Penguin, 1978.

Chapter 5

From Kramnick: Rousseau, 'Children and civic education.' See the selections from pp.181–242.

Martin Fitzpatrick, Peter Jones, Christa Knellwolf & Ian McCalman (eds.), *The Enlightenment World*, Abingdon: Routledge, 2007, chapters 2, 4, 10, 12 & 14.

Chapter 6

From Kramnick: Kant, 'What is Enlightenment?' Condorcet, 'The future progress of the human mind.' Bacon, 'The new science.' Locke, 'A letter concerning toleration.' Shaftesbury, 'On enthusiasm.' 'The American declaration of independence.' Frederick the Great, 'Benevolent despotism.' 'The declaration of the rights of man and the citizen.' Kant, 'The difference between the races.' Encyclopaedia Britannica, 'Negro.' See the selections on pp. 351–670.

Maurice Cranston, *Philosophers and Pamphleteers: Political Theorists of the Enlightenment*, Oxford: Oxford University Press, 1986.

William Doyle, *The French Revolution: A Very Short Introduction*, Oxford: Oxford University Press, 2001.

John Dunn, *Setting the People Free: The Story of Democracy*, London: Atlantic Books, 2005.

Martin Fitzpatrick, Peter Jones, Christa Knellwolf & Ian McCalman (eds.), *The Enlightenment World*, Abingdon: Routledge, 2007, chapters 5, 16, 25, 26, 27, 28, 29, 30, 35 & 36.

Jonathan I. Israel, *Enlightenment Contested: Philosophy, Modernity, and the Emancipation of Man 1670–1752*, Oxford: Oxford University Press, 2006.

Paul A. Rahe, *Republics Ancient and Modern* Volume III: *Inventions of Prudence: Constituting the American Regime*, Chapel Hill: University of North Carolina Press, 1994.

Simon Schama, *Citizens: A Chronicle of the French Revolution*, London: Penguin, 2004.

Hugh Thomas, *The Slave Trade: History of the Atlantic Slave Trade 1440–1870*, New York: Simon & Schuster, 1997.

Chapter 7

From Kramnick: see the selections on pp.39–74.

Carl B. Boyer, *A History of Mathematics*, New York: John Wiley & Sons, 1968, 367–543.

Martin Fitzpatrick, Peter Jones, Christa Knellwolf & Ian McCalman (eds.), *The Enlightenment World*, Abingdon: Routledge, 2007, chapters 1 & 15.

James Gleick, *Isaac Newton*, London: HarperPerennial, 2004.

John Gribbin, *Science: A History*, London: Penguin, 2003.

William Kneale & Martha Kneale, *The Development of Logic*, Oxford: Clarendon Press, 1984, 320–350.

John Losee, *A Historical Introduction to the Philosophy of Science*, 4th edition, Oxford: Oxford University Press, 2001, 46–102.

Colin A. Ronan, *The Cambridge Illustrated History of the World's Science*, Cambridge: Cambridge University Press, 334–418.

Chapter 8

From Kramnick: Shaftesbury, 'On enthusiasm.' Newton, 'The argument for a deity.' See the selections on pp.75–180.

Derek Beales, *Prosperity and Plunder: European Catholic Monasteries in the Age of Revolution 1650–1815*, Cambridge: Cambridge University Press, 2003.

Owen Chadwick, *The Popes and European Revolution*, Oxford: Oxford University Press, 1980.

Martin Fitzpatrick, Peter Jones, Christa Knellwolf & Ian McCalman (eds.), *The Enlightenment World*, Abingdon: Routledge, 2007, chapter 3.

John McManners, *Church and Society in Eighteenth-Century France Volume 2: The Religion of the People and the Politics of Religion*, Oxford: Oxford University Press, 1998.

Jeffrey R. Wigelsworth, *Deism in Enlightenment England: Theology, Politics and Newtonian Public Science*, Manchester: Manchester University Press, 2009.

Chapter 9

From Kramnick: Beaumarchais, *Le Mariage de Figaro*. Mozart, *The Magic Flute*. Burke, 'The sublime.' See selections from pp.314–350.

Martin Fitzpatrick, Peter Jones, Christa Knellwolf & Ian McCalman (eds.), *The Enlightenment World*, Abingdon: Routledge, 2007, chapters 18, 19 & 20.

Boris Ford (ed.), *The New Pelican Guide to English Literature* Vol. 4: *From Dryden to Johnson*, Harmondsworth: Penguin, 1982.

Robert W. Gutman, *Mozart: A Cultural Biography*, San Diego: Harcourt, 1999.

Michael Levey, *From Rococo to Revolution: Major Trends in Eighteenth-Century Painting*, London: Thames & Hudson, 1966.

Susan Manning, 'Literature and society in colonial America', in Boris Ford (ed.), *The New Pelican Guide to English Literature Vol. 9: American Literature*, London: Penguin, 1988, 3–26.

John Summerson, *The Architecture of the Eighteenth Century*, London: Thames & Hudson, 1986.

Christoph Wolff, *Johann Sebastian Bach: The Learned Musician*, Oxford: Oxford University Press, 2001.

Architecture

I suggest only a very few of the many great architectural works of the Enlightenment that can be visited in Europe and Britain, but visits to all or any of them will add to a rounder picture of the Enlightenment world. Extravagant palaces and stately homes abound:

Blenheim Palace (Oxfordshire, UK) built by John Vanbrugh (c1664-1726) for Lord Marlborough;

The Sanssouci Palace and other buildings built in Potsdam by Georg von Knobelsdorff (1699-1753) for Frederick II;

The Imperial Palace of Schönbrunn, near Vienna, built by Fischer von Erlach (1656-1723) for Emperor Leopold I;

The Royal Palace of Stockholm, built by Nicodemus Tessin the Younger (1654-1728) for Charles XII (his second palace on this site – the first burned down soon after completion);

The Grand Peterhof Palace, Peterhof Palace Chapels, Smolny

Convent, Vorontsov Palace and the Winter Palace by Bartolomeo Rastrelli for Tsar Peter the Great and his successor Elizabeth in St Petersburg.

There are also splendid churches, cathedrals and abbeys throughout Europe:

The Karlskirche in Vienna;
St Sulpice and Ste Geneviève, now the Panthéon in Paris;
St Mary le Strand, St John's, Smith Square and St Martin in the Fields in London;
Banz Abbey (now Banz Castle) in Bavaria, Germany;
Melk Abbey in Austria.

As well as those neo-classical buildings mentioned in the text, consider visits to:

The Palace of Versailles, the extension by Jacques-Ange Gabriel (sometimes called Ange-Jacques Gabriel, 1698-1782), and the same architect's Château of the Petit Trianon;
The Rotonde de la Villette, Place de Stalingrad, Paris, by Claude-Nicolas Ledoux (1736-1806), originally part of the city wall of Paris;
Chiswick House and gardens, by Lord Burlington;
Monticello, the University of Virginia and the Virginia State Capitol by Thomas Jefferson.

Art

A number of galleries have good collections of Enlightenment works, some highlights are listed below. However, galleries rotate their collections so all works might not be on display at all times.
The Louvre, Paris. Boucher: *Mme de Pompadour, Odalisque*. David: *The Death of Marat* (copy from David's studio – the original is in the

Royal Museum of Fine Arts, Brussels), *The Oath of the Horatii, The Lictors Bring the Body of Brutus to His Sons.* Tiepolo: *Virgin and Child.* Watteau: *Departure from the Island of Cythera, Pierrot.*

The Frick Collection, New York. See in particular the Fragonard room, where four large canvases from the series *The Progress of Love* are complemented by contemporary porcelains, furniture, sculptures and fittings, and the Boucher room where his series *The Arts and Sciences* is shown. The collection also includes Boucher's *The Four Seasons* and works by Reynolds, Gainsborough and Hogarth.

The Metropolitan Museum of Art, New York. David: *The Death of Socrates.* Fragonard: *The Stolen Kiss.* Fuseli: *The Night-Hag Visiting Lapland Witches.* Tiepolo: *The Glorification of the Barbaro Family.* Watteau: *Mezzetin.*

The Derby Museum and Art Gallery. Contains the largest collection of works by Joseph Wright.

The National Gallery, London. Boucher: *Pan and Syrinx.* Gainsborough: *Mr and Mrs Andrews.* Hogarth: *Marriage-à-la-Mode* (1–6). Stubbs: *Whistlejacket.* Tiepolo: *An Allegory With Venus and Time.* Wright: *An Experiment on a Bird in an Air Pump.*

The National Portrait Gallery, London.

Sir John Soane's Museum, London. Has a particularly good collection of works by Hogarth.

The Wallace Collection, London. Has a number of works by Boucher, Watteau, and Gainsborough among others.

The Scottish National Gallery, Edinburgh. Has a collection of works by British and Scottish Enlightenment artists.

The National Museum of Western Art, Tokyo. See the *Apotheosis of Admiral Vettor Pisani* by Giovanni Battista Tiepolo and the splendidly icy *Madonna and Child with Three Saints* by his son Giovanni Domenico Tiepolo, as well as works by Fuseli, Fragonard and Boucher, and some excellent pieces by a range of lesser artists.

Gallerie dell'Accademia, Venice. Houses a collection of works by Venetian artists.

Music

C.P.E. Bach, *Die Auferstehung und Himmelfahrt Jesu* (*The Resurrection and Ascension of Jesus*), H777, Sigiswald Kuijken, Hyperion, CDA67364.

C.P.E. Bach, J.C.F. Bach & J.C. Bach, *Sonatas and Fantasies/Chamber Music*, Andreas Staier, Deutsche Harmonia Mundi, 82876 67374 2.

J.S. Bach, *Christmas Oratorio*, John Eliot Gardiner, Archiv, 423 232–2.

J.S. Bach, *Mass in B Minor*, John Eliot Gardiner, Archiv, 415 514–2.

J.S. Bach, *Matthäus-Passion* (*St Matthew Passion*), Nikolaus Harnoncourt, Teldec, 8573–81036–2.

J.S. Bach, *St John Passion*, John Eliot Gardiner, Archiv, 419 324–2.

C.W. Gluck, *Orfeo ed Eurydice* (*Orpheus and Eurydice*), René Jacobs, Harmonia Mundi, HMC 901742.43.

G.F. Handel, *Giulio Cesare*, René Jacobs, Harmonia Mundi, HMC 901385.87.

G.F. Handel, *Israel in Egypt*, Andrew Parrott, Virgin Veritas, 7243 5 61350 2 4.

G.F. Handel, *Orchestral Works*, Trevor Pinnock, Archiv, 423 149–2.

J. Haydn, *The Seasons*, René Jacobs, Harmonia Mundi, HMX 296 1829.30.

J. Haydn, *The Paris Symphonies 82–87*, Sigiswald Kuijken, Virgin Veritas, 7243 5 61659 2 2.

J. Haydn, *String Quartets Vols.1 & 2*, The Lindsays, ASV, CD QS 6144 & CD QS 6145.

W.A. Mozart, *Le Nozze di Figaro* (*The Marriage of Figaro*), Vittorio Gui, EMI Classics, 7243 5 73845 2 0. For the libretto (not included) see *The Marriage of Figaro* (English National Opera Guide 17), London: Calder Publications, 1983.

W.A. Mozart, *Piano Concertos Nos.17 & 21*, Maria João Pires & Claudio Abbado, Deutsche Grammophon, 439 941–2.

W.A, Mozart, *Symphonies 25, 29, 38 & 40*, Benjamin Britten, Decca, 444 323–2.

W.A. Mozart, *Die Zauberflöte* (*The Magic Flute*), Karl Böhm, Deutsche Grammophon, 449 749–2.

Chapter 10

From Kramnick: Kant, 'What is Enlightenment?' Diderot, '*Encyclopédie*'. Beaumarchais, *Le Mariage de Figaro*.

Theodor W. Adorno & Max Horkheimer, *Dialectic of Enlightenment*, John Cumming (trans.), London: Verso, 1997.

Isaiah Berlin, 'The Counter-Enlightenment', in *Against the Current: Essays in the History of Ideas*, London: Pimlico, 1999, 1–25.

Andrew Collier, *Marx*, Oneworld: Oxford, 2004.

Richard Dawkins, *The God Delusion*, London: Bantam Press, 2006.

Martin Fitzpatrick, Peter Jones, Christa Knellwolf & Ian McCalman (eds.), *The Enlightenment World*, Abingdon: Routledge, 2007, chapters 37, 38 & 39.

Francis Fukuyama, *The End of History and the Last Man*, London: Penguin, 1992.

John Gray, *Enlightenment's Wake: Politics and Culture at the Close of the Modern Age*, London: Routledge, 1995.

F.A. Hayek, *The Constitution of Liberty*, London: Routledge & Kegan Paul, 1960.

Dan Hind, *The Threat to Reason: How the Enlightenment Was Hijacked and How We Can Reclaim It*, Cambridge: Verso, 2007.

R.J. Hollingdale (ed.), *A Nietzsche Reader*, Harmondsworth: Penguin, 1977.

Eugene Kamenka (ed.), *The Portable Karl Marx*, New York: Viking Penguin, 1983.

Darrin M. McMahon, *Enemies of the Enlightenment: The French Counter-Enlightenment and the Making of Modernity*, New York: Oxford University Press, 2001.

John Stuart Mill, *On Liberty and Other Essays*, Oxford: Oxford University Press, 1991.

John Rawls, *A Theory of Justice*, Oxford: Oxford University Press, 1972.

Civilisation: A Personal View by Lord Clark: The Complete Series, BBC DVD, 2 Entertain Video. See episode 11 for the transition to Romanticism.

Index

A Beginner's Guide to The French Revolution

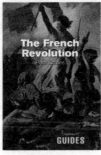

9781851686933
£9.99/ $14.95

Blending narrative with analysis, Peter Davies explores a time of obscene opulence, mass starvation, and ground-breaking ideals; where the streets of Paris ran red with blood, and the numbers requiring execution precipitated the invention of the guillotine.

Davies brings the subject up to date by considering the legacy of the revolution and how it continues to resonate in today's France.

PETER DAVIES is senior lecturer in History at the University of Huddersfield. His previous books include 'The Debate about the French Revolution' and 'The Extreme Right in France: From de Maistre to Le Pen'. He has also written about fascism, the far right, small-group teaching and learning, and the social history of cricket.

Browse further titles at
www.oneworld-publications.com

A Beginner's Guide to History of Science

9781851686810
£9.99/ $14.95

Sean Johnston weaves together intellectual history, philosophy, and social studies to offer a unique appraisal of the nature of this evolving discipline. This book demonstrates that science is a continually evolving activity that both influences and is influenced by its cultural context.

"Lucidly and engagingly written ... Johnston has managed to cover an impressive range of material, making it readily accessible to newcomers." **Patricia Fara** – author of *Science: A Four Thousand Year History*

"Clearly written without being patronising, this is a first-rate introduction to the history of science! " **Dr Peter Morris** – Head of Research at the Science Museum, London

SEAN F. JOHNSTON is Reader in the History of Science and Technology at the University of Glasgow. He is also a Fellow of the Higher Education Academy with a prior career as a physicist and systems engineer.

Browse further titles at
www.oneworld-publications.com

A Beginner's Guide to Philosophy of Science

9781851686841
£9.99/ $14.95

Geoffrey Gorham considers explores the social and ethical implications of science by linking them to issues facing scientists today: human extinction, extraterrestrial intelligence, space colonization, and more.

"Lively, accessible, and clear-headed. Good for the beginning student and for anyone wishing guidance on how to start thinking philosophically about science."
Helen Longino – Clarence Irving Lewis Professor of Philosophy at Stanford University

GEOFFREY GORHAM has been teaching and researching philosophy of science for 15 years, and is currently Associate Professor of Philosophy at Macalester College in St. Paul, Minnesota.

A Beginner's Guide to Philosophy of Religion

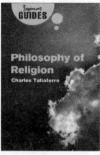

Assuming no prior knowledge of philosophy from the reader, Taliaferro provides a clear exploration of the discipline, introducing a wide range of philosophers and covering the topics of morality and religion, evil, the afterlife, prayer, and miracles.

9781851686506
£9.99/ $14.95

"Brimming with arguments, the material is cutting edge, and the selection of topics is superb."
J.P. Moreland – Professor of Philosophy, St Olaf College, Minnesota

"Covers all the most important issues in a way that is always fair-minded, and manages to be accessible without over-simplifying" **John Cottingham** – President of the British Society for the Philosophy of Religion and Professor Emeritus of Philosophy, Reading University

CHARLES TALIAFERRO is Professor of Philosophy at St. Olaf College, Minnesota, USA. He is the author or editor of numerous books on the philosophy of religion including as co-editor of *The Blackwell Companion to Philosophy of Religion*.

Browse further titles at
www.oneworld-publications.com

A Beginner's Guide to Philosophy of Mind

9781851684786
£9.99/ $14.95

In this lively and entertaining introduction to the philosophy of mind, Edward Feser explores the questions central to the discipline; such as 'do computers think?', and 'what is consciousness?'; and gives an account of all the most important and significant attempts that have been made to answer them.

"A splendid, highly accessible and lucid introduction. The arguments are engaging and provide a refreshing challenge to some of the conventional assumptions in the field."
Charles Taliaferro – Professor of Philosophy, St Olaf College, Minnesota

"Fesar has a feel for the enduring problems…an excellent introduction."
John Haldane – Professor of Philosophy, University of St Andrews

EDWARD FESER is Visiting Assistant Professor of Philosophy at Loyola Marymount University, California, and the author of On Nozick. He has taught and written widely in the areas of philosophy of mind, and his most recent research has focused on new solutions to the mind/body problem

Browse further titles at
www.oneworld-publications.com

Beginners
GUIDES

A Beginner's Guide to Humanism

978-1-85168-589-9
£9.99/ $14.95

Showing how humanists make sense of the world using reason, experience, and sensitivity, Cave emphasizes that we can, and should, flourish without God. Lively, provocative, and refreshingly rant-free, this book is essential reading for all – whether atheist, agnostic, believer, or of no view – who wish better to understand what it means to be human.

"An admirable guide for all those non-religious who may wake up to the fact that they are humanists." **Sir Bernard Crick** – Emeritus Professor of Birkbeck College, University of London, and author of *Democracy: A Very Short Introduction*

"Humanism is loving, sharing and caring and above all an intelligent philosophical way to make the best of our own and our neighbours' lives. I could not commend it more." **Clare Rayner** – Broadcaster, writer and Vice President of the British Humanist Association

Writer and broadcaster Peter Cave teaches philosophy for The Open University and City University London. Author of the bestselling *Can A Robot Be Human?*, he chairs the Humanist Philosophers' Group, frequently contributes to philosophy journals and magazines, and has presented several philosophy programmes for the BBC. He lives in London.

Browse further titles at
www.oneworld-publications.com

A Beginner's Guide to Democracy

978-1-85168-363-5
£9.99/ $14.95

David Beetham offers new insights into the role of the citizen and how large corporations affect democracy as well as contemplating the future of democracy in the developed and developing worlds.

"Beetham's book should stimulate anyone, beginner or expert, who is interested in the survival and renewal of democracy in the era of globalization." **Peter Singer** – Author of *The President Of Good And Evil: Taking George Bush Seriously*

"A strong and shrewd mixture of analysis and polemic...If more was not to come, I would call this the author's crowning achievement." **Sir Bernard Crick** – Advisor on citizenship to the UK government

DAVID BEETHAM is Professor Emeritus of Politics at the University of Leeds, a Fellow of the Human Rights Centre at the University of Essex, and Associate Director of the UK Democratic Audit.

Browse further titles at
www.oneworld-publications.com

A Beginner's Guide to Feminism

9781851687121
£9.99/ $14.95

By highlighting the themes that form the enduring nexuses between its various strands, taking powerful examples from feminist campaigns, and tackling timely issues such as genocide and war rape, Scholtz invites us to join in with the lively debates and always germane challenges of feminism.

"This book is written so clearly, cogently, and cleverly that anyone who reads it carefully will be persuaded that all societies should become more feminist." **Rosemarie Tong** – Distinguished Professor in Health Care Ethics, University of North Carolina at Charlotte

"Cleverly combines a broad range of topics with careful scholarship, all laid out in friendly and accessible prose." **Hilde Lindemann** – Professor of Philosophy, Michigan State University.

SALLY J. SCHOLZ is is Professor of Philosophy at Villanova University, Pennsylvania, and faculty-in-residence at its Center for Peace and Justice Studies.

Browse further titles at
www.oneworld-publications.com

A Beginner's Guide to Anarchism

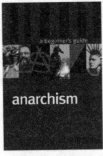

In this clear and penetrating study, Ruth Kinna goes right to the heart of the ideology, explaining the influences that have shaped anarchism, and the tactics and strategies that anarchists have used to bring about their goals.

978-1-85168-370-4
£9.99 / $14.95

"Kinna is an ideal guide and has written an exemplary work of clarification and explanation. This book deserves to be read very widely." **David Goodway** – Senior Lecturer In Political Theory, University of Leeds

"A valuable contribution to our understanding of this much misunderstood philosophy." **Howard Zinn** – Author of *A People's History Of The United States*

RUTH KINNA is Lecturer in Politics at Loughborough University, UK. She is the author of *William Morris: The Art of Socialism* and co-editor of the journal *Anarchist Studies*. Her research focuses on socialism and anarchism in 19th century Britain.

Browse further titles at
www.oneworld-publications.com

A Beginner's Guide to Racism

Provocative and intelligent reading for the newcomer and expert alike, this invaluable resource exposes the roots of racial thought and demonstrates why it has remained crucial to our everyday lives.

978-1-85168-543-1
£9.99/ $14.95

"Clearly and convincingly written." **David Theo Goldberg** – Director of the University of California Humanities Research Institute

"I've learned an enormous lot from Alana Lentin's book. I only regret that a guide like this was not in existence when sixty years ago I started to study that phenomenon, one of the most insidious and complex of our times." **Zygmunt Bauman** – Emeritus Professor of Sociology at the University of Leeds

ALANA LENTIN is a lecturer in sociology at the University of Sussex. She is the author of *Racism and Anti-Racism in Europe* (2004) and is a regular contributor to openDemocracy.net

Browse further titles at
www.oneworld-publications.com